PRO BASKETBALL STATISTICS

Basketball is a veritable ballet—most people don't realize what tremendous athletes basketball players are.

—Al McGuire

But he was in no way able to submit himself to the discipline, the hard labor, the acceptance of defeat and failure that make a good athlete; he wanted always to win, he wanted always to be the general, the heroic spear-head of victory. And after that, he wanted to be loved.

—Thomas Wolfe,
Look Homeward, Angel

PRO BASKETBALL STATISTICS

Top Players and Teams by Game, Season and Career

by

Martin Taragano

McFarland & Company, Inc., Publishers
Jefferson, North Carolina, and London

Also by Martin Taragano:
BASKETBALL BIOGRAPHIES (McFarland)

British Library Cataloguing-in-Publication data are available

Library of Congress Cataloguing-in-Publication Data

Taragano, Martin, 1959–
Pro basketball statistics : top players and teams by game, season and career / Martin Taragano.
p. cm.
Includes bibliographical references (p.) and index.
ISBN 0-89950-804-9 (lib. bdg. : 50# alk. paper)
1. 1. Basketball players—United States—Statistics. 2. Basketball—United States—Statistics. 3. Basketball—United States—Records. I. Title.
GV885.55.T37 1993
796.323'64'0973021—dc20 92-51094
CIP

Manufactured in the United States of America

McFarland & Company, Inc., Publishers
Box 611, Jefferson, North Carolina

TO MY HELPERS:

Helene, a colossal beauty of a woman, who carved and battled her way to become Queen of my Mountain.

Goody, a gargantuan talent of a man, whose magnificent honesty makes me often doubt dishonesty's very existence.

Steve, a young man who looks at the world with a wise man's tolerance and an even wiser man's acceptance.

Berdie, whose tender innocence makes me humble to possess any knowledge at all.

And to Coal, a woman who never demanded of me, never refused to share, never had the need to cure any of my foibles.

Acknowledgments

A man named Bill Mokray, whom I never met, must be thanked for one single reason: born in 1907, Mokray is unarguably considered the father of basketball statistics; he invented them in the 1940s and then splashed them across the nation until stats became a popular and officially documented science. He died in 1974.

I thank the authors of the myriad reference books that I had to use in writing this book. So to them (see bibliography), I extend my heartiest acknowledgments. They too are in love with the game.

Thanks to the Professional Basketball Writers Association of America, especially to Don Greenburg, Jan Hubbard, and Bill Halls; to Joseph R. Vancisin, executive director of the National Association of Basketball Coaches of the United States and to Joe O'Brien at the Naismith Memorial Basketball Hall of Fame; and to Jerry Krause, Ed.D. of NABC.

A special amount of gratitude to the inventor of the game of basketball, James Naismith, a Canadian denizen, an orphan, a one-time high school dropout, a minister and a doctor who was born on November 6, 1861, and died 78 years later on November 28.

To "Pistol" Pete Maravich for playing the sport of life with more brilliance than the game of basketball. He's my all time favorite player, but I cannot omit extending thanks to Dr. J., Rick Barry, Bob Cousy, Wilt Chamberlain, Bob McAdoo, Oscar Robertson, George Gervin, Michael Jordan, Larry Bird, Magic Johnson, Bob Pettit and Elgin Baylor for their colossal basketball artistry.

Contents

List of Abbreviations

Many of the abbreviations in this book are common enough to be self-explanatory. However, the listing below explains those as well as some that might not be so readily apparent.

Statistical Terminology

avg — average
boards — rebounds
FG — field goals
FG% — field goal percentage
FT — free throws
FT% — free throw percentage
MVP — Most Valuable Player (also known in the NBA as the Maurice Podoloff Trophy, in honor of the former league commissioner)
no — number
PCT or **Per** or **%** — percentage
rebs — rebounds
rpg — rebounds per game
stats — statistics

General League and Team Abbreviations Used in the Pro Game

ABA — American Basketball Association
ABL — American Basketball League
BAA — Basketball Association of America
CBA — Continental Basketball Association
EBL — Eastern Basketball League
NBA — National Basketball Association
NBL — National Basketball League
Pro — Professional

Teams in the NBA (Past and Present)

Atl — Atlanta Hawks
Balt — Baltimore Bullets
Bost — Boston Celtics
Char — Charlotte Hornets
Chi — Chicago Bulls
Cin — Cincinnati Royals

Dal—Dallas Mavericks
Den—Denver Nuggets
Det—Detroit Pistons
G. S.—Golden State Warriors
Hou—Houston Rockets
Ind—Indiana Pacers
KC—Kansas City-Omaha Kings
LA—Los Angeles Lakers or Los Angeles Clippers
Minn—Minnesota Timberwolves
Milw—Milwaukee Bucks
NJ—New Jersey Nets
NY—New York Knickerbockers
Phi—Philadelphia 76ers
Phoe—Phoenix Suns
Por—Portland Trail Blazers
Sea—Seattle SuperSonics
SA—San Antonio Spurs
SD—San Diego Clippers
SF—San Francisco Warriors (later Golden State Warriors)
St. Lou—St. Louis Hawks
UT—Utah Jazz
Wash—Washington Bullets

Teams from the ABA

Amigos—Anaheim Amigos
Americans—New Jersey Americans
Buccaneers—New Orleans Buccaneers
Braves—Buffalo Braves
Chaparrals—Dallas Chaparrals or Texas Chaparrals
Condors—Pittsburgh Condors
Conquistadors—San Diego Conquistadors
Capitols—Washington Capitols
Cougars—Carolina Cougars
Colonels—Kentucky Colonels
Floridians—Miami Floridians
Mavs or Mavericks—Houston Mavericks
Muskies—Minnesota Muskies
Nets—New York Nets
Nuggets—Denver Nuggets
Oaks—Oakland Oaks
Pacers—Indiana Pacers
Pipers—Minnesota Pipers or Pittsburgh Pipers
Rockets—Denver Rockets
Sounds—Memphis Sounds
Sails—San Diego Sails
Spirits—Spirits of St. Louis
Squires—Virginia Squires
Spurs—San Antonio Spurs
Stars—Los Angeles Stars or Utah Stars

List of Tables

Preface

When analyzed properly, statistics cannot lie; stats are one of the foundations for understanding any sport. Without adequate statistics, no sport can be translated to the fans. *Watching* basketball games rarely fulfills the fascination of fans. That's why stat books like this are needed—and desired. But not all stat books are the same.

There have been many previous basketball reference books over the years but most of them require the reader to scrounge through several other books, side by side, in an effort to compare player-by-player. That is tedious and takes the enjoyment out of what should be an entertaining endeavor.

This book will not require such page flipping. Each section is clearly defined. Want to learn how Wilt Chamberlain compares game-by-game to Moses Malone or Kareem Abdul-Jabbar? Chapter 2 is a concise, comparative compilation of individual statistical categories.

I chose the fundamental, obvious and time-worn stat categories in order to rank the all-time greatest pro players in basketball history: stats such as points, rebounds, assists, FG%, FT%, steals, blocked shots. Any fan can identify and understand these standards.

The reader will discover dozens of entirely new, originally compiled statistical charts, and side by side player comparison tables; the majority do not repeat material from any previous basketball stat book. They are included to shed new light on the accomplishments of pro basketball's finest athletes.

A brief note on the statistical tables in the early sections of this book: the most enjoyable way to understand, analyze and compare these stats is to first look at each heading on top to see what categories are being compared (e.g. "All NBA" simply means the number of seasons each player earned a nominated berth on the All NBA team; or "MVP" simply means the number of seasons, if any, that each player in the column listed was named a league Most Valuable Player, and so on).

At the back of the book are two appendices: an up-to-date and accurate directory of the essential addresses of basketball teams, and an exhaustive listing of birthdays of great players and influential contributors. This section, I feel, will be especially useful to the journalist, researcher, college or high school coach and young student.

A bibliography is provided for those readers absorbed in pursuing supplemental basketball reading.

I ranked the greatest players with objective statistical highlights and in-depth analysis not only overall, but *by position* (guards, forwards and centers).

As for the book's accuracy, I spent thousands of hours researching, rechecking, cross-checking, and then checking once again a myriad of sources to be certain everything was as accurate as possible. But in a work of this scope and depth, it's inevitable that a small degree of oversight will have crept in and I beg the indulgence of the reader if, after all, some minor errors do surface.

In your hands then is what I hope will be the most critically objective basketball stats book ever compiled in a single volume. Its goal is to reveal, once and for all, in a statistically oriented methodology, who the all-time greatest players were.

Introduction

An orphan who felt he never belonged, a high school dropout who eventually became a medical doctor—but never treated a single patient—and an ordained Presbyterian minister, who never maintained a pastorate, James Naismith singlehandedly created what is perhaps the greatest American athletic invention: basketball.

Born on November 6, 1861, in Altmonte, Ontario, Canada, he had to walk two-and-a-half miles to school each morning, often through thick, driving snowstorms and bone-chilling cold. He was a fighter early on, getting into fisticuffs with anyone who would punch back.

Eight years after he was born, both his parents died. After dropping out of high school for several years, he returned and finally obtained his diploma. Then it was on to McGill University in Montreal where he played on the football team.

At McGill, he taught gym after earning his degree. Around 1890, he matriculated at Springfield College in Massachusetts. Before he entered Gross Medical School in Denver, Colorado, in 1894 (now known as the University of Colorado Medical School), he invented an indoor, winter sport with 13 original rules, and he called it basketball simply because the idea was to toss a ball into a peach basket.

Statistics were not kept back then. Nobody knew anything about stats or FG% . Naismith was teaching physical education at the time and also conducting daily chapel exercises.

The year was 1891. He never was good at the game he invented, preferring to coach it, to teach it, and to watch it spread throughout the world, until, by 1936, his idea became an official international sport played by teams from all over the world in the Olympic Games.

In a 1939 article in *The Rotarian,* Naismith said, "Invention of the game of basketball was not an accident. It was developed to meet a need. Basketball, finally, is a popular spectator's game. How many millions the world over gather to cheer their favorite team is beyond a guess. But this much is certain:

in the United States, for several years, basketball has attracted more customers than either football or baseball, amateur or professional combined. Collectors of statistics say that some 90 million admissions were paid to see the youth of the nation perform on basketball courts last year alone and the years ahead will probably witness even a higher total."

In 1959, he was the first electee/nominee to the Hall of Fame. After inventing basketball, Naismith coached in France during the First World War. Two years after he retired from Kansas University, and seven years before the NBA was formed, on November 28, 1939, he died. But basketball continues to live.

The public's fascination with the sport of basketball is ceaseless. Basketball, according to *Sports Marketplace* is the tenth most popular sport in the entire United States in terms of player participation—significantly ahead of either baseball or football. (Bowling is number one.)

There are, at last count, 23 million officially documented people—boys and girls, men and women—who participate in regular leagues on all levels, including the almost 20,000 high school teams, over 12,000 men's college teams, more than 10,000 women's college teams, 10 Continental Basketball Association (CBA) teams and 27 National Basketball Association (NBA) pro teams and this is just in the United States.

Fan attendance in 1991 surged to a reported 47 million and close to $100 million was spent for basketball-related equipment such as baskets, backboards, nets, floorings, timers, clocks, uniforms and, of course, basketballs. The NBA's gross revenues in the 1991 season bulged to a staggering $1.1 *billion.*

The CBA alone boasted over one million paid fans in 1991. More than 80 percent of the televised pro games were broadcast via the major networks and by the cable industries. That does not include the hundreds more featured by local and regional broadcasters. Basketball ranks third of all the major sports as far as television ratings. Finally, regarding television, no fewer than 690,000 persons/households tuned in to watch a recent NBA all star game; that is tantamount to a 10 percent ratings share. Another all star game, at the Houston Astrodome, packed in a record 44,725 fans.

All in all, the future of Dr. Naismith's cherished game appears to be surging towards the stratosphere as fans cannot seem to get enough of pro basketball.

Chapter 1

The All Time Top 100 Pro Players: Statistical Rankings

He rarely smiled when he played yet when he did play he made everyone who was watching smile back. He stood 6'5" and weighed a muscular 210 pounds. Many who played before were taller or faster, could leap higher, dunked better, swooped more gracefully or dribbled fancier. He entered the NBA in 1960, at age 22, and, before he left 14 years later, Oscar Robertson, basketball's most versatile player ever, singlehandedly revolutionized the concept of just how great an NBA guard could be.

This section deals with the pro game's all time greatest players, ranking the legends on the basis of comparative statistical accomplishments. By these criteria, Robertson ranks as the best ever.

Chamberlain, also ranked here in the listing of the ten greatest pro players in history, was the better scorer and rebounder without question but despite Chamberlain's scoring prowess, he failed to have as *versatile* seasons in basketball's three major categories (points, rebounds and assists) as Robertson.

Robertson is, moreover, the all time highest scoring guard in professional basketball history with 26,710 points.

This chapter will look at the top 100 pro players, taking an in-depth look at the individual statistics of the top 20 players (broken down into Top 10 and Second Team).

Table 1.1—The Top 100 Players

1. Oscar Robertson*
2. Wilt Chamberlain*
3. Bob Pettit*
4. Elgin Baylor*
5. Kareem Abdul-Jabbar
6. Julius Erving
7. Jerry West*
8. Rick Barry*
9. Bob Cousy*
10. Bill Russell*
11. Michael Jordan**
12. Larry Bird
13. George Mikan*
14. John Havlicek*
15. Moses Malone**

Table 1.1—The Top 100 Players *(cont.)*

16. Magic Johnson
17. Dolph Schayes*
18. Elvin Hayes*
19. Neil Johnston*
20. Paul Arizin*
21. George Gervin
22. Bob McAdoo
23. Walt Bellamy
24. Hal Greer*
25. Chet Walker
26. Dan Issel
27. Dave Bing*
28. Artis Gilmore
29. Bob Lanier*
30. Nate Archibald*
31. Pete Maravich*
32. Isiah Thomas**
33. Earl Monroe*
34. Walt Frazier*
35. Willis Reed*
36. Ed Macauley*
37. Nate Thurmond*
38. Billy Cunningham*
39. Calvin Murphy
40. Bill Sharman*
41. Guy Rodgers
42. David Thompson
43. Gail Goodrich
44. Lenny Wilkens*
45. Lou Hudson
46. Sam Jones*
47. Spencer Haywood
48. George McGinnis
49. Alex English
50. Adrian Dantley
51. Jerry Lucas*
52. Bob Davies*
53. Frank Ramsey*
54. K. C. Jones*
55. Slater Martin*
56. Bob Lanier*
57. Al Cervi*
58. Andy Phillip*
59. Bill Bradley*
60. Cliff Hagan*
61. Tom Heinsohn*
62. Jack Twyman*
63. Jim Pollard*
64. Joe Fulks*
65. Dave DeBusschere*
66. Tom Gola*
67. Clyde Lovellette*
68. Hakeem Olajuwon**
69. Ralph Sampson
70. Dominique Wilkins**
71. Charles Barkley**
72. Bernard King**
73. Gus Johnson
74. Vern Mikkelsen
75. Johnny Kerr
76. Dave Cowens*
77. Bill Walton
78. Harry Gallatin*
79. Max Zaslofsky
80. Jo Jo White
81. Larry Costello
82. World B. Free
83. Kevin Porter
84. Louie Dampier
85. Paul Westphal
86. Gene Shue
87. Norm Van Lier
88. Carl Braun
89. Bernhard Borgman*
90. Bill Bridges
91. Bailey Howell
92. Paul Silas
93. George Yardley
94. Richie Guerin
95. Mel Daniels
96. Connie Hawkins*
97. Maurice Stokes
98. Alex Groza
99. Larry Foust
100. Bob Feerick

*Indicates player is in Hall of Fame (as of February 1992).
**Indicates player is still active as of 1993.

Table 1.2—The Top 100 Players in Their Positions

Guards	Forwards	Centers
Oscar Robertson	Bob Pettit	Wilt Chamberlain
Jerry West	Elgin Baylor	Kareem Abdul-Jabbar
Earvin "Magic" Johnson	Julius Erving	Bill Russell
Michael Jordan	Rick Barry	Willis Reed
Bob Cousy	Larry Bird	Neil Johnston
Pete Maravich	Dolph Schayes	Elvin Hayes
Isiah Thomas	John Havlicek	Dan Issel
Nate Archibald	Paul Arizin	Artis Gilmore
George Gervin	Spencer Haywood	Bob McAdoo
Earl Monroe	George McGinnis	Bob Lanier

Oscar Robertson is statistically the greatest basketball player ever. (Photo courtesy of Naismith Memorial Basketball Hall of Fame.)

Guards	Forwards	Centers
Walt Frazier	Ed Macauley	Moses Malone
Calvin Murphy	Alex English	George Mikan
Guy Rodgers	Adrian Dantley	Nate Thurmond
Bill Sharman	Billy Cunningham	Walt Bellamy
Hal Greer	Carl Braun	Wes Unseld
David Thompson	Bailey Howell	Jerry Lucas
Gail Goodrich	Chet Walker	Clyde Lovellette
Lenny Wilkens	Bill Bradley	Dave Cowens
Lou Hudson	Cliff Hagan	Bill Walton
Sam Jones	Tom Heinsohn	Harry Gallatin

Table 1.2—The Top 100 Players in Their Positions *(cont.)*

Guards	Forwards	Centers
Bob Davies	Bill Bridges	Johnny Kerr
Frank Ramsey	Jim Pollard	Vern Mikkelsen
K. C. Jones	Jack Twyman	Gus Johnson
Slater Martin	Paul Silas	Larry Foust
Bobby Wanzer	George Yardley	Zelmo Beatty
Al Cervi	Dave DeBusschere	Hakeem Olajuwon
Andy Phillip	Joe Fulks	Ralph Sampson
Max Zaslofsky	Tom Gola	
Jo Jo White	Richie Guerin	
Dave Bing	Mel Daniels	
Charlie Scott	Connie Hawkins	
Kevin Porter	Maurice Stokes	
Louie Dampier	Bob Feerick	
Paul Westphal	Alex Groza	
Gene Shue	Charles Barkley	
Norm Van Lier	Bernard King	
	Dominique Wilkins	

There are 36 guards, 37 forwards and 27 centers. Some were swingmen and played two positions, but are listed here by the position most fans recognize them as having played for the majority of their respective careers.

The Top 10 Players

The following players, in order from best-rated to tenth, have been selected as the most skilled offensive players in basketball history in terms of possessing more mastery of every fundamental—shooting, passing, rebounding, defense, and scoring than any other players before or since.

With the sole exception here of former Boston Celtic Bill Russell, the nine others have amassed significantly higher honors in every basketball category than anyone else. Russell, however, must be included for what he did to *defensive* basketball as far as quite literally controlling the very pace of the game itself with his presence.

Table 1.3—Top 10: Career Achievements (Regular Season)

	Times Named:		
Player	All NBA	All Star	MVP
Kareem Abdul-Jabbar	15	18	6
Rick Barry	10	11	Never

Player	All NBA	Times Named: All Star	MVP
Elgin Baylor	10	11	Never
Wilt Chamberlain	10	13	4
Bob Cousy	12	13	1
Julius Erving	12	16	4
Bob Pettit	11	11	2
Oscar Robertson	11	12	1
Bill Russell	11	12	5
Jerry West	12	12	Never

To be named to these teams and to capture the MVP award signify greatness among one's peers; to be so honored many times signifies greatness among all the players who ever played in any era. Only four players ever played in 13 all star games. They were: Cousy, Chamberlain and John Havlicek along with Abdul-Jabbar's record 18 games. Other stars like Oscar Robertson or Jerry West only got in an even dozen.

Kareem Abdul-Jabbar never won an all star game MVP despite playing in a record 18 contests during his 20 NBA seasons.

Barry's and Erving's totals include their ABA days as well, which in no way should reflect negatively. They were, perhaps, the two greatest ABA players in that league's history.

All NBA numbers include both first and second team selections.

Table 1.4—Top 10: Playoff and All Star Game MVP Awards Won

Player	Times Named: MVP in Playoffs	MVP in All Star Game
Abdul-Jabbar	2	Never
Barry	1	1
Baylor	Never*	1
Chamberlain	1	1
Cousy	Never*	2
Erving	2	2
Pettit	Never*	4
Robertson	Never*	3
Russell	Never*	1
West	1	1

*Indicates that the award for the playoff MVP was not officially given until 1969; thus, many of these greats didn't have the chance to win it in their primes—such as Robertson, Cousy, Pettit, Baylor and Russell.

The categories that follow were selected for side by side comparisons to best determine all-around skills and achievements earned. Versatility is the key when determining the very best ever list, as is ultimate dominance in one area, such as scoring or rebounding. To rank in the top 10 with one's peers every season is another mark of superiority.

Table 1.5—Top 10 Postseason Achievements: Rookie of the Year, Scoring and Rebounds

		Times Named:	
Player	Rookie of the Year	Scoring Champ	Rebounds Champ
Abdul-Jabbar	Yes	2	1
Barry	Yes	2*	Never
Baylor	Yes	Never	Never
Chamberlain	Yes	7	11
Cousy	No	Never	Never
Erving	No	3*	Never
Pettit	Yes	2	1
Robertson	Yes	Never	Never
Russell	No	Never	4
West	No	1	Never

*Indicates both NBA and ABA careers.

Forwards and guards are not usually among the rebounding leaders. Pettit's rebounding crown is all the more significant—even if he played some center that season—since he wasn't a great jumper. But he had the required timing and instinctive sense to grab many boards *below* the rim.

It may surprise many to learn that neither Baylor nor Robertson ever captured a scoring title. However, they were close many seasons.

Table 1.6—Top 10 Postseason Achievements: Assists, Steals and Blocked Shots

		Times Named:	
Player	Assists Champ	Steals Champ	Blocked Shots Champ
Abdul-Jabbar	Never	Never	4†
Barry	Never	1	Never
Baylor	Never	Never*	Never*
Chamberlain	1	Never*	Never*
Cousy	8	Never*	Never
Erving	Never	Never*	Never
Pettit	Never	Never*	Never*

Wilt Chamberlain, ranked second to Oscar Robertson, established 14 NBA records and once scored 100 points in a single game. (Photo courtesy of Naismith Memorial Basketball Hall of Fame.)

		Times Named:	
Player	Assists Champ	Steals Champ	Blocked Shots Champ
Robertson	6	Never*	Never
Russell	Never	Never*	Never*
West	1	Never*	Never

*Indicates that these categories were not officially recorded during that player's career or during his peak seasons. Steals and blocks began to be marked down for the first time in the 1973-74 season.

†Only two players have ever totaled more than 3,000 career blocked shots: Artis Gilmore leads the way with 3,178 and Kareem Abdul-Jabbar ranks second with 3,104. Wayne "Tree" Rollins is in third with 2,283.

Russell and Chamberlain would have led the entire league as often as possible since Russell, especially, was known as the best shot blocker of all time, despite the lack of stats. He practically invented the block, much as Erving invented the dunk.

Also, assist titles are usually reserved for the guards, since that's one of their main roles. Thus, for Chamberlain to have led the league is truly extraordinary. He is also the tallest player to ever win the assist title at 7′1″ in 1968.

Table 1.7—Top 10 Postseason Achievements: FT%, FG% and Minutes

Player		Times Named:	
	FT% Champ	FG% Champ	Minutes Leader
Abdul-Jabbar	Never	1	1
Barry	9*	Never	Never
Baylor	Never	Never	Never
Chamberlain	Never	9	7
Cousy	Never	Never	Never
Erving	Never	Never	Never
Pettit	Never	Never	Never
Robertson	1	Never	Never
Russell	Never	Never	2
West	Never	Never	Never

*Indicates Barry's total in both the ABA and NBA.

Just because a player hasn't led the league in FT% and FG% doesn't mean he couldn't shoot: it simply indicates that he wasn't the very best. However, it does indicate if a player dominated one category of shooting—either from the field or from the foul line.

Barry is generally regarded as the best from the line, although some others amassed very similar seasonal percentages, such as Dolph Schayes, Calvin Murphy and Larry Bird. Chamberlain was the most dominant FG shooter ever with nine titles. Centers rarely have as high FT%s as guards, who being shorter, possess softer touches. Also, guards and forwards shoot further away from the basket, thus lower FG%s are the result.

Table 1.8—Top 10 Postseason Achievements: First Team NBA and Defense

Player	Times Named:	
	First Team All NBA	First Team Defense
Abdul-Jabbar	10	10
Barry	4**	Never

Player	Times Named: First Team All NBA	First Team Defense
Baylor	10	Never*
Chamberlain	7	2
Cousy	10	Never*
Erving	9**	Never
Pettit	11	Never*
Robertson	9	Never*
Russell	3	1*
West	10	4

*The All Defensive team selections began in 1968. Many greats never had a chance to be considered for this honor since they played before it was even awarded.

**Includes both ABA and NBA totals.

Erving and West had big steals numbers in their primes. West, for example, once had 10 in a single game while Erving is ranked second in all time career steals, so their defensive abilities should go unchallenged. (Maurice Cheeks is the NBA's all time steals leader. Cheeks was a teammate of Erving on the potent Philadelphia 76ers squads of the 1980s.)

Table 1.9—Top 10: Career Scoring Accomplishments

Player	Seasons at 30 Points a Game	50 + Point Games
Abdul-Jabbar	4	2
Barry	4*	14
Baylor	3	17
Chamberlain	7	121*
Cousy	None	1*
Erving	1*	3
Pettit	1	6
Robertson	6	2
Russell	None	None
West	4	3

*Indicates both NBA and ABA careers for Barry and Erving. Also indicates that Chamberlain's colossal total includes three playoff games and that Cousy's only 50 point game in his career came in a playoff contest.

Thirty points a game is obviously indicative of offensive greatness and shooting mastery. Most pros have *never* averaged 30 a game even once. Russell's and Cousy's failures to do so may reflect the era rather than their talent. (The player with the second highest number of career 50+ point games is Michael Jordan.)

Table 1.10 — Top 10: Team Titles Won

Player	Team Championships in Career
Abdul-Jabbar	6
Barry	1
Baylor	1
Chamberlain	2
Cousy	6
Erving	3
Pettit	1
Robertson	1
Russell	11
West	1

Team titles are obviously not the work of only one star player; however, to win many does impact on a player's overall contributions.

Table 1.11 — Top 10: Championship Teams

Abdul-Jabbar	Milwaukee (1971) and Los Angeles (1980, 1982, 1985, 1987–88)
Baylor	Los Angeles Lakers (1972)
Barry	Golden State Warriors (1975)
Chamberlain	Philadelphia (1967) and Los Angeles (1972)
Cousy	Boston Celtics (1957, 1959–63)
Erving	New York Nets/ABA (1974 and 1976) and Philadelphia 76ers (1983)
Pettit	St. Louis Hawks (1958)
Robertson	Milwaukee Bucks (1971)
Russell	Boston Celtics (1957, 1959–66, 1968–69)
West	Los Angeles Lakers (1972)

Table 1.12 — Top 10: Number of Seasons Each Was Among the League's Top 10

Player	Points	Rebs	Asst	FT%	FG%	Seasons Played
Abdul-Jabbar	13	12	None	None	18	20
Barry	8	1	5	14	1	14
Baylor	10	7	4	3	None	14
Chamberlain	9	13	4	None	13	14

Player	Points	Rebs	Asst	FT%	FG%	Seasons Played
Cousy	7	None	13	8	None	14†
Erving*	8	5	None	None	None	16
Pettit	10	10	None	1	3	11
Robertson	9	1	11	8	8	14
Russell	None	13	4	None	4	13
West	7	None	8	8	4	14

*NBA career (see Chapter 5 for more on Erving).

†Cousy played only seven games in his last year. He was a player/coach from 1969 to 1970 at 41 years of age.

This chart shows how the ten best fared among each other. This comparison is perhaps the best indication of who is the best out of the ten.

They were competing head-to-head at similar positions, and, if given equal minutes, the chart shows where their talents lie.

Only Barry and Robertson have ranked in the end-of-season top 10 at least once in every statistical category.

Table 1.13—Top 10: Career Per Game Averages (Regular Season)

Player	Points	Rebounds	Assists	FT%	FG%
Abdul-Jabbar	25.3	11.5	3.8	72.1	56.1
Barry	26.9	7.0	4.6	89.0	47.1
Baylor	27.4	13.6	4.3	78.0	43.1
Chamberlain	30.1	22.9	4.4	51.1	54.0
Cousy	18.4	5.2	7.6	80.3	37.5
Erving	25.4	9.4	4.4	77.8	50.8
Pettit	26.4	16.2	3.0	76.1	43.6
Robertson	25.7	7.5	9.5	83.8	48.5
Russell	15.1	22.5	4.3	56.1	44.0
West	27.0	5.8	6.7	81.4	47.4

Chamberlain was one of the few players in NBA history to actually have a higher FG shooting percentage than his FT% mark. Most amazing are Chamberlain's and Russell's rebounding figures. Don't forget, these are per *game* marks. Also, Cousy shot below 40 percent on his career, despite being a top scorer. Robertson averaged close to 10 assists a game in his 14 year career. Pettit's rebounds—and that he had more than high-jumping Baylor or even Erving—are also surprising.

Baylor averaged an amazing 34.8 points per game in the 1960-61 season, his second pro season, but came in second to Chamberlain's 38.4.

The first player to average 20 points per game in the NBA was Mel Riebe of Cleveland who did it in 1945. He posted 20.2 points per game when the league was known as the National Basketball League (NBL).

The first player to shoot over 50 percent from the field was Chamberlain of Philadelphia. In 1961 he shot 50.9 percent.

The first player to shoot over 90 percent from the foul line was Rochester's Bobby Wanzer in 1952. His mark was 90.4 percent.

The first player to average over 10 assists per game was Robertson who dished out 11.4 in 1961 for Cincinnati.

The first player to average more than 20 rebounds per game was Bill Russell. His 22.7 per game mark was accomplished for the Boston Celtics in 1958.

The best FT% mark for a season was 95.8 set in 1981 by 5'9" guard Calvin Murphy.

Table 1.14 – Top 10: Career Per Game Averages (Playoffs)

Player	Points	Rebounds	Assists	FT%	FG%
Abdul-Jabbar	25.2	10.9	3.4	74.1	53.5
Barry	29.2	6.9	4.1	87.6	46.0
Baylor	27.0	12.9	4.0	76.9	43.9
Chamberlain	22.5	24.5	4.2	46.5	52.2
Cousy	18.5	5.0	8.6	80.1	32.6
Erving	26.5	10.0	4.7	78.7	50.8
Pettit	25.5	14.8	2.7	77.4	41.8
Robertson	22.2	6.7	8.9	85.5	46.0
Russell	16.2	24.9	4.7	60.3	43.0
West	29.1	6.3	5.6	80.5	46.9

Playoff stats tell that a star can rise to the occasion when his team depends on his greatness most. Peak performance must be delivered when it's needed most, as in a short playoff series.

Barry and West have the best averages. Barry's mark combines both his ABA and NBA playoff seasons. Robertson was close to 9 assists a game – the highest, but not far ahead of Cousy's 8.6 mark per outing (only Magic Johnson's assist average was higher than these two greats. See the second team top 10 comparative charts for more).

Table 1.15 – Top 10: Career Per Game Averages (All Star Games)

Player	Points	Rebounds	Assists	FT%	FG%
Abdul-Jabbar	13.9	8.3	3.0	81.3	50.2
Barry	14.7	5.1	4.5	84.5	45.9

Player	Points	Rebounds	Assists	FT%	FG%
Baylor	14.7	9.0	3.5	79.6	42.7
Chamberlain	14.7	15.6	2.8	50.0	59.0
Cousy	11.3	6.0	6.6	84.3	32.9
Erving	20.1	6.8	4.0	78.6	50.7
Pettit	20.4	16.2	2.1	77.5	42.0
Robertson	20.5	5.6	6.8	71.4	51.2
Russell	10.0	11.6	3.3	52.9	45.9
West	13.3	3.9	4.6	72.0	45.3

All star game averages are always *lower* than either regular season or playoff averages, not because of inferior play quality, but simply due to fewer minutes given to each player. Coaches in these games have to jockey all the selectees so the fans—who voted for them—will be satisfied. Nevertheless, comparisons are an excellent barometer of who performs best in these star-studded contests.

Michael Jordan has the highest all star game career average with 21.5 points in four games, while Wilt Chamberlain scored the most in a single game with 42 points.

Table 1.16—Top 10: Individual Game Scoring Highs

Player	Most Points in a: Regular Season Game	Playoff Game	All Star Game
Abdul-Jabbar	55	46	25
Barry	64	55	38
Baylor	71	61	32
Chamberlain	100	56	42
Cousy	50	50	20
Erving	63*	45	30
Pettit	57	50	29
Robertson	56	43	28
Russell	39	31	24
West	63	53	22

This comparison chart can be viewed a couple of ways. One can either compare the three centers with each other and do the same for the four forwards and three guards, or one can decide to compare regardless of position played.

Cousy's 50 points in a playoff game happened in a quadruple overtime match, while Baylor's 61 points in the playoffs stood as a record for 25 years until Michael Jordan broke it with 63 in 1986 (in double overtime).

Robert Cousy was voted NBA's Greatest Player in a sports poll in 1963. (Photo courtesy of Naismith Memorial Basketball Hall of Fame.)

Table 1.17 – Top 10: Highest Season Marks in Three Shooting Areas

Player	Top Season Average	Best FT%	Best FG%
Abdul-Jabbar	34.8 Points	78.3	60.4
Barry	35.6	94.7	51.4
Baylor	38.3	83.7	48.6
Chamberlain	50.4	61.3	72.7
Cousy	21.3	85.5	39.7
Erving	31.9	84.5	54.6
Pettit	31.1	82.0	46.3
Robertson	31.4	87.3	51.8
Russell	18.9	61.2	46.7
West	31.3	87.8	51.4

Bill Russell is the second player ever to haul down over 50 rebounds in one game. (Photo courtesy of Naismith Memorial Basketball Hall of Fame.)

Chamberlain's 72.7 FG% mark is simply uncanny; for a player to be so accurate over an entire season is hard to believe. It led the league in 1973. Baylor's 38.3 season scoring figure was in 1962, which was his fourth NBA season, but he only played in 48 regular season games because of an injury.

Robertson led the league in 1968 with an 87.3 FT% mark, yet 20 years later in 1988, he would have failed to even make the league top 10! Despite the above players' greatness, four of the 10 failed to shoot over 50 percent from the field even in their very best season. Russell's is especially peculiar since he was a center.

Table 1.18: Top 10: Most Assists, Rebounds and FTs in a Single Game

Player	Assists	Rebounds	FTs Made
Abdul-Jabbar	14	34	20
Barry	16	18	21
Baylor	14	28	20
Chamberlain	20	55	28
Cousy	28	11	19
Erving	12	18	17
Pettit	11	35	19
Robertson	22	17	22
Russell	12	51	15
West	23	13	20

Chamberlain holds two all time records from the above list: most rebounds and most free throws made in a single NBA game. Russell's 51 rebounds make him only the second player ever to grab more than 50 in a game.

Over 20 assists in a single game is considered brilliant. Robertson twice had 22 (and also made 22 free throws in three different games); Cousy's 28 is the third best ever—Kevin Porter's 29 is second. Scott Skiles holds the record (30 assists).

A player's versatility, and hence greatness, can be apparent from his non-scoring contributions such as assists and rebounds. Chamberlain is the only one from the above list to amass over 20 in each category, and the only center to dish out 20 assists in a single game.

Table 1.19—Top 10 Career Totals: Points, Rebounds, Assists, Minutes and Games

Player	Points	Rebounds	Assists	Minutes	Games
Abdul-Jabbar	38,387	17,440	5,660	57,446	1,560*
Barry	25,279	6,863	4,952	38,153	1,020
Baylor	23,149	11,463	3,650	33,863	846
Chamberlain	31,419	23,924	4,643	47,859	1,045
Cousy	16,960	4,786	6,955	32,805	924
Erving	30,026	10,525	5,176	45,227	1,243
Pettit	20,880	12,849	2,369	30,690	792
Robertson	26,710	7,804	9,887	43,866	1,040
Russell	14,522	21,620	4,100	40,726	963
West	25,192	5,376	6,238	36,571	932

*Abdul-Jabbar holds the all time career record for most points, most games, most seasons (20), and ranks third in rebounds. He is also first in minutes played as well as in several other career categories (see appropriate areas in the other chapters for more on all time career leaders).

Robertson has the most career points, rebounds and assists of any guard in history. Chamberlain has the most career rebounds while Pettit's career totals are all the more remarkable considering he played less than 800 games in his 11 seasons. Baylor's totals are similarly brilliant considering he only starred in 54 more games than Pettit.

Only four players ever totaled more career rebounds than career points: Wes Unseld with 13,769 rebounds and only 10,624 points; Paul Silas with 12,357 rebounds and only 11,782 points; Nate Thurmond with 14,464 rebounds and 14,437 points; Bill Bridges with 11,054 rebounds and 11,012 points.

Moreover, only three players in history have amassed more than 30,000 points, over 10,000 rebounds *and* starred in more than 1,000 games in their careers: Chamberlain, Abdul-Jabbar and Erving.

Table 1.20—Top 10 Career Totals: FGs and FTs

Player	FG Attempted	FG Made	FT Attempted	FT Made
Abdul-Jabbar	28,307	15,837	9,304	6,712
Barry	20,911	9,592	6,397	5,713
Baylor	20,171	8,693	7,391	5,763
Chamberlain	23,497	12,681	11,862	6,057
Cousy	19,620	6,168	5,756	4,624
Erving	23,097	11,730	8,052	6,256
Pettit	16,872	7,349	8,119	6,182
Robertson	19,620	9,508	9,185	7,694
Russell	12,930	5,687	5,614	3,148
West	19,032	9,016	8,801	7,160

Chamberlain and Abdul-Jabbar took the most shots from the field, and, accordingly sank the most. The same can be said for Erving. However, only Chamberlain and Moses Malone have tried 10,000 or more free throws in their careers. Only Robertson, West and Moses Malone have made over 7,000 career free throws. Malone is on the second best team ever list.

The list reflects the combined NBA/ABA totals.

The Second Team

The superstars who follow are ranked as the second top 10 players of all time. It was incredibly difficult to put any of these mega-talents on *any* second team since they had such outstanding careers; however, a dividing line had to be drawn somewhere.

Table 1.21—The Second Team Top 10 (in order)

1—Michael Jordan	6—Earvin "Magic" Johnson
2—Larry Bird	7—Dolph Schayes
3—George Mikan	8—Elvin Hayes
4—John Havlicek	9—Neil Johnston
5—Moses Malone	10—Paul Arizin

The hardest players to leave off were George Gervin, Bob McAdoo, Walt Bellamy, Hal Greer, Chet Walker, Dan Issel, Dave Bing, Artis Gilmore, Bob

Lanier and Nate Archibald. They *all* possessed inexhaustible genius and gargantuan mastery of the sport. Their career stats and overall skills are almost as brilliant and mind-boggling as the other 20.

Table 1.22—Second Team: Career Achievements (Regular Season)

Player	All NBA	Times Named: All Star	MVP	Years
Arizin	4	11	Never	1950–62
Bird	10	9	3	1979–1992
Havlicek	11	13	Never	1962–78
Hayes	6	12	Never	1968–84
Johnson	8	9	2	1979–92
Johnston	5	6*	Never*	1951–59
Jordan	6	6	2	1984–Present
Malone	8	12**	3	1974–Present
Mikan	6	4*	Never*	1946–56
Schayes	12	11	Never	1948–64

*Some of these great players were in their prime before the NBA Most Valuable Player was officially awarded. Its first year was in 1956, Pettit was the winner.

The same can be said of the All Star team selections, which wasn't until 1951, although non–all star game teams were chosen in the earlier leagues such as the BAA and NBL. See appropriate sections for more information. Jordan and Malone are still active (1993).

**Indicates Malone's NBA seasons only.

Additionally, only 16 players in NBA history have ever won the prestigious MVP award for the regular season and all but five are on the Top 20 Best Ever List. For various reasons, the following five were omitted from the list despite having won the MVP. They each won the award one time: Wes Unseld, Willis Reed, Dave Cowens, Bob McAdoo and Bill Walton.

The main reasons for omitting these five superstars, who are either already in the Hall of Fame or will eventually be inducted, was a lack of long-term, consistently brilliant seasons. They did not amass the huge career stats nor the regularly top echelon years—or at least not nearly as many as the other players in the Top 20 List.

Unseld was an all star only five of his 13 seasons and barely scored over 10,000 career points while only making All NBA once. Reed, who played 10 injury plagued seasons, made the All Star team seven times and was All NBA five times. He accrued over 12,000 career points and close to 8,500 rebounds, yet despite his value to his NY Knick teams, he never truly dominated a league as did the players in the top 20 with their high stats.

Dave Cowens made the All Star squads seven out of his 11 seasons and made the All NBA Second Team three times. However, his pro years were plagued by injuries and he only posted a 20-point season average twice. Despite his more than 10,000 career rebounds, Cowens also failed to dominate the league with either his scoring or rebounding figures.

The three-time NBA scoring champ certainly dominated the points category as well as any player who ever played, but Bob McAdoo only starred in six full seasons. His other eight were minimum efforts simply due to part-time play from injuries. He did manage to score almost 19,000 career points—certainly brilliant—but made the All Star team only five times and the All NBA team only two times.

Finally, Bill Walton, the 1978 League MVP, was the ultimate example of how injuries can destroy greatness; in 10 NBA seasons, he only managed to play in 468 games. That's a ridiculously low 47 games per 82 game season. How could he possibly have been able to muster big career or season numbers with such few chances of playing opportunities? The answer is, of course, that it was impossible. He only played in one of the two All Star games in which he was selected to participate and was only a two-time All NBA choice.

That's why these five players failed to make the list.

Table 1.23—Second Team: Playoff and All Star Game MVP Awards Won

	Times Named:	
Player	MVP in Playoffs	MVP in All Star Game
Arizin	Never*	1
Bird	2	1
Havlicek	Never	Never
Hayes	Never	Never
Johnson	2	2
Johnston	Never*	Never
Jordan	1	1
Malone	1	Never
Mikan	Never*	1
Schayes	Never*	Never

*Indicates that the Playoff MVP award wasn't officially given out until 1969, when Jerry West first won it. Thus, Mikan, Schayes, Johnston and Arizin never even had the opportunity to capture the honor. But they all had tremendous games as well. (Magic won his all star MVP awards in 1990 and in 1992.)

Just because most of these great players did not win these two major NBA awards does not mean that they failed to have outstanding games in both the postseason and the All Star games. In fact, Magic Johnson had brilliant assist games in both contests while Havlicek and Hayes had 20-plus point outbursts in the playoffs and the inter-league contests.

Moses Malone is one of only six players in history to capture three MVP awards in the regular season; this indicates his dominance among the all-time greats, as well as his superior value to his teams.

Table 1.24—Second Team Postseason Achievements: Rookie of the Year, Scoring and Rebounds

Player	Rookie of the Year	Times Named: Scoring Champ	Rebounds Champ
Arizin	No	2	Never
Bird	Yes	Never	Never
Havlicek	No	Never	Never
Hayes	No	1	2
Johnson	No	Never	Never
Johnston	No*	3	1
Jordan	Yes	6	Never
Malone	No	Never	6
Mikan	No*	3	1
Schayes	No	Never	1

*Indicates that the award wasn't yet officially given.

The Rookie of the Year Award began in the 1952-53 season. Don Meineke won it. Mikan was a rookie in 1946-47 with Chicago in the NBL. He did, however, lead the league in scoring that year. Neil Johnston was a Philadelphia rookie in 1952 and was a teammate of Arizin, who was in his third year. Mikan, Johnston, Schayes and Arizin dominated the early NBA—which began in 1946—along with Ed Macauley of Boston, Jim Pollard of Minneapolis, a teammate of Mikan's, as well as Vern Mikkelsen. Other dominant stars of this era included Bobby Wanzer and Bob Davies of Rochester, Andy Phillip of Philadelphia, Harry Gallatin and Carl Braun of New York, Slater Martin, also of Minneapolis, and, of course, the greats, Pettit, Cousy and a bit later, Russell and teammate Bill Sharman.

These stars were regularly selected to the All NBA teams and the All Star teams and laid the foundation for the rapid, surging growth of the NBA.

Before 1960, the NBA was only an eight-team league. Teams averaged a high-scoring 110 points a game and played a 72-game season. The playoffs consisted of a semifinal between the four best teams in the two divisions (Eastern and Western), a seven-game final, and a seven-game world championship series.

The set-shot was still being used as were hook shots and one-handers,

Neil Johnston (left) is one of only three players to be the scoring champ and FG% champ in the same season. (Photo courtesy of Naismith Memorial Basketball Hall of Fame.)

while a dunk was a rarity. But the game—through the aforementioned men—was grabbing much needed national attention and media coverage. Such media attention forced it to germinate into today's monumental sports institution.

The only six players to win the regular season MVP a minimum of three times were: Russell (five times); Chamberlain (four times); Abdul-Jabbar (six times); Malone (three times); Bird (three times); and finally, Magic Johnson (three times).

Table 1.25—Second Team Postseason Achievements: Assists, FT%, FG% and Minutes

	Times Named:			
Player	Assists Champ	FT% Champ	FG% Champ	Minutes Leader
Arizin	Never	Never	1	2
Bird	Never	3	Never	Never
Havlicek	Never	Never	Never	2
Hayes	Never	Never	Never	3
Johnson	4	1	Never	Never
Johnston	Never	Never	3	2
Jordan	Never	Never	Never	3
Malone	Never	Never	Never	2
Mikan	Never	Never	Never	Never
Schayes	Never	3	Never	2

Being the league leader in minutes played indicates enormous value to one's team, and hence, one's greatness. Magic, in 1992, surpassed Robertson's career assist total with over 10,000. Schayes, at 6′8″, was a tremendous FT shooter, and aside from Bird and Rick Barry, was the greatest free throw shooting big man of all time. Bird is 6′9″, and Barry is 6′7″.

Neil Johnston not only was a scoring champ three times but also was a FG% champ three times, which demonstrates his ability to maneuver for and pour in appropriate shots. In fact, aside from Chamberlain and Bob McAdoo, Johnston was the only scoring champ to also be a FG% champ in the same season (1953).

Table 1.26—Second Team Postseason Achievements: First Team NBA and Defense and Defensive Player of the Year

		Times Named:	
Player	First Team All NBA	First Team Defense	Defensive Player of Year
Arizin	4	Never*	Never*
Bird	9	Never	Never
Havlicek	11	5	Never
Hayes	6	Never	Never
Johnson	8	Never	Never
Johnston	5	Never*	Never*
Jordan	6	5	1
Malone	8	1	Never

Player	First Team All NBA	Times Named: First Team Defense	Defensive Player of Year
Mikan	6	Never*	Never*
Schayes	12	Never*	Never*

*Indicates that these categories were not yet officially awarded (see Top 10 comments). Again, it's very unfortunate that the NBA failed to recognize the importance of great defensive efforts.

Havlicek proved his versatility with many offensive and defensive team selections, yet never won the defensive player of the year honor. Magic Johnson, despite leading the NBA in steals twice—the same as Michael Jordan—failed to earn the defensive player of the year award as well.

Table 1.27—Second Team: Career Scoring Accomplishments

Player	Seasons at 30 Points a Game	50+ Points
Arizin	Never	Never
Bird	Never	6
Havlicek	Never	1
Hayes	Never	1
Johnson	Never	Never
Johnston	Never	2
Jordan	5	22
Malone	1	5
Mikan	Never	2
Schayes	Never	Never

For a player such as Mikan or Neil Johnston to score 50 points in a single game is tantamount to Jordan scoring at least 75 or 80. Why? Because in their era—the early 1950s—*teams* rarely scored more than 80 points in a game. So their high games possess even more significance.

Mikan was by far the dominant scorer of his day; the 6′10″ giant posted over 27 PPG for three seasons. Schayes averaged over 22 a game four seasons, while Johnston did the same five, and Arizin six seasons.

Jordan's astonishing twenty-two 50 point-plus games include four playoff games; two of his 50-point efforts were in back-to-back games, an unprecedented accomplishment. Magic, as great as he was, never hit for 50.

Table 1.28 – Second Team: Team Titles Won

Player	Team Championships in Career
Arizin	1
Bird	3
Havlicek	8
Hayes	1
Johnson	5
Johnston	1
Jordan	2
Malone	1
Mikan	7
Schayes	1

Table 1.29 – Second Team: Championship Teams

Arizin	Philadephia Warriors (1956)
Bird	Boston (1981, 1984, 1986)
Havlicek	Boston (1963–66, 1968–69, 1974, 1976)
Hayes	Washington Bullets (1978)
Johnson	Los Angeles (1980, 1982, 1985, 1987–88)
Johnston	Philadelphia Warriors (1956)
Jordan	Chicago Bulls (1991–92)
Malone	Philadelpia 76ers (1983)
Mikan	Chicago (1947) and Minnesota (1948–50 and 1952–54)
Schayes	Syracuse Nationals (1955)

Table 1.30 – Second Team: Number of Seasons Each Was Among the League's Top 10

Player	Points	Rebs	Asst	FT%	FG%	Seasons Played
Arizin	9	2	None	6	5	12
Bird	6	7	None	8	None	10
Havlicek	5	None	8	7	None	16
Hayes	7	13	None	None	None	16
Johnson	1	None	8	2	None	10
Johnston	6	5	None	2	6	8
Jordan	6	None	1	None	None	8
Malone	8	13	None	None	None	15
Mikan	8	6	2	1	5	9
Schayes	11	11	4	10	None	16

It would be very rare indeed for a guard to be among the league's year-end top 10 in FG%, due to the very nature of the guard's shot attempts—

mostly outside, except for drives. Mikan's first two pro seasons were in the NBL—not the NBA—and rebounds were not yet tabulated, so he would have had two more years in the top 10, hypothetically at least.

In fact, rebounds were not recorded officially for Mikan's first four pro seasons (two in the NBL and two in the NBA). Yet Mikan is the only player without a "None" in any column, which is proof of his true versatility and talent.

Table 1.31—Second Team: Career Per Game Averages (Regular Season)

Player	Points	Rebounds	Assists	FT%	FG%
Arizin	22.8	8.6	2.3	81.0	42.1
Bird	25.0	10.2	6.1	87.9	50.3
Havlicek	20.8	6.3	4.8	81.5	43.9
Hayes	21.0	12.4	1.8	67.0	45.2
Johnson	19.1	7.3	11.0	82.3	52.3
Johnston	19.4	11.3	2.5	76.8	44.4
Jordan	32.7	5.6	5.3	84.8	50.6
Malone	20.4	13.4	1.3	69.6	52.4
Mikan	22.6	13.4	2.8	77.8	40.1
Schayes	18.2	10.6	2.9	84.4	38.0

These ten players ripped the league apart during their respective reigns, and in their heyday too their stats just kept hurrying into the NBA record-books.

Jordan is the best scorer; Mikan and Malone tie for the best rebounder; Magic is by far the best passer; Bird is the top FT shooter, while Malone narrowly edges Magic as the standout FG shooter.

Table 1.32—Second Team: Career Per Game Averages (Playoffs)

Player	Points	Rebounds	Assists	FT%	FG%
Arizin	24.2	8.2	2.6	82.9	41.1
Bird	24.5	10.7	6.4	89.2	47.6
Havlicek	22.0	6.9	4.8	83.6	43.6
Hayes	22.9	13.0	1.9	65.2	46.4
Johnson	19.0	12.5	7.9	81.8	52.0
Johnston	15.0	11.2	3.3	73.4	39.0
Jordan	35.9	6.7	5.8	86.4	49.3
Malone	23.0	14.1	1.5	71.2	56.0
Mikan	23.5	13.9	2.0	76.7	40.3
Schayes	19.2	10.2	2.5	82.2	39.0

Jordan's scoring average (through the 1992 season) is the highest in playoff history. As if his phenomenal scoring in the regular season isn't enough, he seems to be able to reach an even higher plateau in postseason play, when his team needs it most.

Magic is the all time leader in total playoff assists; he had 1,800 as of this writing. He also ranks the closest to averaging a "Triple-Double" in the playoffs above anyone else, including Robertson (see Top 10 team charts). However, Magic does have over 100 triple-double games to his career.

Table 1.33—Second Team: Career Per Game Averages (All Star Games)

Player	Points	Rebounds	Assists	FT%	FG%
Arizin	15.2	5.2	0.7	82.9	46.6
Bird	14.0	7.9	4.2	83.3	42.6
Havlicek	13.8	3.5	1.5	75.6	48.1
Hayes	10.5	7.7	1.4	64.7	40.3
Johnson	14.1	5.3	13.9	89.5	44.3
Johnston	11.7	8.7	1.0	69.6	42.9
Jordan	21.5	2.5	2.8	68.8	48.6
Malone	9.0	10.0	1.5	48.9	56.4
Mikan	19.5	10.2	1.4	81.5	35.0
Schayes	12.5	9.5	1.5	84.0	44.0

Magic seems to be the only player who doesn't mind passing the ball in these heated ego battles; in fact, his per game assist average is much higher than Robertson's or Cousy's (see Top 10 team charts). He's the only player on either list, and of all time, to have amassed over 100 assists in these games. He also holds the single game record of 22.

Havlicek is one of only four players to have played in 13 All Star contests. Hayes and Schayes were in 12, as were Robertson and West. If one counts their ABA years, then Erving was in 16 games, while George Gervin and Barry were in 12, and Malone was in 13 contests.

Table 1.34—Second Team: Individual Game Scoring Highs

	Most Points in a:		
Player	Regular Season Game	Playoff Game	All Star Game
Arizin	44	38	26
Bird	60	43	23
Havlicek	54	54	26
Hayes	54	46	24
Johnson	46	42	21

John Havlicek had a career average of 13.8 points in his thirteen All Star games. (Photo courtesy of Naismith Memorial Basketball Hall of Fame.)

Player	Most Points in a: Regular Season Game	Playoff Game	All Star Game
Johnston	50	39	19
Jordan	69*	63**	40
Malone	53	42	27
Mikan	61	45	26
Schayes	46	41	21

**Indicates the all time record for a playoff game.

Obviously all these superstars could score a lot of points—even Arizin and Schayes were known as top scorers despite not reaching the elite 50-point mark in a single game. Nevertheless, one would be hard pressed to find more prolific offensive players than the 10 above (other than the Top 10 or George Gervin, Bob McAdoo, Dominique Wilkins and Adrian Dantley).

Table 1.35—Second Team: Highest Season Marks in Three Shooting Areas

Player	Top Season Average	Best FT%	Best FG%
Arizin	26.4	83.2	44.8
Bird	29.9	91.6	52.7
Havlicek	28.9	87.0	46.4

Table 1.35—Second Team: Highest Season Marks in Three Shooting Areas *(cont.)*

Player	Top Season Average	Best FT%	Best FG%
Hayes	28.7	76.6	50.1
Johnson	23.9	91.1	56.5
Johnston	24.4	82.6	47.6
Jordan	37.1	85.7	53.5
Malone	31.1	82.4	57.2
Mikan	28.4	80.3	42.8
Schayes	24.9	90.4	40.1

Hayes' 28.7 points per game was third in the league in 1971; however, as a rookie in 1969, he led the NBA in scoring—yet had a lower average of 28.4 a game. He was one of only a handful of rookies to lead the NBA in scoring (see Remarkable Rookies list in scoring section).

Malone's 31.1 ranked second in the entire league in 1982—Gervin was first at 32.2.

While the above stars from the 1950s era shot just about as well from the line as today's greats, their field accuracy—due to low percentage set-shots versus jump shots—was very poor. Few reached 50 percent in a year.

Table 1.36—Second Team: Most Assists, Rebounds and FTs in a Single Game

Player	Most Rebounds	Most Assists	Most FTs Made
Arizin	16	13	16
Bird	21	17	16
Havlicek	19	17	18
Hayes	35	11	17
Johnson	18	23	17
Johnston	39	8	14
Jordan	17	16	26
Malone	37	7	21
Mikan	31	9	20
Schayes	24	13	23

Wilt Chamberlain holds the single game rebound record with 55. Scott Skiles, in 1991, with 30 assists, shattered Kevin Porter's 29 mark. Chamberlain, along with Adrian Dantley, holds the free throws made in a single game record with 28.

Four of the above 10 players came quite close to amassing over 20 in each category. Havlicek, Bird, Johnson and Jordan had the best three figures in each area. Only Havlicek and Arizin failed to post 20 in at least one category while Schayes, Mikan and Malone were the only three to have at least 20 in two of the three categories.

Table 1.37 – Second Team Career Totals: Points, Rebounds, Assists, Minutes and Games

Player	Points	Rebounds	Assists	Minutes	Games
Arizin	16,266	6,129	1,665	24,897	713
Bird	20,109	8,799	5,609	28,786	847
Havlicek	26,395	8,007	6,114	46,471	1,270
Hayes	27,313	16,279	2,398	50,000	1,303
Johnson	15,390	6,344	10,000 +	27,849	859
Johnston	10,023	5,856	1,269	18,298	516
Jordan	16,726†	3,768	3,896	16,883	591
Malone	27,500†	16,729	2,981	43,707	1,318
Mikan	11,764	4,167*	1,245*	8,350*	520
Schayes	19,249	11,256	3,072	29,800	1,059

*Indicates that, unfortunately, Mikan's rebound, assist and minutes totals are not as high as they should be since those categories were not officially recorded when he broke into the pros in the late 1940s. However, to be fair, his totals are the closest accurate estimates considering the lack of complete stats on him. Mikan had about 1,000 rebounds a season when they were recorded, and so a projection would give him a far more accurate 9,000-plus career rebounds for his nine seasons.

†Means that these players' totals are increasing even more as this book goes to print (they are still active players).

Totals are through the end of the 1992 season. Only one player has amassed more than 1,000 career playoff assists: Magic Johnson with 1,800. Jerry West is second with 970.

In addition, consider that Mikan and Johnston only played *half* as many career games as Havlicek, Schayes, Hayes and Malone. That's interesting in relation to their respective point totals.

Again, if projected with an equal number of games as the others, both Mikan and Johnston may have easily amassed over 20,000 career points. But, aside from this hypothetical, there can be no question whatsoever that these two giants deserve to be ranked as high as they are.

Considering that two of the players – Malone and Jordan – are still active, their career totals are even more impressive. Malone, for example, is but one of only 11 in all of NBA history to have totaled 25,000-plus points.

Table 1.38—Overview of the Top 20 (in order): Comparative Career Honors and Single Game Highs

Player	All NBA	All Star	Most Points	Best Season
Robertson	11	12	56	31.4
Chamberlain	10	13	100	50.4
Pettit	11	11	57	31.1
Baylor	10	11	71	38.3
Abdul-Jabbar	15	18	55	34.8
Erving	12	16	63	31.9
West	12	13	63	31.3
Barry	10	12	64	35.6
Cousy	12	13	50	21.7
Russell	11	12	39	18.9
Jordan	7	7	69	37.2
Bird	11	11	60	29.9
Mikan	6	4	61	28.4
Havlicek	11	13	54	28.9
Malone	8	12	53	31.1
Johnson	10	11	46	23.9
Schayes	12	11	46	24.9
Hayes	6	12	54	28.7
Johnston	5	6	50	24.4
Arizin	4	11	44	26.4

Chapter 2

Top Centers

Table 2.1—The Top 16 Centers

Wilt Chamberlain	Bob McAdoo
Kareem Abdul-Jabbar	Bob Lanier
Bill Russell	Moses Malone*
Willis Reed	George Mikan
Neil Johnston	Nate Thurmond
Elvin Hayes	Walt Bellamy
Dan Issel	Wes Unseld
Artis Gilmore	Jerry Lucas

*Indicates player is still active (as of 1993).

Table 2.2—Second String Centers

Clyde Lovellette	Gus Johnson
Dave Cowens	Larry Foust
Bill Walton	Zelmo Beatty
Harry Gallatin	Hakeem Olajuwon*
Johnny Kerr	Ralph Sampson
Vern Mikkelsen	

*Indicates player is still active (as of 1993).

Some players, during their careers with different teams, also played the forward position; however, Elvin Hayes, Bob McAdoo, Willis Reed and Jerry Lucas, for example, are primarily known and recognized as centers since they played that position for the vast majority of their careers.

There can be no doubt that Abdul-Jabbar and McAdoo and Gilmore will eventually be inducted into the Hall of Fame thus securing their status among the all time greats.

Other Hall of Fame centers *not* on this list include: Dutch Dehnert, Bob Houbregs, Bob Kurland and Moose Krause. Among these three, only Houbregs, a 6′8″, 225 lb. center during the 1950s, played in the NBA (with several teams, including Milwaukee, Baltimore and Ft. Wayne, among others). However, Houbregs is not on my list due to the level of play during his 281 game NBA career; he was an all–American, dominant center at Washington and guided his squad to the NCAA final four in 1953, when he poured in 30 points per game that season. He is considered to have possessed the greatest hook shot in basketball history, but he just was not the standout player at the professional level that he was when wearing number 25 for his Huskies.

Clyde Lovellette is in the Hall of Fame. The 6′9″ former Kansas star posted NBA per game season marks of 20 plus points no less than six of his 11 seasons.

The NBA's two top centers today—David Robinson and Patrick Ewing—did not, as of this book's compilation, play in enough seasons (minimum of five) nor chalk up enough "great" seasons to qualify for inclusion among the game's all time best centers.

Table 2.3—Biographical Information

Player	Height	Weight	Birthdate	Year Drafted	Seasons Played	College
Abdul-Jabbar	7′ 2″	265	4/16/47		1970–89	UCLA
Beatty	6′ 9″	235	10/25/39	1962	1963–75	Prairie View
Bellamy	6′11″	245	7/24/39		1962–75	Indiana
Chamberlain	7′ 1″	275	8/21/36		1960–73	Kansas
Cowens	6′ 9″	230	10/25/48	1970	1970–83	Florida State
Foust	6′ 9″	250	6/24/28	1950	1951–62	LaSalle
Gallatin	6′ 6″	215	4/26/27	1948	1949–58	N.E. Miss.
Gilmore	7′ 2″	265	11/21/49		1972–88	Jacksonville
Hayes	6′ 9″	235	12/17/45		1969–84	Houston
Issel	6′ 9″	240	10/25/48		1971–85	Kentucky
Johnson	6′ 6″	230	12/13/38	1963	1964–73	Idaho
Johnston	6′ 8″	210	2/ 4/29		1952–59	Ohio State
Kerr	6′ 9″	230	8/17/32	1954	1955–66	Illinois
Lanier	6′11″	265	9/10/48		1971–84	St. Bonaventure
Lovellette	6′ 9″	235	9/27/29	1953	1954–64	Kansas
Lucas	6′ 8″	235	3/30/40		1964–74	Ohio State
McAdoo	6′10″	225	11/25/51		1973–86	North Carolina
Malone	6′10″	255	3/23/55		1975–Present	None
Mikan	6′10″	245	6/18/24		1947–56	DePaul
Mikkelsen	6′ 7″	230	10/21/28	1949	1950–59	Hamline
Olajuwon	7′ 0″	250	1/21/63	1984	1984–Present	Houston
Reed	6′ 9″	240	6/25/42		1965–74	Grambling

Player	Height	Weight	Birthdate	Year Drafted	Seasons Played	College
Russell	6' 9"	220	2/12/34		1957–69	San Francisco
Sampson	7' 4"	230	7/ 7/60	1983	1983–Present	Virginia
Thurmond	6'11"	235	7/25/41		1964–77	Bowling Green
Unseld	6' 7"	245	3/14/46		1969–81	Louisville
Walton	6'11"	235	11/ 5/52	1974	1975–87	UCLA

Table 2.4—Career Achievements: All NBA and All Star

Player	Times Named: All NBA	All Star
Abdul-Jabbar	15	18
Beatty	2*	5*
Bellamy	Never	4
Chamberlain	10	13
Cowens	3	7
Foust	2	8
Gallatin	2	7
Gilmore	5*	11*
Hayes	6	12
Issel	5*	7*
Johnson	4	5
Johnston	5	6
Kerr	Never	3
Lanier	Never	8
Lovellette	1	6
Lucas	Never	7
McAdoo	2	5
Malone	8	12
Mikan	6	4
Mikkelsen	4	6
Olajuwon	5	6
Reed	5	7
Russell	11	12
Sampson	1	3
Thurmond	Never	7
Unseld	1	5
Walton	2	2

*Indicates both NBA and ABA careers.

Mikan's totals would have been more had he not played *before* the official team selections were made. The game's premier centers—known here as "The Big 3"—were Wilt Chamberlain, Bill Russell and Kareem Abdul-Jabbar. No other centers in pro basketball history compiled more impressive game per game, season per season and overall career stats.

Table 2.5—The Top 16 Career Achievements: MVP and Rookie of the Year

Player	Times Named: MVP	All Star MVP	Playoff MVP	Rookie of Year
Abdul-Jabbar	6	Never	2	Yes
Bellamy	Never	Never	Never	Yes
Chamberlain	4	1	1	Yes
Gilmore	Yes*	1	Never	Yes*
Hayes	Never	Never	Never	No
Issel	Never	1	Never	Yes*
Johnston	Never	Never	Never	No
Lanier	Never	1	Never	No
Lucas	Never	1	Never	Yes
McAdoo	Yes	Never	Never	Yes
Malone	3	Never	1	No
Mikan	Never*	1	Never	No*
Reed	1	1	2	Yes
Russell	5	1	Never	No
Thurmond	Never	Never	Never	No
Unseld	1	Never	1	Yes

*Indicates award wasn't yet officially given out. Also, Gilmore and Issel won their awards in the ABA rather than the NBA.

McAdoo was also the league scoring champ in his 1975 MVP season. Only Pettit, Chamberlain and Abdul-Jabbar have done that along with Jordan, who did it in 1988.

Table 2.6—The Top 16 Career Achievements: Scoring, Rebounds, Blocks and FG% Champ

Player	Times Named: Scoring Champ	Rebound Champ	Block Champ	FG% Champ
Abdul-Jabbar	2	1	4	1
Bellamy	Never	Never	Never	1
Chamberlain	7	11	Never	9
Gilmore	Never	4*	2*	6*
Hayes	1	2	Never	Never
Issel	1	Never	Never	Never
Johnston	3	1	Never	1
Lanier	Never	Never	Never	Never
Lucas	Never	Never	Never	1

Jerry Lucas was a rookie when he won the FG% crown. (Photo courtesy of Naismith Memorial Basketball Hall of Fame.)

	Times Named:			
Player	Scoring Champ	Rebound Champ	Block Champ	FG% Champ
McAdoo	3	Never	Never	1
Malone	Never	6	Never	Never
Mikan	3	1	Never	Never
Reed	Never	Never	Never	Never
Russell	Never	4	Never	Never
Thurmond	Never	Never	Never	Never
Unseld	Never	1	Never	1

*Indicates in both his NBA and ABA careers.

Lucas won the FG% crown as a rookie in 1964 while Gilmore's six FG% titles were won four times in the NBA and two times in the ABA. Also, his two rebound titles were both in the ABA, as were his blocked shot titles.

Mark Eaton and Kareem Abdul-Jabbar were the only players ever to lead the NBA in blocked shots four times. Chamberlain's nine FG% titles make him, without a doubt, the best ever in that category. Malone's six rebounding crowns are second only to Chamberlain's 11 as the best ever. McAdoo was one of only five players to ever capture the league scoring title three times.

Neil Johnston and George Mikan played before blocks were an official category: however, they were so big for their eras—6′8″ and 6′10″—that surely they would have been among the league leaders had the category been recorded.

While Russell amassed more rebounds per game in his career than Malone, Malone, nevertheless, has two more career titles than Russell. Bellamy was third in league rebounding in both 1962 and 1963, behind Chamberlain and Russell. That is the closest the talented Chicago Zephyr ever came to capturing a rebounds crown.

Thurmond was second in the NBA in rebounds in 1973 at 17.1 per game. That was his best ranking ever. Chamberlain was first again that year—his last—at 18.6. Reed was regularly in the league top 10 in rebounds and had a career best ranking of fifth in 1965 as Rookie of the Year. He posted a solid 14.7 per game mark. Lanier was in the top 10 in rebounds, blocks, and FG% in 1974.

Table 2.7—The Top 16: Career Per Game Averages (Regular Season)

Player	Points	Rebounds	Assists	FT%	FG%
Abdul-Jabbar	25.3	11.5	3.8	72.1	56.1
Bellamy	20.1	13.7	2.4	63.2	51.6
Chamberlain	30.1	22.9	4.4	51.1	54.0
Gilmore	20.0	13.6	2.5	69.1	57.9
Hayes	21.0	12.4	1.8	67.0	45.2
Issel	23.0	9.4	2.4	79.7	49.9
Johnston	19.4	11.3	2.5	76.8	44.4
Lanier	20.1	10.1	3.1	76.7	51.4
Lucas	17.0	15.6	3.3	78.3	49.9
McAdoo	22.1	9.5	2.3	75.4	50.3
Malone	20.4	13.4	1.3	69.6	52.4
Mikan	22.6	13.4	2.8	77.8	40.1
Reed	18.7	12.9	1.8	74.7	47.6
Russell	15.1	22.5	4.3	56.1	44.0
Thurmond	15.0	15.0	2.7	66.7	42.1
Unseld	10.8	14.0	3.9	63.3	50.9

Chamberlain, obviously, was the most prolific scorer; he also nudged Russell in the rebounds category. Similarly, he beat out Russell by a mere tenth of a point in per game assists. However, the greatest FG shooter on the list is clearly Gilmore, while the best free throw marksman was Dan Issel by a significant margin.

Table 2.8—The Top 16: Career Per Game Averages (Playoffs)

Player	Points	Rebounds	Assists	FT%	FG%
Abdul-Jabbar	25.2	10.9	3.4	74.1	53.5
Bellamy	18.5	14.8	3.0	64.2	47.1
Chamberlain	22.5	24.5	4.2	46.7	52.2
Gilmore	16.9	9.9	2.2	68.5	56.7
Hayes	22.9	13.0	1.9	65.2	46.4
Issel	21.6	9.7	2.2	82.4	49.1
Johnston	15.0	11.2	3.3	73.4	39.0
Lanier	18.6	9.6	3.5	76.8	53.2
Lucas	12.4	10.0	3.0	78.6	46.7
McAdoo	18.3	7.6	1.4	72.4	49.1
Malone	23.0	14.1	1.5	71.2	56.0
Mikan	23.5	13.9	2.0	76.7	40.3
Reed	17.4	10.3	1.9	76.5	47.4
Russell	16.2	24.9	4.7	60.3	43.0
Thurmond	11.9	13.6	2.8	62.1	41.6
Unseld	10.6	14.9	3.8	60.8	49.3

The best playoff scorer was Abdul-Jabbar while Russell was the top rebounder per game. Russell was the top passer; Issel, the best FT shooter; and Gilmore was the highest FG% shooter in the playoffs.

Table 2.9—The Top 16: Career Per Game Averages (All Star Games)

Player	Points	Rebounds	Assists	FT%	FG%
Abdul-Jabbar	13.9	8.3	3.0	81.3	50.2
Bellamy	12.0	7.5	1.0	52.6	50.0
Chamberlain	14.7	15.2	2.8	50.0	59.0
Gilmore	11.0	7.5	1.3	69.5	61.1
Hayes	10.5	7.7	1.4	64.7	40.3
Issel	8.6	3.9	1.4	73.1	53.2
Johnston	11.7	8.7	1.0	69.6	42.9
Lanier	9.3	5.6	1.5	83.3	58.2
Lucas	12.7	9.1	1.7	90.5	54.7
McAdoo	17.6	6.0	1.2	73.7	57.8
Malone	9.0	10.0	1.5	48.9	56.4

Workhorse Willis Reed totaled 12,183 points in 10 injury plagued seasons. (Photo courtesy of Naismith Memorial Basketball Hall of Fame.)

Table 2.9—The Top 16: Career Per Game Averages (All Star Games) *(cont.)*

Player	Points	Rebounds	Assists	FT%	FG%
Mikan	19.5	10.2	1.4	81.5	35.0
Reed	12.6	8.3	1.0	75.0	45.2
Russell	10.0	11.6	3.3	52.9	45.9
Thurmond	6.2	8.8	0.4	37.5	32.6
Unseld	6.2	7.2	1.2	60.0	50.0

The eight players to win the All Star game MVP award from this group were: Issel and Gilmore (both in the ABA), Mikan, Lucas, Reed, Lanier, Chamberlain and Russell. No one won it more than once.

Table 2.10—The Top 16 Career Highs: Season Average, Points a Game, FT% and FG%

Player	Best Season Average	Most Points a Game	FT%	FG%
Abdul-Jabbar	34.8	55	78.3	60.4
Bellamy	31.6	44	67.4	54.4
Chamberlain	50.4	100	61.3	72.7
Gilmore	24.6	42	76.8	67.0
Hayes	28.7	54	76.6	50.1
Issel	30.6	47	85.0	51.6

Player	Best Season Average	Most Points a Game	FT%	FG%
Johnston	24.4	50	82.6	47.2
Lanier	25.7	48	81.8	57.2
Lucas	21.5	42	81.4	55.1
McAdoo	34.5	52	80.5	54.7
Malone	31.1	53	82.4	57.2
Mikan	28.4	61	80.3	42.8
Reed	21.7	41	78.5	52.1
Russell	18.9	39	61.2	46.7
Thurmond	21.9	36	75.4	44.6
Unseld	16.2	33	70.3	57.7

A center has won the scoring title six times since 1947. Chamberlain holds the highest scoring marks by a center, while the best FT shooter was Issel with a career mark of 79.7 percent. Mikan shot 77.8 percent, and Lanier shot 76.7 percent.

Table 2.11—The Top 16 Career Highs: Most Points (All Star and Playoff Game), Assists and Rebounds

Player	Most Points in a: All Star Game	Playoff Game	Assists	Rebounds
Abdul-Jabbar	25	46	14	34
Bellamy	23	41	11	34
Chamberlain	42	56	20	55
Gilmore	18	27	9	40*
Hayes	24	46	11	35
Issel	21	36	10	21
Johnston	19	39	8	39
Lanier	24	38	12	33
Lucas	25	41	11	40
McAdoo	30	50	10	29
Malone	27	42	11	37
Mikan	26	45	9	31
Reed	21	39	12	34
Russell	24	31	12	51
Thurmond	16	31	8	32
Unseld	11	30	12	35

*Indicates Gilmore grabbed 40 in an ABA game.

Chamberlain's 56 points is the all time record for a center. Chamberlain's 42 points is also the record for a center in an All Star game. Kareem

Abdul-Jabbar, as great as he was, never had even 50 points in a playoff contest. In fact, only 13 players in history ever did.

Table 2.12—The Top 16: All Defensive and NBA Championship Teams

Player	All Defensive Team	NBA Championship Team
Abdul-Jabbar	11	Milwaukee (1971) and Los Angeles (1980, 1982, 1985, 1987–88)
Bellamy	Never	Never
Chamberlain	2	Philadelphia (1967) and Los Angeles (1972)
Gilmore	1	Kentucky Colonels (1975)
Hayes	2	Washington Bullets (1978)
Issel	Never	Kentucky Colonels (1975)
Johnston	Never*	Philadelphia Warriors (1956)
Lanier	Never	Never
Lucas	Never	NY Knicks (1973)
McAdoo	Never	Los Angeles (1982 and 1985)
Malone	2	Philadelphia 76ers (1983)
Mikan	Never*	Chicago (1947) and Minnesota (1948–50 and 1952–54)
Reed	Never	NY Knicks (1970 and 1973)
Russell	1*	Boston Celtics (1957, 1959–66, 1968–69)
Thurmond	5	Never
Unseld	Never	Washington Bullets (1978)

*The All Defensive team selection officially began in 1968 so Russell, Mikan, Johnston—and even Thurmond and Chamberlain for parts of their careers—failed to get a fair shot at the team while in their primes. Abdul-Jabbar's 11 times include 10 times on the first team and once on the second.

Table 2.13—The Top 16 Career Totals: Points, Rebounds, Assists, Minutes and Games

Player	Points	Rebounds	Assists	Minutes	Games
Abdul-Jabbar	38,387	17,440	5,660	57,446	1,560
Bellamy	20,941	14,241	2,544	38,940	1,043
Chamberlain	31,410	23,924	4,643	47,859	1,045
Gilmore	24,941	16,330	3,050	47,134	1,329
Hayes	27,313	16,279	2,398	50,000	1,303
Issel	27,482	11,133	2,907	41,786	1,218
Johnston	10,023	5,586	1,269	18,298	516
Lanier	19,248	9,698	3,007	32,103	959
Lucas	14,053	12,942	2,730	32,131	829

Dave Cowens was selected as Co-Rookie of the Year in 1971. (Photo courtesy of Naismith Memorial Basketball Hall of Fame.)

Player	Points	Rebounds	Assists	Minutes	Games
McAdoo	19,787	8,048	1,951	28,327	852
Malone	27,500	16,729	2,981	43,707	1,318
Mikan	11,764	4,167*	1,245*	8,350*	520
Reed	12,183	8,414	1,186	23,073	650
Russell	14,522	21,620	4,100	40,726	963
Thurmond	14,437	14,464	2,575	35,875	964
Unseld	10,624	13,769	3,822	35,832	984

*Indicates Mikan's totals are the closest accurate estimates from the record books since some of his categories weren't yet recorded in his early seasons. Thus, his totals are on the conservative side. Malone is the only active player on the list.

Table 2.14—The Second String: Total Points and Scoring Average

Player	Total Points	Scoring Average
Beatty	13,490	18.3
Cowens	13,516	17.6

Table 2.14—The Second String: Total Points and Scoring Average *(cont.)*

Player	Total Points	Scoring Average
Foust	11,198	13.7
Gallatin	8,843	13.0
Johnson	9,944	17.1
Kerr	12,480	13.8
Lovellette	11,947	17.0
Mikkelsen	10,063	14.4
Olajuwon	9,783	22.5
Sampson	8,049	19.3
Walton	6,215	13.3

*Indicates Beatty's NBA and ABA career figures.

Table 2.15—The Second String: Individual Shooting Highs

Player	Highest Scoring Average	Best FT%	Best FG%
Beatty	23.6	83	57
Cowens	20.5	84	49
Foust	17.0	82	49
Gallatin	15.0	81	44
Johnson	20.7	74	47
Kerr	17.8	77	47
Lovellette	23.4	86	47
Mikkelsen	18.7	81	44
Olajuwon	23.5	67	51
Sampson	22.1	65	52
Walton	18.9	72	56

Don't let the fact that none of these centers ever posted a 30 point per game season average fool you. Remember, Lovellette, Cowens and Gallatin are all Hall of Famers—and the remainder of this list's members will, in time, most certainly be inducted.

Table 2.16—The Second String: Playoff Points, Playoff Average, and All Star Average

Player	Total Playoff Points	Playoff Average	All Star Game Average
Beatty	2,062	18.0	9.5
Cowens	1,684	18.9	12.7
Foust	902	12.4	7.0
Gallatin	768	12.0	8.1
Johnson	494*	7.9	13.4

Player	Total Playoff Points	Playoff Average	All Star Game Average
Kerr	933	12.3	4.3
Lovellette	963	14.0	13.3
Mikkelsen	1,141	13.4	11.2
Olajuwon	1,186	27.6	10.4
Sampson	711	18.7	16.3
Walton	528	10.8	15.0

*Indicates that Johnson's totals and stats are combined from both NBA and ABA.

Ralph Sampson's career was ruined by back and leg injuries after but a few years in the NBA. However, those seasons were enough for him, when healthy, to showcase his considerable scoring and offensive prowess. Olajuwon was, in the mid to late 1980s, considered the premier center in the NBA until the NY Knicks' Patrick Ewing and San Antonio's David Robinson—both 7-footers—came along. But they haven't played enough seasons yet to warrant inclusion on a greatest centers list.

Chapter 3

Top Forwards

There were, as of February 1992, more forwards in the Naismith Hall of Fame than either guards or centers. Maybe the reason for this is that to perform as a brilliant forward in the NBA requires possessing the most versatile basketball skills of all the positions.

Centers are rarely expected to be skilled dribblers or passers while guards are equally unexpected to manifest credible rebounding or blocked shot skills. The NBA forwards, or frontcourt players, are always expected to not only shoot and score but to help rebound, to help move the ball up court (passing and dribbling skills) and to protect their hoop.

The forward in basketball is similar to the catcher in baseball: the only player who must play both offense and defense simultaneously, though guards are also required to handle both ends of the court (although not with as much specific court coverage area as the frontcourtmen).

Most of the forwards on the Top Forward list are already in the Hall of Fame—a tribute to their monumental basketball skills.

Table 3.1—The Top 14 Forwards

Bob Pettit	Paul Arizin
Elgin Baylor	Spencer Haywood
Julius Erving	George McGinnis
Rick Barry	Ed Macauley
Larry Bird	Alex English
Dolph Schayes	Adrian Dantley
John Havlicek	Billy Cunningham

Table 3.2—Second String Forwards

Carl Braun	Bill Bradley
Bailey Howell	Cliff Hagan
Chet Walker	Tom Heinsohn

Table 3.2 — Second String Forwards *(cont.)*

Bill Bridges	Mel Daniels
Jim Pollard	Connie Hawkins
Jack Twyman	Maurice Stokes
Paul Silas	Bob Feerick
George Yardley	Alex Groza
Dave DeBusschere	Charles Barkley*
Joe Fulks	Bernard King*
Tom Gola	Dominique Wilkins*
Richie Guerin	

*Indicates player is still active (as of 1993).

Table 3.3 — Biographical Information

Player	Height	Weight	Birthdate	Year Drafted	Seasons Played	College
Arizin	6'4"	200	4/ 9/28		1951–62	Villanova
Barkley	6'6"	265	2/20/63	1984	1985–Present	Auburn
Barry	6'7"	220	3/28/44		1969–80	Miami
Baylor	6'5"	225	9/16/34		1959–72	Seattle
Bird	6'9"	220	12/ 7/56		1980–92	Indiana St.
Bradley	6'5"	205	7/28/43	1966	1968–77	Princeton
Braun	6'5"	180	9/25/27	1947	1948–62	Colgate
Bridges	6'6"	235	4/ 4/39	1961	1962–75	Kansas
Cunningham	6'5"	210	6/ 3/43		1966–76	North Carolina
Daniels	6'9"	225	7/20/44	1967	1967–77	New Mexico
Dantley	6'5"	210	2/28/56		1977–92	Notre Dame
DeBusschere	6'6"	225	10/16/40	1962	1963–74	Detroit
English	6'8"	190	1/ 5/54		1977–92	South Carolina
Erving	6'7"	210	2/22/50		1972–87	Massachusetts
Feerick	6'3"	190	1/ 2/20	1945	1946–50	Santa Clara
Fulks	6'5"	190	10/26/21	1946	1947–54	Murray State
Gola	6'6"	205	11/13/33	1955	1956–66	LaSalle
Groza	6'7"	220	10/ 7/26	1949	1950–51	Kentucky
Guerin	6'4"	215	5/29/32	1956	1957–70	Iowa
Hagan	6'4"	215	12/ 9/31	1956	1957–70	Kentucky
Havlicek	6'5"	205	4/ 8/40		1963–78	Ohio State
Hawkins	6'8"	215	7/17/42	1967	1968–76	Iowa
Haywood	6'8"	225	4/22/49		1970–83	Detroit
Heinsohn	6'7"	215	8/26/34	1956	1957–65	Holy Cross
Howell	6'7"	220	1/20/37	1959	1960–71	Miss. State
King	6'7"	205	12/ 4/56	1977	1977–Present	Tennessee
Macauley	6'8"	190	3/22/28		1950–59	St. Louis
McGinnis	6'8"	235	8/12/50		1972–82	Indiana
Pettit	6'9"	215	12/12/32		1955–65	LSU
Pollard	6'4"	190	7/ 9/22	1947	1948–55	Stanford

Player	Height	Weight	Birthdate	Year Drafted	Seasons Played	College
Schayes	6'8"	220	5/19/28		1949–64	NYU
Silas	6'7"	230	7/12/43	1964	1965–80	Creighton
Stokes	6'7"	240	6/17/33	1955	1956–58	Saint Francis
Twyman	6'6"	210	5/11/34	1956	1956–66	Cincinnati
Walker	6'6"	215	2/20/40	1962	1963–75	Bradley
Wilkins	6'8"	200	1/12/60	1982	1982–Present	Georgia
Yardley	6'5"	195	11/ 3/28	1953	1954–60	Stanford

Table 3.4—Career Achievements: All NBA and All Star

Player	Times Named: All NBA	All Star
Arizin	4	11
Barkley	4	5
Barry	10	12
Baylor	10	11
Bird	10	9
Bradley	Never	1
Braun	2	3
Bridges	Never	3
Cunningham	4	5
Daniels	5*	6*
Dantley	2	6
DeBusschere	1	8
English	3	7
Erving	12	16
Feerick	3	3
Fulks	3	5
Gola	Never	5
Groza	2	2
Guerin	3	6
Hagan	2	6*
Havlicek	11	13
Hawkins	3*	5
Haywood	5	5
Heinsohn	4	6
Howell	1	6
King	3	3
Macauley	4	7
McGinnis	5	6
Pettit	11	11
Pollard	3	6
Schayes	12	11
Silas	Never	7
Stokes	3	3

Table 3.4—Career Achievements: All NBA and All Star *(cont.)*

Player	Times Named: All NBA	All Star
Twyman	2	6
Walker	Never	7
Wilkins	4	4
Yardley	2	6

*Indicates both NBA and ABA or just ABA, for Daniels.

McGinnis' and Haywood's careers include both NBA and ABA figures. Schayes was selected for 12 All Star games but only played in 11. Dantley and English both have over 22,500 career points, which ranks them among the top 15 players in history.

Table 3.5—The Top 14 Career Achievements: MVP and Rookie of the Year

	Times Named:			
Player	MVP	All Star MVP	Playoff MVP	Rookie of the Year
Arizin	Never	1	Never*	No
Barry	Never	1	1	Yes
Baylor	Never	1	Never*	Yes
Bird	3	1	2	Yes
Cunningham	1*	Never	Never	Never
Dantley	Never	Never	Never	No
Erving	4	2	1	No
English	Never	Never	Never	No
Havlicek	Never	Never	1	No
Haywood	1	1	Never	Yes*
Macauley	Never	1	Never*	No
McGinnis	1*	Never	Never	No
Pettit	2	4	Never*	Yes
Schayes	Never	Never	Never*	No

*Haywood, McGinnis and Cunningham won their awards in the ABA. Also indicates that for Schayes, Arizin, Baylor, Macauley and Pettit, the Playoff MVP award wasn't officially given out during their careers or was awarded at the tailend of their careers, after their prime.

Erving won three MVP awards in the ABA and one in the NBA.

Table 3.6 — The Top 14 Career Achievements: Scoring, Rebounds, FT% and FG% Champ

Player	Times Named: Scoring Champ	Rebound Champ	FT% Champ	FG% Champ
Arizin	1	1	Never	Never
Barry	2	Never	9	Never
Baylor	Never	Never	Never	Never
Bird	Never	Never	3	Never
Cunningham	Never	Never	Never	Never
Dantley	2	Never	Never	Never
English	1	Never	Never	Never
Erving	3	Never	Never	Never
Havlicek	Never	Never	Never	Never
Haywood	1	1	Never	Never
Macauley	Never	Never	Never	1
McGinnis	1	Never	Never	Never
Pettit	2	1	Never	Never
Schayes	Never	1	3	Never

Only six forwards have ever won the rebounding title: Schayes, Pettit, Maurice Stokes, Truck Robinson, Charles Barkley and Michael Cage. A forward has never won the league assist title. Haywood's title was in the ABA in 1970.

Table 3.7 — The Top 14: Career Per Game Averages (Regular Season)

Player	Points	Rebounds	Assists	FT%	FG%
Arizin	22.8	8.6	2.3	81.0	42.1
Barry	26.9	7.0	4.6	89.0	47.1
Baylor	27.4	13.6	4.3	78.0	43.1
Bird	25.0	10.2	6.1	87.9	50.3
Cunningham	22.0	10.9	5.0	75.6	46.8
Dantley	25.5	6.0	3.1	82.0	54.6
English	22.3	6.0	3.8	82.7	51.2
Erving	25.4	9.4	4.4	77.8	50.8
Havlicek	20.8	6.3	4.8	81.5	43.9
Haywood	24.6	14.4	2.1	78.8	48.1
Macauley	17.5	7.5	3.2	76.1	43.6
McGinnis	21.0	11.3	3.8	66.7	46.3
Pettit	26.4	16.2	3.0	76.1	43.6
Schayes	18.2	10.6	2.9	84.4	38.0

Of the top 14 forwards, Elgin Baylor has the highest points per game average with 27.4. (Photo courtesy of Naismith Memorial Basketball Hall of Fame.)

Barry's and Erving's averages are combined from their NBA and ABA careers. Erving was a tremendous rebounder in his early ABA seasons. Baylor can be seen as the top scorer; Pettit is the best rebounder; the best passer of the bunch is Bird. Barry also wins the FT% mark while Dantley is the most accurate (FG%) shooter of the lot.

Table 3.8—The Top 14: Career Per Game Averages (Playoffs)

Player	Points	Rebounds	Assists	FT%	FG%
Arizin	24.2	8.2	2.6	82.9	41.1
Barry	29.2	6.9	4.1	87.6	46.0
Baylor	27.0	12.9	4.0	76.9	43.9
Bird	24.5	10.7	6.4	89.2	47.6
Cunningham	19.9	9.9	3.9	69.0	45.6
Dantley	22.2	5.6	2.4	79.6	52.7
English	24.6	5.6	4.4	86.3	50.0
Erving	26.5	10.0	4.7	78.7	50.8
Havlicek	22.0	6.9	4.8	83.6	43.6
Haywood	13.4	5.7	1.2	78.9	44.8
Macauley	13.8	6.8	2.9	72.9	43.7
McGinnis	19.2	11.3	3.8	66.9	42.9
Pettit	25.5	14.8	2.7	77.4	41.8
Schayes	19.2	10.2	2.5	82.2	39.0

Bird is both the best assist man and the top FT shooter on the list. Barry is the high scorer, while Dantley has the highest FG%.

Table 3.9 — The Top 14: Career Per Game Averages (All Star Games)

Player	Points	Rebounds	Assists	FT%	FG%
Arizin	15.2	5.2	0.7	82.9	46.6
Barry	14.0	5.1	4.5	84.5	45.9
Baylor	19.8	9.0	3.5	79.6	42.7
Bird	14.0	7.9	4.2	83.3	42.6
Cunningham	15.0	3.4	3.4	80.0	61.2
Dantley	12.6	4.6	1.4	89.5	42.6
English	8.1	2.1	1.6	50.0	47.5
Erving	20.1	6.8	4.0	78.6	50.7
Havlicek	13.8	3.5	1.5	75.6	48.1
Haywood	12.0	7.8	1.5	88.9	43.5
Macauley	11.9	4.6	2.6	85.4	38.7
McGinnis	14.2	9.7	2.5	50.0	42.3
Pettit	20.4	16.2	2.1	77.5	42.0
Schayes	12.5	9.5	1.5	84.0	44.0

All Star averages are usually very low due to much fewer minutes allowed to each player. Nevertheless, Pettit is the big winner in points and rebounds, and his four MVP awards prove that he has been the most dominant all star ever.

Table 3.10 — The Top 14 Career Highs: Season Average, Points a Game, FT% and FG%

Player	Best Season Average	Most Points a Game	FT%	FG%
Arizin	26.4	44	83.2	44.8
Barry	35.6	64	94.7	51.4
Baylor	38.3	71	83.7	48.6
Bird	29.9	60	91.6	52.7
Cunningham	26.1	50*	79.7	49.3
Dantley	30.7	57	86.0	58.0
English	29.8	47	86.2	55.1
Erving	31.9	63	84.5	52.1
Havlicek	28.9	54	87.0	46.4
Haywood	30.0	47	84.2	49.6
Macauley	20.4	46	79.9	48.6
McGinnis	29.8	58	74.0	49.9
Pettit	31.1	57	82.0	46.3
Schayes	24.9	46	90.4	40.1

Barry is the *only* player to belong to the exclusive 30–90–50 club: that is, to average over 30 points a game, shoot over 90 percent from the foul line,

Larry Bird, who retired in 1992, ranks as the best assists man on the top forwards list.

and 50 percent from the field in a single season. Bird came very close but his season average of 29.9 points was one-tenth of a point too little.

Table 3.11—The Top 14 Career Highs: Most Points (All Star and Playoff Game), Assists and Rebounds

Player	Most Points in a: All Star Game	Playoff Game	Assists	Rebounds
Arizin	26	38	13	16
Barry	38	55	16	18
Baylor	32	61	14	28
Bird	23	43	17	21
Cunningham	19	50	12	24
Dantley	23	46	11	19
English	16	42	16	20
Erving	30	45	12	18
Havlicek	26	54	17	19
Haywood	23	43	9	25
Macauley	20	39	10	19
McGinnis	23	42	10	23
Pettit	29	50	11	35
Schayes	21	41	8	24

The most points ever scored in a playoff game by a forward was Baylor's 61. The most points in an All Star game by a forward was Barry's 38 points.

Haywood's and McGinnis' rebounding and assist figures are for their

Billy Cunningham played for the Philadelphia 76ers—a team he would later coach. (Photo courtesy of Naismith Memorial Basketball Hall of Fame.)

NBA careers only. Haywood was the Rookie of the Year, scoring champ, rebounding champ, MVP and All Star game MVP all in the same fabulous 1970 ABA season with the Denver Nuggets (see Greatest Seasons chapter). McGinnis was the 1975 ABA scoring champ at 29.8 points a game and he also won his league MVP that year.

Arizin was sixth in league rebounding in 1952 at 11.3, his second pro season. In 1956, he ranked second in league scoring (for the second time, in addition to his scoring title) at 24.2 points, second in FG% at 45 percent and seventh in FT% at 81 percent. That is how versatile he was.

Bird, who regularly ranked in the league top 10 in rebounds and among the top five in FT% and points, had his best rebounding ranking in 1981. He was fourth with a solid 10.9 mark. Havlicek was never in the top 10 in league rebounding—he was only 6′5″ and not a brilliant leaper. However, his best assist season was in 1971 with a 7.5 per game figure and a fourth place ranking, behind three guards.

McGinnis also ranked eighth in NBA rebounding in 1977 at 11.5 a contest. "Easy" Ed Macauley was sixth in assists in 1953 at 4.1 as well as ranking fourth in points at 20.3 and second in FG% at 45 percent.

Cunningham, ranked third in league scoring at 24.8 in 1969 as well as tenth in rebounds with a healthy 12.8 average. Also, he was fourth in scoring at 26.1 and seventh in rebounding at 13.6 per game in 1970 for the Philadelphia 76ers—the team he would later coach.

Dantley and English are considered small forwards and were not required to rebound very much as part of their team roles. However, they were both high scorers. Dantley, in addition to leading the NBA twice (in 1981 and 1983) with a 30.7 and a 30.6 mark, also ranked in the league top three, in three other seasons. English ranked in the league top five no less than six times in addition to his 28.4 (points per game) NBA crown in 1983.

Table 3.12—The Top 14: All Defensive and NBA Championship Teams

Player	All Defensive Team	NBA Championship Team
Arizin	Never*	Philadelphia Warriors (1956)
Barry	Never	Golden State Warriors (1975)
Baylor	Never*	Los Angeles (1972)
Bird	3	Boston Celtics (1981, 1984 and 1986)
Cunningham	Never	Philadelphia 76ers (1967)
Dantley	Never	Detroit Pistons (1989)
English	Never	Never
Erving	Never	New York Nets/ABA (1974 and 1976)† and Philadelphia 76ers (1983)
Havlicek	8	Boston Celtics (1963–66, 1968–69, 1974, 1976)
Haywood	Never	Los Angeles (1980)
Macauley	Never*	St. Louis Hawks (1958)
McGinnis	Never	Indiana Pacers (1972–73)†
Pettit	Never*	St. Louis Hawks (1958)
Schayes	Never*	Syracuse Nets (1955)

*Indicates that the selection of All Defensive teams did not officially begin until after their careers were over or past their primes. Surprisingly, even though Barry led the entire NBA in steals in 1975, he failed to be named to either the first or second teams. Bird's three includes all second team selections. Havlicek's totals include five first team and three second team selections. McGinnis and Erving also were high in steals and deserved inclusion.

†Indicates ABA team for McGinnis and Erving (Nets).

Table 3.13—The Top 14 Career Totals: Points, Rebounds, Assists, Minutes and Games

Player	Points	Rebounds	Assists	Minutes	Games
Arizin	16,266	6,129	1,665	24,897	713
Barry	25,279	6,863	4,952	38,153	1,020
Baylor	23,149	11,463	3,650	33,863	846
Bird	17,899	7,319	4,396	27,560	717
Cunningham	16,310	7,981	3,305	26,844	770
Dantley	22,597	5,270	2,741	32,845	904
English	23,417	5,998	4,021	34,104	1,034
Erving	30,026	10,525	5,176	45,227	1,243
Havlicek	26,395	8,007	6,114	46,471	1,270
Haywood	17,111	8,675	1,541	29,408	844
Macauley	11,234	4,325	2,079	18,071	641
McGinnis	17,009	9,233	3,179	28,179	847
Pettit	20,880	12,849	2,389	30,690	792
Schayes	19,249	11,256	3,072	29,800	1,059

Table 3.14—The Second String: Total Points and Scoring Average

Player	Total Points	Scoring Average
Barkley	6,579	21.1
Bradley	9,217	12.4
Braun	10,652	13.5
Bridges	11,012	11.9
Daniels	11,107*	18.9*
DeBusschere	14,053	16.1
Feerick	3,134	13.0
Fulks	8,003	16.4
Gola	7,871	11.3
Groza	2,925	22.5
Guerin	14,676	17.3
Hagan	13,447	18.0
Hawkins	9,599	18.9
Heinsohn	12,194	18.6
Howell	17,770	18.7
King	15,778	22.7
Pollard	6,522	13.1
Silas	14,437	15.0
Stokes	3,315	16.4
Twyman	15,840	19.2
Walker	18,831	18.2
Wilkins	14,557	26.0
Yardley	9,065	19.2

*Indicates just ABA.

Table 3.15 — The Second String: Individual Shooting Highs

Player	Highest Scoring Average	Best FT%	Best FG%
Barkley	28.3	75	59
Bradley	16.1	88	46
Braun	16.5	85	47
Bridges	29.2*	78*	49*
Daniels	24.0	77	51
DeBusschere	18.1	77	46
Feerick	16.8	86	40
Fulks	26.0	86	35
Gola	15.0	79	46
Groza	23.4	79	48
Guerin	29.5	85	45
Hagan	24.8	85	51
Hawkins	30.2	82	52
Heinsohn	22.3	84	43
Howell	23.6	81	51
King	32.9	82	59
Pollard	15.5	81	40
Silas	17.5	78	47
Stokes	16.9	71	35
Twyman	31.2	83	49
Walker	22.0 (twice)	86	51
Wilkens	30.7	84	48
Yardley	27.8	82	45

*Indicates Bridges' marks were achieved in the ABL.

Bob Feerick was the NBA's FG% champ for the 1946-47 season. At 6'3", Feerick is the shortest player ever to win the award.

Table 3.16 — The Second String: Career Totals and Shooting Percentages

Player	Rebounds	Assists	FT%	FG%	Games	Seasons Played
Barkley	6,742	1,911	74	58	451	7
Bradley	2,354	2,533	84	45	742	10
Braun	2,122	2,892	80	38	788	13
Bridges	12,550*	2,821	72	47	1,034	14
Daniels	9,528*	1,138	62	42	639	9**
DeBusschere	9,618	2,497	70	43	875	12
Feerick	†	440	81	36	242	5
Fulks	1,379	587	77	30	489	8
Gola	5,605	2,953	76	43	698	10
Groza	709	318	76	47	130	2

Player	Rebounds	Assists	FT%	FG%	Games	Seasons Played
Guerin	4,278	4,211	78	42	847	13
Hagan	5,458*	2,640	80	47	840	13
Hawkins	5,450	2,556	78	49	616	9*
Heinsohn	5,749	1,318	79	40	654	9
Howell	9,383	1,853	76	48	951	12
King	4,807	2,507	72	53	857	13
Pollard	2,487	1,417	75	36	497	8
Silas	12,357	2,572	67	43	1,254	16
Stokes	3,492	1,062	70	35	202	3
Twyman	5,421	1,969	78	45	823	11
Walker	7,314	2,126	80	47	1,032	13
Wilkens	4,694	1,719	81	47	718	9
Yardley	4,220	815	78	42	472	7

*Indicates ABA and NBA career totals.

**Indicates Daniels didn't play during the 1975-76 season due to injury.

†Feerick's rebounds weren't yet officially recorded due to the early era in which he played.

Table 3.17 — The Second String: Playoff Points, Playoff Average and All Star Average

Player	Total Playoff Points	Playoff Average	All Star Game Average
Barkley	698	21.2	9.3
Bradley	1,222	12.9	4.0
Braun	561	14.0	7.5
Bridges	1,185	10.5	9.3
Daniels	1,901	17.4	18.9
DeBusschere	1,536	16.0	9.6
Feerick	101	11.2	†
Fulks	588	19.0	12.5
Gola	432	11.1	7.3
Groza	234	26.0	17.0
Guerin	654	15.6	10.5
Hagan	1,889*	15.7*	7.7
Hawkins	825*	23.8	6.7
Heinsohn	2,058	19.8	10.2
Howell	1,401	16.3	5.3
King	679	27.2	12.3
Pollard	977	13.6	12.0
Silas	1,124	6.9	4.0
Stokes	12	12.0	13.0
Twyman	621	18.3	14.8

Table 3.17—The Second String: Playoff Points, Playoff Average and All Star Average *(cont.)*

Player	Total Playoff Points	Playoff Average	All Star Game Average
Walker	1,916	18.2	8.1
Wilkens	1,151	26.8	15.3
Yardley	933	20.3	10.7

*Indicates career totals for both ABA and NBA.

†Bob Feerick played before all star totals were kept. Moreover, he never played in even one contest. Groza's averages are quite high solely due to having played in just one all star contest and in just one playoff series (consisting of only nine games).

Table 3.18—NBA and ABA Forwards with the Greatest Rookie Seasons

Player	Year	Team	Points	Rebs	Asst	FT%	FG%	All Star	All NBA
Bob Pettit	1955	Milw	20.4	13.8	3.2	75	41	Yes	Yes
Elgin Baylor	1959	Minn	24.9	15.0	4.1	78	41	Yes	Yes
Rick Barry	1966	S.D.	25.7	10.6	2.2	86	44	Yes	Yes
Spencer Haywood	1970	Den	30.0	19.5	2.3	78	49	Yes	Yes*
Sidney Wicks	1972	Por	24.5	11.5	4.3	71	43	Yes	No
Bob McAdoo	1973	Buff	18.0	12.4	2.5	77	45	No	No
Keith Wilkes	1975	G.St.	14.2	8.2	2.2	73	44	No	No
Adrian Dantley	1977	Buff	20.3	7.6	1.9	82	52	No	No
Larry Bird	1980	Bost	21.3	10.4	4.5	84	47	Yes	Yes
Terry Cummings	1983	S.D.	23.7	10.6	2.5	71	52	No	No

*Haywood captured the rookie of the year award in the ABA.

It is much more difficult, and hence, more prestigious, to earn a spot on the All NBA team as opposed to the All Star. Why? For one thing, there are fewer slots open on the All NBA squad (only 10). Secondly, all star berths, especially for rookies, are often reserved for the more exciting and flamboyant and higher-scoring players, as opposed to the most versatile.

However, in the last two years, the NBA has expanded its All NBA selections to three teams; this means, 15 players will be picked (not 10). This innovation will allow heretofore "lesser" players to be chosen.

It is a toss up between Baylor and Barry as to which frontcourtman posted the most prolific individual rookie campaign. Baylor also captured the prestigious All Star game MVP award that season as well.

But it's worth noting too that Haywood also was awarded both the regular season MVP award and the All Star game MVP trophy in the ABA in 1970.

Chapter 4

Top Guards

Fourteen guards have captured the league free throw title, while six forwards and only one center have done it (Jack Sikma was the center who won it in 1988).

The scoring title has been won by a guard twelve times. They were: Max Zaslofsky (1948); Dave Bing (1968); Jerry West (1970); Nate Archibald (1973); Pete Maravich (1977); George Gervin (1978–80 and 1982); and Michael Jordan (1987–89), seven players total.

Also, in the ABA, Charlie Scott, a guard for the Virginia Squires in 1972, led his league with a 34.6 per game mark.

The assist title has been won by a guard every year except in 1968, when Wilt Chamberlain won it as a center. The second tallest player to win the title (a guard) was 6′9″ Earvin "Magic" Johnson, who, as the chart indicates, won it four times.

Another four-time NBA assist champ who is not on the list is Kevin Porter, a 5′10″ flashy dynamo. He won the title in 1975, 1978, 1979 and 1981.

A guard has never won an NBA field goal title.

Table 4.1—The Top 20 Guards

Oscar Robertson	Walt Frazier
Jerry West	Calvin Murphy
Magic Johnson	Guy Rodgers
Michael Jordan*	Bill Sharman
Bob Cousy	Hal Greer
Pete Maravich	David Thompson
Isiah Thomas*	Gail Goodrich
Nate Archibald	Len Wilkens
George Gervin	Lou Hudson
Earl Monroe	Sam Jones

*Indicates player is still active (as of 1993).

Table 4.2 – Second String Guards

Bob Davies	Jo Jo White
Frank Ramsey	Dave Bing
K. C. Jones	Charlie Scott
Slater Martin	Kevin Porter
Bobby Wanzer	Louie Dampier
Al Cervi	Paul Westphal
Andy Phillip	Gene Shue
Max Zaslofsky	Norm Van Lier

West was known as a better defensive guard than Robertson (who was a superior assist man as well as a rebounder). West would have earned a spot on the All Defensive teams even more times but the category was not begun until 1968 (in West's eighth season).

The best defensive guards aside from West were Frazier, Jordan, Norm Van Lier, Jerry Sloan, Don Chaney, Slick Watts, Don Buse, Dennis Johnson, and Michael Cooper. However, these guards (aside from West, Frazier and Jordan, of course) were not known as superb offensive players; thus, they can't possibly be considered as among the all time greats.

Robertson was the most versatile guard and player ever. Despite not being awarded a spot on the all defensive squads, opponents will agree that he was far from a poor defensive player; he had instincts, anticipation, timing and quickness to play top notch defense on the league's premier guards.

However, West, Frazier and Jordan were better defenders. But Robertson's stats are head and shoulders above those three (and Cousy) especially in areas of rebounding, assists and FTs made.

There has, moreover, never been another guard, or player, for that matter, who could and did average 30 points, 10 assists and 10 rebounds a game. Jordan (and perhaps West) is as unstoppable offensively; however, not even Jordan has come remotely close to *averaging* 10 rebounds a game.

Table 4.3 – Biographical Information

Player	Height	Weight	Birthdate	Seasons Played	College
Archibald	6′ 1″	165	9/ 2/48	1971–84	UTEP
Bing	6′ 3″	180	11/24/43	1967–78	Syracuse
Cervi	5′11″	175	2/12/17	1938–53	None
Cousy	6′ 1″	175	8/ 9/28	1951–70	Holy Cross
Dampier	6′ 4″	175	11/20/44	1968–79	Kentucky
Davies	6′ 1″	175	1/15/20	1946–55	Seton Hall
Frazier	6′ 4″	205	3/29/45	1968–80	Southern Illinois
Gervin	6′ 7″	185	4/27/52	1973–86	Eastern Michigan

Cat-Quick "Clyde" Walt Frazier was a seven time All Defensive team selection. (Photo courtesy of Naismith Memorial Basketball Hall of Fame.)

Player	Height	Weight	Birthdate	Seasons Played	College
Goodrich	6′ 1″	175	4/23/43	1966–79	UCLA
Greer	6′ 2″	175	6/26/36	1959–73	Marshall
Hudson	6′ 5″	210	7/11/44	1967–79	Minnesota
Johnson	6′ 9″	225	8/14/59	1980–92	Michigan State
K. C. Jones	6′ 1″	200	5/25/32	1959–67	San Francisco
S. Jones	6′ 4″	205	6/24/33	1958–69	N.C. Central
Jordan	6′ 6″	195	2/17/63	1985–Present	North Carolina
Maravich	6′ 5″	200	6/22/47	1971–80	LSU
Martin	5′10″	170	10/22/25	1950–60	Texas
Monroe	6′ 3″	190	11/21/44	1968–80	Winston-Salem
Murphy	5′ 9″	165	5/ 9/48	1971–83	Niagara

Table 4.3—Biographical Information *(cont.)*

Player	Height	Weight	Birthdate	Seasons Played	College
Phillip	6′ 2″	195	3/ 7/22	1948–58	Illinois
Porter	6′ 0″	175	4/17/50	1973–83	Saint Francis
Ramsey	6′ 3″	190	7/13/31	1955–64	Kentucky
Robertson	6′ 5″	220	11/24/38	1961–74	Cincinnati
Rodgers	6′ 0″	185	9/ 1/35	1959–70	Temple
Scott	6′ 5″	175	12/15/48	1971–80	North Carolina
Sharman	6′ 1″	190	5/25/26	1951–61	USC
Shue	6′ 2″	175	12/18/31	1955–64	Maryland
Thomas	6′ 1″	185	4/30/61	1982–Present	Indiana
Thompson	6′ 4″	195	7/13/54	1976–84	N.C. State
Van Lier	6′ 2″	175	4/ 1/47	1970–79	Saint Francis
Wanzer	6′ 0″	170	6/ 4/21	1948–57	Seton Hall
West	6′ 2″	185	5/28/38	1961–74	West Virginia
Westphal	6′ 2″	195	11/30/50	1973–84	USC
White	6′ 3″	190	11/16/46	1970–81	Kansas
Wilkens	6′ 1″	180	10/28/37	1961–75	Providence
Zaslofsky	6′ 2″	170	12/ 7/25	1947–56	St. Johns

Table 4.4—Career Accomplishments: All NBA and All Star

Player	Times Named: All NBA	All Star
Archibald	5	6
Bing	3	7
Cervi	1	3
Cousy	12	13
Dampier	4*	4*
Davies	5	6
Frazier	6	7
Gervin	10	12
Goodrich	1	5
Greer	7	12
Hudson	Never	6
Johnson	8	9
K. C. Jones	Never	Never
S. Jones	3	5
Jordan	6	6
Maravich	Never	5
Martin	5	5
Monroe	1	4
Murphy	Never	1
Phillip	2	5
Porter	Never	Never

Player	Times Named: All NBA	All Star
Ramsey	Never	Never
Robertson	11	12
Rodgers	Never	4
Scott	2*	3*
Sharman	7	8
Shue	2	4
Thomas	5	9
Thompson	1	5
Van Lier	1	3
Wanzer	3	3
West	12	13
Westphal	4	5
White	2	7
Wilkens	Never	9
Zaslofsky	4	6

*Indicates averages and totals for both NBA and ABA years.

West only played in 12 All Star games, like Robertson, but was nominated for a 13th. However, he could not play due to an injury. Robertson made the All NBA first team nine times; West and Cousy made it 10 times.

Table 4.5 – The Top 20 Career Accomplishments: MVP and Rookie of the Year

Player	MVP	Times Named: All Star MVP	Playoff MVP	Rookie of the Year
Archibald	Never	1	Never	No
Cousy	Never	2	Never*	No
Frazier	Never	1	Never	No
Gervin	Never	1	Never	No
Goodrich	Never	Never	Never	No
Greer	Never	Never	Never*	No
Hudson	Never	Never	Never	No
Johnson	2	1	2	No
S. Jones	Never	Never	Never*	No
Jordan	1	1	1	Yes
Maravich	Never	Never	Never	No
Monroe	Never	Never	Never	Yes
Murphy	Never	Never	Never	No
Robertson	1	3	Never	Yes
Rodgers	Never	Never	Never*	No
Sharman	Never	1	Never*	No
Thomas	Never	2	1	No

Table 4.5—The Top 20 Career Accomplishments: MVP and Rookie of the Year *(cont.)*

Player	MVP	Times Named: All Star MVP	Playoff MVP	Rookie of the Year
Thompson	Never	2	Never	Yes†
West	Never	1	1	No
Wilkens	Never	1	Never	No

*Indicates Playoff MVP was not yet officially awarded.
†Thompson's award was in the ABA.

Table 4.6—The Top 20 Career Accomplishments: Scoring, Assists, FT% and Steals Champ

Player	Scoring Champ	Times Named: Assists Champ	FT% Champ	Steals Champ
Archibald	1	1	Never	Never
Cousy	Never	8	Never	Never*
Frazier	Never	Never	Never	Never
Gervin	4	Never	Never	Never
Greer	Never	Never	Never	Never*
Goodrich	Never	Never	Never	Never
Hudson	Never	Never	Never	Never
Johnson	Never	4	1	2
S. Jones	Never	Never	Never	Never*
Jordan	6	Never	Never	2
Maravich	1	Never	Never	Never
Monroe	Never	Never	Never	Never
Murphy	Never	Never	2	Never
Robertson	Never	6	1	Never
Rodgers	Never	2	Never	Never*
Sharman	Never	Never	7	Never*
Thomas	Never	1	Never	Never
Thompson	Never	Never	Never	Never
West	1	1	Never	Never
Wilkens	Never	1	Never	Never

*Indicates that steals weren't an official NBA category until 1973-74, which was after these men played.

Table 4.7—The Top 20: Career Per Game Averages (Regular Season)

Player	Points	Assists	Rebounds	FT%	FG%
Archibald	18.8	7.4	2.3	81.0	46.7
Cousy	18.4	7.6	5.2	80.3	37.5

Player	Points	Assists	Rebounds	FT%	FG%
Frazier	18.9	6.1	5.9	78.6	49.0
Gervin	24.1	2.5	6.0	83.8	50.1
Goodrich	18.6	4.7	3.2	80.7	45.6
Greer	19.2	4.0	5.0	80.1	45.2
Hudson	20.2	2.7	4.4	79.7	48.9
Johnson	19.1	11.0	7.3	82.3	53.3
S. Jones	17.7	2.5	4.9	80.3	45.6
Jordan	32.7	5.3	5.6	84.8	50.6
Maravich	24.2	5.4	4.2	82.0	44.1
Monroe	18.8	3.9	3.0	80.7	46.4
Murphy	17.9	4.4	2.1	89.2	48.2
Robertson	25.7	9.5	7.5	83.8	48.5
Rodgers	11.7	7.8	4.3	72.1	37.8
Sharman	17.8	3.0	3.9	88.3	42.6
Thomas	20.5	10.0	3.8	75.5	46.2
Thompson	24.1	3.5	5.1	78.6	51.2
West	27.0	6.7	5.8	81.4	47.4
Wilkens	16.5	6.7	4.7	77.4	43.2

Table 4.8—The Top 20: Career Per Game Averages (Playoffs)

Player	Points	Assists	Rebounds	FT%	FG%
Archibald	14.2	6.5	1.7	82.6	42.3
Cousy	18.5	8.6	5.0	80.1	32.6
Frazier	20.7	6.4	7.2	75.1	51.1
Gervin	26.1	2.8	7.7	81.7	50.1
Goodrich	18.1	2.7	3.1	81.9	44.2
Greer	20.4	4.3	5.6	81.2	42.5
Hudson	21.3	2.7	5.2	80.4	44.6
Johnson	19.0	7.9	12.5	81.8	52.0
S. Jones	18.9	2.3	4.7	81.1	44.7
Jordan	35.9	5.8	6.7	86.4	49.3
Maravich	18.7	3.8	3.7	78.4	42.3
Monroe	17.9	3.2	3.2	79.1	43.9
Murphy	18.5	4.2	1.5	93.6	47.5
Robertson	22.2	8.9	6.7	85.5	46.0
Rodgers	10.8	6.1	3.7	64.0	35.0
Sharman	18.5	2.6	3.7	91.1	42.6
Thomas	23.2	9.6	4.8	77.7	45.5
Thompson	24.7	3.4	5.5	79.2	50.2
West	29.1	5.6	6.3	80.5	46.9
Wilkens	16.1	5.8	5.8	76.9	39.9

The only player ever to lead the NBA in scoring and assists in the same season was Nate Archibald, who accomplished the feat in 1973. (Photo courtesy of Naismith Memorial Basketball Hall of Fame.)

Table 4.9—The Top 20 Career Highs: Season Average, Points a Game, FT% and FG%

Player	Best Season Average	Most Points a Game	FT%	FG%
Archibald	34.0	55	87.2	49.9
Cousy	21.7	50	85.5	39.7
Frazier	23.2	44	85.0	51.8
Gervin	33.1	63	87.9	54.4
Goodrich	25.9	53	86.4	49.5

Player	Best Season Average	Most Points a Game	FT%	FG%
Greer	24.1	38	83.4	47.8
Hudson	27.1	57	88.7	53.1
Johnson	23.9	46	91.1	56.5
S. Jones	25.9	42	85.7	47.6
Jordan	37.1	69	85.7	53.5
Maravich	31.1	68	87.0	45.8
Monroe	25.8	56	87.5	51.7
Murphy	25.6	57	95.8	52.2
Robertson	31.4	56	87.3	51.8
Rodgers	18.6	36	80.6	39.1
Sharman	22.3	39	92.1	45.6
Thomas	22.9	47	80.9	48.8
Thompson	27.2	73	84.9	53.9
West	31.3	63	87.8	51.4
Wilkens	22.4	37	82.8	46.6

Jordan poured in his 61 points twice with the Chicago Bulls. He also, in 1990, scored 69 points—surpassing Maravich's previous 68 (in 1977, when he was with the New Orleans Jazz).

The all time guard high is, of course, David Thompson's 73 points during the final game of the 1978 campaign when Thompson starred with the Denver Nuggets.

The highest single season scoring average for a guard also belongs to Jordan, with 37.1 in 1988.

Top guards were among the very best all time FT shooters: Calvin Murphy, Magic Johnson and Bobby Wanzer, the latter who shot over 90 percent from the line in 1952.

Also, Larry Costello, a 6'1" guard, of Syracuse and Philadelphia in the mid-1960s shot 88 percent twice in the NBA. Flynn Robinson, Ernie DiGregorio and Kyle Macy were also 90 percenters in their respective heydays.

Table 4.10—The Top 20 Career Highs: Most Points (All Star and Playoff Game) and Assists

Player	Most Points in a: All Star Game	Playoff Game	Assists
Archibald	27	28	23
Cousy	20	50	21
Frazier	30	44	19

Table 4.10—The Top 20 Career Highs: Most Points (All Star and Playoff Game) and Assists *(cont.)*

Player	Most Points in a: All Star Game	Playoff Game	Assists
Gervin	34	46	11
Goodrich	18	41	19
Greer	21	34	16
Hudson	15	44	10
Johnson	21	42	23
S. Jones	16	42	10
Jordan	40	63	17
Maravich	15	45	19
Monroe	21	43	18
Murphy	6	42	18
Robertson	28	43	22
Rodgers	8	31	28
Sharman	17	30	14
Thomas	30	43	25
Thompson	29	40	12
West	22	53	23
Wilkens	21	36	20

Table 4.11—The Top 20: All Defensive and NBA Championship Teams

Player	All Defensive Team	NBA Championship Team
Archibald	Never	Boston Celtics (1981)
Cousy	Never	Boston Celtics (1957, 1959–63)
Frazier	7	NY Knicks (1970 and 1973)
Gervin	Never	Never
Goodrich	Never	Los Angeles (1972)
Greer	Never	Philadelphia 76ers (1967)
Hudson	Never	Never
Johnson	Never	Los Angeles (1980, 1982, 1985, 1987–88)
S. Jones	Never	Boston Celtics
Jordan	5	Chicago Bulls (1991–92)
Maravich	Never	Never
Monroe	Never	NY Knicks (1973)
Murphy	Never	Never
Robertson	Never	Milwaukee Bucks (1971)
Rodgers	Never*	Never
Sharman	Never*	Boston Celtics
Thomas	Never	Detroit Pistons (1989–90)
Thompson	Never	Never
West	5	Los Angeles (1972)
Wilkens	Never	Never

*Indicates award wasn't yet official during their careers. West made the first team four times and the second team once.

During his career, Sam Jones helped his Boston Celtics win 10 NBA championships. (Photo courtesy of Naismith Memorial Basketball Hall of Fame.)

Table 4.12—The Top 20 Career Totals: Points, Rebounds, Assists, Minutes and Games

Player	Points	Rebounds	Assists	Minutes	Games
Archibald	16,481	2,046	6,476	31,159	876
Cousy	16,960	4,786	6,955	32,805	924
Frazier	15,581	4,830	5,040	30,965	825
Gervin	26,595	5,584	2,798	35,597	1,060
Goodrich	19,181	4,805	2,775	33,528	1,031
Greer	21,586	5,665	4,540	39,788	1,122
Hudson	17,940	3,936	2,432	29,794	890

Table 4.12—The Top 20 Career Totals: Points, Rebounds, Assists, Minutes and Games *(cont.)*

Player	Points	Rebounds	Assists	Minutes	Games
Johnson	15,390	6,344	10,000+	27,849	859
S. Jones	15,411	4,305	2,209	24,285	871
Jordan*	16,726	3,768	3,896	16,883	591
Maravich	15,948	2,747	3,563	24,316	658
Monroe	17,454	2,796	3,594	29,636	926
Murphy	17,949	2,103	4,402	30,607	1,002
Robertson	26,710	7,804	9,887	43,866	1,040
Rodgers	10,415	3,791	6,917	28,663	892
Sharman	12,665	2,779	2,101	21,793	711
Thomas*	16,371	3,818	8,309	25,993	864
Thompson	13,422	2,446	1,939	19,402	592
West	25,192	5,376	6,238	36,571	932
Wilkens	17,772	5,030	7,211	38,064	1,077

*Still active as of 1993.

Table 4.13—The Second String: Total Points and Scoring Average

Player	Total Points	Scoring Average
Bing	18,327	20.3
Cervi	3,872	10.2
Dampier	15,093	15.7*
Davies	7,771	13.7
K. C. Jones	4,999	7.4
Martin	6,940	10.2
Phillip	6,384	9.1
Porter	8,645	13.1
Ramsey	8,378	13.4
Scott	14,837	20.6*
Shue	10,068	14.4
Van Lier	8,547	13.1
Wanzer	7,090	11.7
Westphal	12,809	15.6
White	14,399	17.2
Zaslofsky	7,990	14.8

*Indicates averages and totals for both NBA and ABA years.

Earvin "Magic" Johnson is the NBA's all time career assists leader with over 10,000.

Table 4.14—The Second String: Individual Shooting Highs

Player	Highest Scoring Average	Best FT%	Best FG%
Bing	27.1*	82	47
Cervi	14.4	88	44
Dampier	24.8	86	51
Davies	16.2	79	41
K. C. Jones	9.2	69	41
Martin	13.6	83	41
Phillip	12.0	75	40
Porter	15.4	83	53

Table 4.14—The Second String: Individual Shooting Highs *(cont.)*

Player	Highest Scoring Average	Best FT%	Best FG%
Ramsey	16.5	84	45
Scott	34.6*	81	46
Shue	22.8	86	42
Van Lier	16.0	90	45
Wanzer	15.7	90	47
Westphal	25.2	86	53
White	23.1	88	48
Zaslofsky	21.0	86	38

*Indicates player also captured league scoring crown, Bing in the NBA while 6'6" Scott won the ABA scoring title.

Scott was, by far, the most prolific offensive player of this group. Norm Van Lier's 90 percent high in FT shooting was matched only by Bobby Wanzer's mark. And K. C. Jones' high in that category was many players' career *lows*! But he was never paid to be a Boston Celtic shooter. Defensive prowess was his forté.

Table 4.15—The Second String: Career Totals and Shooting Percentages

Player	Rebounds	Assists	FT%	FG%	Games	Seasons Played
Bing	3,420	5,397	78	44	901	12
Cervi	2,610	648	84	36	389*	9
Dampier	2,543	4,687	79	46	960	12
Davies	980	2,050	76	38	569*	10
K. C. Jones	2,399	2,908	63	39	676	9
Martin	2,302	3,160	76	36	745	11
Phillip	2,395	3,759	70	37	701	11
Porter	1,179	5,314	74	48	659	10
Ramsey	3,410	1,136	80	40	623	9
Scott	2,846	3,515	74	45	717	11
Shue	2,856	2,609	81	40	700	10
Van Lier	3,596	5,217	78	41	746	10
Wanzer	1,979	1,830	81	39	608*	10
Westphal	1,580	3,591	82	50	823	12
White	3,345	4,095	83	44	837	12
Zaslofsky	864	1,093	77	34	540	10

*Indicates career totals for these players were in both the NBA and during the earlier years of NBL play—before the NBA began.

Also, notice the much lower FG% for the pioneer guards such as Bob Davies, Slater Martin, Bobby Wanzer and Al Cervi and Max Zaslofsky. None had career averages above 40 percent, which today seems unheard of. For assist totals, the greatest passers in history have managed to amass a minimum of 5,000 career dishes. On this list, the only ones who achieved this were Kevin Porter, Van Lier, and Dave Bing.

Table 4.16—The Second String: Playoff Points, Playoff Average and All Star Average

Player	Total Playoff Points	Playoff Average	All Star Average
Bing	477	15.4	5.9
Cervi	216	8.0	*
Dampier	1,651	10.7	12.6
Davies	506	13.3	12.0
K. C. Jones	668	6.4	†
Martin	924	10.0	5.7
Phillip	428	6.4	6.8
Porter	363	11.0	†
Ramsey	1,331	13.6	*
Scott	824	21.0	7.4
Shue	569	17.8	13.2
Van Lier	530	13.9	1.7
Wanzer	554	14.6	9.2
Westphal	1,337	12.5	19.4
White	1,720	21.5	9.1
Zaslofsky	899	14.3	11.0

*Indicates that Frank Ramsey and Al Cervi played before All Star game records/stats were officially documented.

†Indicates that future Boston Celtic coach K. C. Jones and Kevin Porter, a four-time NBA assist champ, never were selected to play in a single All Star game.

Jo Jo White had the luxury of playing starting guard on many of the dominant Celtic squads, thus his high playoff point total.

Table 4.17—NBA and ABA Guards with the Greatest Rookie Seasons

Player	Year	Team	Points	Rebs	Asst	FT%	FG%	All Star	All NBA
Oscar Robertson	1961	Cin	30.5	10.1	9.7	82	47	Yes	Yes
Terry Dischinger	1963	Chi	25.5	8.0	3.1	77	51	Yes	No

Philadelphia playground legend Earl "The Pearl" Monroe starred for the New York Knicks in the NBA. (Photo courtesy of Naismith Memorial Basketball Hall of Fame.)

Table 4.17 – NBA and ABA Guards with the Greatest Rookie Seasons *(cont.)*

Player	Year	Team	Points	Rebs	Asst	FT%	FG%	All Star	All NBA
Dave Bing	1967	Detr	20.0	4.5	4.1	74	44	No	No
Earl Monroe	1968	Balt	24.3	5.7	4.3	78	45	No	No
Geoff Petrie	1971	Port	24.8	3.4	4.8	77	44	Yes	No
Charlie Scott	1971	VA	27.1	5.2	5.6	75	46	Yes	Yes*
Ernie DiGregorio	1974	Buff	15.2	2.7	8.2	90	42	No	No
Phil Ford	1979	K.C.	15.9	2.3	8.6	81	47	No	Yes

Player	Year	Team	Points	Rebs	Asst	FT%	FG%	All Star	All NBA
Darrell Griffith	1981	Utah	20.6	3.6	2.4	72	46	No	No
Michael Jordan	1985	Chi	28.2	6.5	5.9	85	52	Yes	Yes

*Charlie Scott played in the ABA that season. The highest scoring *rookie* guard in pro basketball history (all leagues) was Robertson with a 30.5 mark. In fact, he's the only rookie guard ever to post a 30-plus point per game mark. Jordan's 28.2 season average is second highest.

Moreover, as far as any rookie posting better than 30 points per game, playing any position, aside from Robertson, only Chamberlain (center), Spencer Haywood (forward in the ABA), and 1962 Rookie of the Year Walt Bellamy (a center) have ever done so.

Chapter 5

The Greatest Pro Games and Seasons

Table 5.1—Players and Their Greatest Games

Kareem Abdul-Jabbar In the 1980 NBA All Star game, Abdul-Jabbar had a terrific all around game with 17 points, 16 rebounds and 9 assists for the West squad. It ranks with Robertson's and Magic's best All Star games, yet Kareem didn't win the MVP award.

Paul Arizin In the 1952 NBA All Star game, the smooth forward scored 26 points and sank all eight of his free throw attempts (a 100% mark) to be named the game's MVP.

Michael Adams, Rick Barry and John Roche These three sharp-shooters all popped for a record eight three pointers in a single game. Barry did it first in 1980 for his Houston Rockets, while Roche did it in 1982 for the Denver Nuggets as did Adams in 1989. Michael Jordan and Larry Bird once made seven three pointers in one game.

Rick Barry On March 26, 1974, the forward for the Golden State Warriors sank 30 field goals in one game against the Portland Trail Blazers. He is the only player aside from Chamberlain to have ever done so. He totaled 64 points in that game. (See also under **Michael Adams**.)

Elgin Baylor On November 15, 1960, the second year phenom trounced the NY Knicks as he scored 71 points for his Los Angeles Lakers. He sank 28 field goals and 15 free throws to amass his mark—the most for any forward.

Larry Bird On March 12, 1985, the Boston Celtic great poured in 60 points against the New Orleans Jazz. He sank 22 field goals and hit on 15 free throws.

Bill Cartwright, Bob Pettit and Adrian Dantley All three talents share the NBA record for sinking 19 free throws in a single game *without a miss*. No one else has ever accomplished that accurate feat.

Wilt Chamberlain On November 2, 1960, the Philadelphia Warrior superstar hauled down a record 55 rebounds against Bill Russell's Boston Celtic team, the most ever in a pro game.

The second highest scoring single game of all time in the NBA also was by the "Big Dipper." Wilt poured in 78 points on December 8, 1961, against the Los Angeles Lakers, who would, ironically, become his future team.

Paul Arizin led the NBA in scoring two years and was named the All Star MVP in 1952. (Photo courtesy of Naismith Memorial Basketball Hall of Fame.)

Table 5.1—Players and Their Greatest Games *(cont.)*

On March 2, 1962, Chamberlain had a 100 point outburst against the NY Knicks. He sank 36 field goals and 28 free throws as his Philadelphia Warriors defeated the Knicks 169–147. The closest scorer on either team was Richie Guerin of the Knicks with 39 points. Wilt had 23 points after the first quarter, 41 at the half, 69 after the third quarter and 31 more by the end of the fourth. Only 4,124 fans witnessed the game!

In the 1962 NBA All Star game, Wilt scored a record 42 points in that talent-laden event. Surprisingly, Bob Pettit captured the MVP award with 25 points.

Bob Cousy On March 21, 1953, against the Syracuse Nationals, Boston's man sank a record 30 free throws in the playoff game. No other player has ever scored 30 points from the FT line.

Wilt Chamberlain and Adrian Dantley Both greats share the record of making 28 free throws in a single game. Wilt amassed 100 points in his game while Dantley totaled 45 points in his. Michael Jordan's best was 26 FTs made in a 1987 contest.

Adrian Dantley see under **Bill Cartwright** and **Wilt Chamberlain**

Julius Erving On February 19, 1975, "Dr. J.," in a contest against the San Diego Conquistadors in the ABA, soared for 63 points. He was with the New York Nets and the game went into quadruple overtime.

Joe Fulks On February 10, 1949, the talented forward exploded for 63 points for his Philadelphia Warriors in a contest against the Indianapolis Olympians. It took until 1961—twelve years later—for another player to top his single game effort, when Wilt Chamberlain had 67.

John Havlicek On April 1, 1973, the Boston Celtic great sank 54 points in a playoff contest against the Atlanta Hawks at Boston Garden. He made 24 field goals and six free throws.

Elvin Hayes The Big E, in the 1970 All Star game, amassed 24 points along with hauling down 15 rebounds. It was among the most dominant All Star performances ever, yet he failed to win the MVP award. It went to Willis Reed.

Earvin "Magic" Johnson In the 1984 All Star game, the superb guard amassed 22 assists, 15 points, and nine rebounds. He came only one rebound shy of recording an All Star game "triple-double."

Neil Johnston On December 4, 1954, the talented Philadelphia Warrior pulled down 39 rebounds in a single game against the Syracuse Nationals. Only four men in history have ever amassed more rebounds in one game.

Michael Jordan On April 20, 1986, the Chicago Bulls star broke Elgin Baylor's 25 year record for most points in a single playoff game. Jordan's 63 point explosion against the Boston Celtics at Boston Garden broke Baylor's 61 point mark by a bucket. The game went into double overtime.

On March 4, 1987, Michael poured in 61 points for his Bulls against the Detroit Pistons. Six weeks later, on April 16, 1987, "Air" matched his total against the Atlanta Hawks. In both games he sank 22 field goals along with 17 free throws.

"Air" exploded for 69 points for his Chicago Bulls on March 28, 1990, sinking 23 of 27 from the field. Only three players in NBA history (Chamberlain, Thompson and Baylor) ever scored more in one game.

Larry Kenon On December 26, 1976, the lanky and lithe forward recorded 11 steals in a single game for his San Antonio Spurs. He was playing against the Kansas City Kings with talented Nate Archibald in the backcourt yet still managed to rack up 11 thefts.

Moses Malone In a 1982 Houston Rockets game, Moses exploded for 53 points. While in the 1987 All Star game, the dominant center amassed 27 points along with 18 rebounds in 35 minutes of action.

Pete Maravich On February 25, 1977, the New Orleans Jazz superstar exploded for 68 points in a single game against the NY Knicks. It was the third highest point total by a guard in NBA history.

George Mikan On January 20, 1952, the center scorched the ropes for 61 points against the Rochester Royals. Aside from Joe Fulks, Mikan was the first man ever to top 60 points in one game. He was a Minneapolis Laker when he did it.

Pete Maravich was named to five All Star teams. (Photo courtesy of Naismith Memorial Basketball Hall of Fame.)

Table 5.1—Players and Their Greatest Games *(cont.)*

Bob Pettit The superstar forward grabbed 27 rebounds as he won the All Star game MVP award in 1962. (See also under **Bill Cartwright**.)

Kevin Porter The flashy and ultra-quick guard for the New Jersey Nets passed off for a record 29 assists in a single game against the Houston Rockets on February 24, 1978.

Willis Reed In the 1970 All Star contest, the bulky center totaled 21 points and 11 rebounds in 30 minutes of action, as he led the East squad to a victory.

Oscar Robertson In the 1961 inter-league event, Robertson scored 23 points, passed off for 14 assists and hauled down nine rebounds. He was just one board shy of recording a "triple-double" in an All Star game.

In the 1964 All Star game, the Big O poured in 26 points, grabbed 14 rebounds and dished off for eight assists in 42 minutes of action. He also won the game's MVP award.

John Roche see under **Michael Adams**

Bill Russell On February 8, 1960, the legendary Celtic grabbed an astounding 51 rebounds in a single contest against the Syracuse Nats. Only Chamberlain ever had more.

Dolph Schayes On January 17, 1952, the versatile frontcourtman for the Syracuse Nationals sank 23 free throws in a game. Only four players have ever made more.

On February 15, 1953, Schayes also made 21 free throws in a game against the NY Knicks.

Elmore Smith On October 28, 1973, the towering seven-foot Los Angeles Laker blocked a record 17 shots in a single NBA contest against the Portland Trail Blazers.

David Thompson On April 9, 1978, the final day of the season, Thompson poured in 73 points for his Denver Nuggets in a game against the Detroit Pistons. It was not only the most prolific performance in history by a guard, but was also the second greatest total by a player behind Wilt Chamberlain.

Jerry West On January 17, 1962, the Los Angeles Laker guard in a game against the NY Knicks scored 63 points, as he sank 22 field goals along with 19 FTs.

Table 5.2 — Players and Their Greatest Seasons

Kareem Abdul-Jabbar Perhaps his finest season was in 1970-71 when he captured the league MVP award; was the scoring champ at 31.7 a game; ranked second in FG% at 57.7 percent; ranked fourth in rebounds at 16.0 per game; and won the playoff MVP award and a team title with the Milwaukee Bucks. He was an NBA All Star and a first team All NBA selection.

In 1975-76 with the Los Angeles Lakers, Kareem captured the league rebounding title at 16.9; the blocked shots crown with 4.1 per game; and was second in league scoring at 27.7 points while being fifth in FG% at 52.9 percent. Also, he was the NBA MVP award winner and the minutes leader. This was at a time prior to the Lakers' league dominance.

Charles Barkley The burly forward from the 76ers, in 1987-88, ranked fourth in league scoring at 28.3 points a game; third in FG% at 58.7 percent; and sixth in rebounds at 11.9 a contest. He was, moreover, a first team All NBA choice and an All Star. He ranked in the top 10 in three of the eight year-end categories.

Rick Barry In the 1968-69 season with the Oakland Oaks of the ABA, Barry led the league in scoring at 34.0 per outing and in FT% at 88.8 percent. Moreover, the slick forward led his Oaks to the league championship and was named a first team All ABA member and an All Star game starter. The MVP award, however, went to Mel Daniels.

In 1974-75, the golden star of the Warriors was the NBA FT% champ at 90.4 percent; the steals champ at 2.9 per game as well as the playoff MVP. Moreover, the All Star and All NBA star led his Golden State club to the NBA title. The sharp-shooting forward was also sixth in the league in assists at 6.2 a game, and was the only forward to rank in the top 10 that year.

Table 5.2—Players and Their Greatest Seasons *(cont.)*

Elgin Baylor In the 1960-61 season, the Los Angeles Laker ranked second in scoring at 34.8 points; fourth in rebounds at 19.8 a game; ninth in assists at 5.1; and scored 49 points in a playoff game as well as 71 points in a regular season contest. He also had 56 and 57 points in two other games that year and was named a first team All NBA choice as well as an All Star. But no MVP.

In the 1962-63 season Baylor came as close as anyone could come to being named an MVP. He ranked second in league scoring with a 34.0 average; was third in FT% at 83.7; and fifth in league rebounding at 14.3 per game. He made the All NBA first team at forward; had 17 points and 14 boards in the All Star game and ranked fifth in league assists at 4.8 per contest. He was in the league top five—not top 10—in four year-end categories, yet the MVP award went to Bill Russell.

Dave Bing In 1967-68, the talented Detroit Piston guard was the league scoring champ at 27.1 points per contest; ranked fourth in assists at 6.4 a game; and was an All NBA first teamer as well as an All Star.

Larry Bird In 1983-84, Larry was the league MVP; the playoff MVP; the league FT% champ and won a team title. Moreover, he ranked seventh in scoring at 24.2 points and tenth in league rebounding with 10.1 a contest. He was unanimously chosen as an All NBA and an All Star.

In 1985-86, he was the NBA FT% champ at 89.6; the MVP; the playoff MVP and captured another team title. Furthermore, he ranked fourth in scoring at 25.8 a game; ninth in steals at 2.02 and fourth in three-point FG% with a mark of 42.3 percent. He was also seventh in rebounding with a 9.8 per game average. He was in the top 10 in four categories and named All NBA and an All Star.

Don Buse In 1976-77, the Indiana Pacer guard led the NBA in both assists and steals. His numbers were 8.5 and 3.5 per game, respectively. Like Slick Watts, Buse also made the NBA's first team All Defensive squad.

Wilt Chamberlain As a rookie in 1959-60, he showed his versatility by becoming the NBA scoring champ at 37.6 a game; the rebounding champ at 27.0; and was sixth in FG% at 46.1. Moreover, he was the All Star game MVP with his 23 points and 25 rebounds.

In 1960-61, he was the scoring champ at 38.4 points; the rebounding champ at 27.2 per and the FG% champ at 50.9. Needless to say in this—and all of the following seasons—he was an All Star and a first team All NBA selection.

In 1962-63, he again repeated the three above titles with numbers including: 44.8 points a game; 24.3 boards and a field goal mark of 52.8 percent.

In 1965-66, he again repeated his scoring, rebounding and FG% titles with 33.5 points; 24.6 boards and a 54.0 FG% mark. He also won the league MVP award as well and ranked seventh in league assists with 5.2 per contest.

In 1966-67, he was the rebounds champ at 23.8 a contest; third in scoring at 24.1 a game; third in assists with a 7.8 per game figure; and the league FG% champ at 59.5. Also, he won the MVP award, and his toned-down scoring produced an NBA team championship with the Philadelphia 76ers.

In 1967-68, Wilt was the MVP; the rebounding champ at 23.8 per; the FG% champ at 59.5; third in scoring at 24.3 points; and the minutes leader. His 76ers won 62 games and, he led the entire league in assists with 8.6 per.

In 1971-72 with the Los Angeles Lakers, Wilt was the rebounding champ at 19.2 per; the FG% champ with a 64.9 mark; and the playoff MVP as well as capturing another team title.

Bob Cousy In 1956-57, the Boston Celtic star won the league assists title with 7.5 a game; was the All Star game MVP with 10 points, seven assists and five boards; and was All NBA. Moreover, the "Houdini of the Hardwood" was the league MVP—the first guard ever to win it—and won a team championship. He was also eighth in league scoring at 20.6 points a game and sixth in league FT% at 82.1. He was in the league top 10 in no less than three categories.

Dave Cowens In 1972-73, Cowens made the second team All NBA squad as a result of his ranking of third in league rebounds at 16.2 a game. He was not in the top 10 in any other category. He only scored 20.5 points a game, but his Celtics made the Eastern Conference finals.

Louie Dampier In 1969-70, with the Kentucky Colonels of the ABA, the great guard led the league in three-point field goal percentage; ranked fifth in league scoring at 25.9 a game and ranked fifth in assists at 5.5 per contest. He led his Colonels to the semifinals of the league playoffs.

Mel Daniels In 1968-69, Daniels was the league rebounding champ at a whopping 16.5 per game mark and was in the top 10 in scoring at 22.3 a game. Also, the Indiana Pacer superstar led his team to the ABA finals against Barry's Oaks, and was a first team All ABA selection and an All Star starter.

In 1970-71, he was the league rebounding champ at 18.0; the All Star game MVP with 26 points and 17 rebounds; and the league MVP. He was a first team All ABA choice.

Ernie DiGregorio The remarkable rookie with the Buffalo Braves in 1973-74 led the league in assists with 8.1 a game and in FT% at 90.2. He was also the Rookie of the Year. He had 25 assists in one game that year.

Julius Erving His greatest pro seasons were, unquestionably, in the American Basketball Association. The "Doctor" ripped that league wide open, tearing apart and dominating just about every offensive category imaginable.

He soared and starred in that league for five seasons, from 1972 to 1976, with both the Virginia Squires and the New York Nets. He then entered the NBA with the 76ers.

Perhaps the all time greatest regular season in that colorful league's short history—and unarguably one of the finest in *any* professional league—was Dr. J.'s final ABA campaign.

In 1975-76, he ranked first in scoring (29.3 ppg); fifth in rebounds (11.0); ninth in FG% (51 percent); sixth in three-point FG% (33 percent); seventh in assists (5.0); tenth in FT% (80 percent); third in steals (2.5); and seventh in league blocked shots (1.9). Dr. J., amazingly, ranked in the league top ten that year in no less than all eight year-end statistical categories. This accomplishment has never been equaled in the 100 year annals of professional basketball.

A few seasons earlier, in 1973-74, Dr. J. ranked in the top 10 in six of the eight categories: first in scoring (27.4); ninth in FG% (51 percent); seventh in boards (10.7); sixth in assists (5.2); third in blocks (2.4); and third in steals (2.3 per game).

Bob Feerick The versatile star of the Washington Capitols had a brilliant season in 1946-47. He ranked in the league top 10 in every conceivable category. Bob was second in scoring at 16.3; the FG% champ at 40.1; fourth in FT% at 76.2; and ninth in league assists with 1.3 a game. The numbers were much lower compared to today, but nevertheless, he was among the elite players to rank in the league top 10 in every category in the same season.

Table 5.2—Players and Their Greatest Seasons *(cont.)*

Walt Frazier In 1969-70, Frazier delivered an NBA championship to his NY Knicks and was a first team All NBA selection as well as an All Star and an All Defensive first teamer. Frazier ranked second in league assists at 8.2 per game and ninth in FG% with a mark of 51.8 percent.

George Gervin In 1979-80, the Iceman led the league in scoring—for the third time—at 33.1 per game; poured in 55 points in a single game; was named a first team All NBA choice and was the All Star game MVP with 34 points and 10 rebounds.

Artis Gilmore In 1971-72 for the Kentucky Colonels of the ABA, the towering center was the Rookie of the Year, the league rebounding champ and the MVP. His boards mark was 17.8 a game. He was an ABA All Star and an All ABA team selection as well.

The 1973-74 season was even better—if that is possible. That year, Artis was again the league rebounding champ at 18.3 and the All Star game MVP with 18 points and 13 boards. Moreover, his Colonels won the team championship and he earned another All ABA team selection.

Cliff Hagan Thirteen years after Feerick's dominant season, St. Louis Hawk Cliff Hagan, in 1959-60, duplicated Feerick's top 10 ranking in every possible league category. Hagan ranked fifth in scoring at 24.8; fifth in FG% at 46.4; ninth in FT% at 80.3; tenth in rebounding with a solid 10.7 mark; and, finally, tenth in assists with a 4.0 per game figure. The 6'4" forward was also an All Star but, surprisingly, failed to be named to either the first or second All NBA team that year.

Note: Robertson, Chamberlain and Baylor all had seasons where they ranked in the top 10 in four of the five categories, and years in which they covered every category to be in the top 10; however none of them ever did it in the same season.

Chamberlain always fell short in FT%, while Baylor usually missed out in assists, and Robertson in rebounds.

John Havlicek In 1971-72, "Hondo" ranked third in NBA scoring at 27.5 per; fifth in assists at 7.5; seventh in FT% with an 83.4 mark; and was the league minutes leader. He was named a first team All Defensive choice and a first team All NBA selection as well as an All Star.

Connie Hawkins In 1967-68, the "Hawk" soared for his Pittsburgh Pipers in the ABA like a man possessed; Hawkins, in that league's first season ever, was the scoring champ at 26.8 points a contest; ranked second in league rebounding at 13.5 per and was a first team All ABA choice and an All Star starter as well. Moreover, the Hawk led his Pipers to capture the ABA championship and was the league MVP. He also ranked fourth in league assists with 4.6 a game.

Elvin Hayes As a 1968-69 rookie for the San Diego Rockets, he led the entire league in scoring with his 28.4 average and ranked fourth in rebounding with 17.1 grabs per outing. He was an All Star but lost out on the Rookie of the Year Award to Wes Unseld.

The Big E, in 1973-74, was the NBA champ in rebounding with his huge 18.1 per game mark; fifth in blocked shots at 3.0 per; and the league minutes leader. He was a second team All NBA member and an All Star. Also, he was on the NBA's All Defensive team.

Spencer Haywood In 1969-70, he had one of the most dominant pro seasons in recorded history. The fact that he was only a 20 year old rookie makes it even more astonishing. Haywood was the ABA scoring champ at 30.0 a game; the league rebounding champ at 19.5 a contest; the All Star game MVP; and the regular season

Cliff Hagan ranked in the top 10 of every league category in the 1959-60 season. (Photo courtesy of Naismith Memorial Basketball Hall of Fame.)

MVP. Of course, the Denver Nugget was also an All ABA first team choice and the Rookie of the Year.

Dan Issel In 1970-71, Issel was a rookie with the ABA's Kentucky Colonels. He led the entire league in scoring with his 29.9 points a game; was the Rookie of the Year and led the Colonels to a place in the ABA championships against Utah. He was a first team All ABA selection and an All Star starter as well.

Earvin "Magic" Johnson In 1986-87, Johnson won the league MVP award; the playoff MVP; a team title with his Los Angeles Lakers; and was the NBA assists champ at 12.2 per. He was tenth in scoring at 23.9 points as well and was All NBA and an All Star.

Michael Jordan In 1987-88, the Chicago Bulls superstar guard had one of the most dominant single seasons in NBA history: He was the league scoring champ at 35.0 PPG, the steals champ at 3.2, the defensive player of the year and the minutes leader. He was also named MVP for both the regular season and the all star game. In that game he grabbed eight rebounds, made four steals and blocked four shots in addition to his 40 points. He also won the game's slam-dunk contest that season. Moreover, he became the first player ever to amass over 200 steals and over 100 blocked shots in a single season. Oscar, West or Magic have never been such intimidating defensive forces. Jordan's overall scoring, defense and high-wire exploits generated one of the greatest seasons in NBA history.

Bernard King In 1984-85, the NY Knick led the NBA in scoring at 32.9 points a game; scorched the ropes for 60 points in one contest; and was a first team All NBA selection. He was, furthermore, an All Star game starter as well. He had consecutive 50 point games in one stretch of the year on top of that.

Bob Lanier In 1973-74, the Detroit Piston center ranked tenth in league scoring with a 22.5 mark; ninth in FG% at 50.4 percent; fourth in blocked shots with 3.04 an outing; and ninth in league boards at 13.3 per. Moreover, big Bob was the All Star game MVP with 24 points and 10 rebounds.

Table 5.2—Players and Their Greatest Seasons *(cont.)*

Jerry Lucas In 1967-68, the talented star of the Cincinnati Royals ranked second in rebounding at 19.0 a game; third in FG% with a 51.9 mark; and eighth in scoring at 21.4 points per contest. He was named as a first team All NBA member and an All Star.

Bob McAdoo Big Mac, in 1973-74, was the NBA scoring champ at 30.6 as well as the FG% winner at 54.7 percent. Moreover, during his second year as a pro, he was third in league rebounding at 15.1 and third in blocked shots at a 3.32 mark. He was in the top 10 in four categories.

In 1974-75, he topped his previous season with the league MVP award; another scoring title at 34.5 a game; a fifth place ranking in FG accuracy at 51.2 percent; and a fourth place ranking in rebounding at 14.1. Moreover, he also was sixth in blocks at 2.12 per contest. He was All NBA and an All Star both seasons.

George McGinnis In 1974-75, in the ABA, he ranked in the top 10 in five of the eight league stat categories: first in scoring (29.8); second in steals (2.6); third in assists (6.3); fifth in boards (14.3); and fourth in three-point FG% (35 percent). This was one of the ABA's all time greatest single seasons.

Moses Malone In the 1982-83 season, Moses was the NBA rebounding champ at 15.3; ranked fifth in scoring with his 24.5 average; and was tenth in blocked shots at 2.0. Also, he was the league MVP, a first team All Defensive team pick and an All NBA selection as well as an All Star. His Philadelphia 76ers won the NBA title, and he was the playoff MVP as well.

Pete Maravich In 1976-77, with the New Orleans Jazz, the Pistol led the NBA in scoring at 31.1 points a game; hit for an explosive 68 points in a single contest; and was named a first team All NBA member and an All Star starter.

George Mikan In 1948-49, he won the league scoring title at 28.3 points a game; was second in FG% at 41.6; and seventh in league assists at 3.6 a game. He was an NBA first team selection and his Lakers won their first NBA team championship. No MVP awards were given out at that time. Rebounds also were not yet recorded.

In 1950-51 Mikan was again the league scoring champ at 28.4 points a game; was second in league boards at 14.1 per; sixth in assists at 4.4; and third in FG% at 42.8. His free throw mark of just 80.3 percent missed the league top 10—it ranked 11th—or else he would have ranked in the NBA top 10 in every conceivable category that season. He was a first team All NBA pick and an All Star, and his Lakers squad just narrowly missed a spot in the NBA finals.

Hakeem Olajuwon The spectacular center from the Rockets, in 1987-88, matched Barkley's achievements when Hakeem ranked tenth in points at 22.8; third in rebounds at 12.1 a contest; and fourth in blocked shots with 2.71 per. He was also an All Star and a first team All Defensive choice as well as a first team All NBA member.

Bob Pettit In 1955-56, Pettit led the NBA in scoring at 25.7 a game; led the league in rebounds at 16.2 per; and was named the league MVP. Moreover, he was All NBA and the All Star game MVP, with his 24 points, 24 boards and seven assists. He was also ninth in FG accuracy at 42.9.

In 1958-59, he was the league MVP; the All Star game MVP with 25 points and 16 rebounds; a first team All NBA choice and ranked first in scoring at 29.2 a game; second in boards with a healthy 16.4 mark; seventh in FG% at .438; and reached the NBA Western Division finals.

Willis Reed In 1969-70, the NY Knick big man was the league MVP; the All Star game MVP with 21 points and 11 rebounds; the playoff MVP; and he won a team championship. Moreover, he was sixth in league rebounding with 13.9.

Michael Ray Richardson In 1979-80, the talented guard was the league assists champ at 10.1 a game and the steals champ with a 3.2 per game mark. The NY Knick was an All Star and a first team All Defensive team pick.

Oscar Robertson In the 1960-61 campaign, when he was just a raw rookie, he posted the following rankings: third in league scoring at 30.5 points a game; the assists champ at 9.7 dishes a game; ninth in FT% at 82.2; eighth in rebounds with 12.5 an outing and a fourth place FG% figure at 47.3. If that wasn't enough, he also captured the All Star game MVP award—that's right, as a rookie—as he hit for 23 points, 14 assists and nine rebounds. He was also a first team All NBA guard, along with Bob Cousy. He also averaged a "Triple-Double" for the entire season—a feat that has never been duplicated.

In 1963-64, he was second in scoring at 31.4 a contest; the league assists champ at 11.0; the league FT% champ at 85.3; and the NBA MVP. Also, he was All NBA and the All Star game MVP with 26 points, 14 rebounds and eight assists. It was a brilliant season.

Bill Russell In 1962-63, Big Russ was the League MVP; the All Star game MVP with 19 points and 24 rebounds; and won an NBA team title with his Boston Celtics. He also beat out Chamberlain for the first team All NBA center choice. He was, moreover, seventh in league assists at 4.5 a game and ranked second in rebounds at 23.0 a contest.

In 1964-65, Russell did even better. He was again the NBA MVP; led the entire league in rebounding at 24.1 a game; won another team championship; and was also on the first team All NBA squad. He was fifth in league assists at 5.3 a game and hauled down an awesome 49 rebounds in a single game that year as well. He was an All Star both seasons.

Dolph Schayes In the 1957-58 season, the versatile Syracuse National ranked first in league FT% with a 90.4 percent figure; was second in league scoring at 24.9 a game; fourth in rebounds at 14.2 per; and tenth in league assists with a 3.3 mark. Also, Dolph was the league minutes leader and a first team All NBA choice as well as an All Star. He lost the MVP award to Bill Russell.

John Stockton In 1988-89, the Utah Jazz sensation led the NBA in steals at 3.21 per and in assists at a whopping 13.6 a game. He was All NBA and a West squad All Star. Also, he ranked fourth in league FG% at 57.4 and was the only guard in the top 10 in that area.

Maurice Stokes As a Rochester Royal rookie in 1955-56, the gracefully talented forward was second in league rebounds—behind Pettit—at 16.3 a game; eleventh in scoring at 16.8; and ninth in NBA assists at 4.9. He was an All Star and an All NBA team selection as well as the Rookie of the Year. He also grabbed an awesome 38 rebounds in one game.

Wes Unseld In 1968-69, Baltimore Bullets rookie Wes Unseld scored 13.8 points a game and ranked in the league top 10 in only one category—rebounding. He was second at 18.2 a game.

Bill Walton In 1976-77, the Mountain man was the league rebounding champ at 14.4 per game and the blocked shots title winner with his 3.3 average. Also he ranked eighth in FG% at 52.8 and made the All Defensive first team.

The very next season, in 1977-78, Walton topped his past one. He was the league

Wes Unseld was the MVP and Rookie of the Year in 1969. (Photo courtesy of Naismith Memorial Basketball Hall of Fame.)

Table 5.2—Players and Their Greatest Seasons *(cont.)*

MVP; the fourth best blocked shots man at 2.52 a game; and All NBA, this time on the first team. Moreover, his Portland Trailblazers captured the league championship in 1977, and he was named the NBA playoff MVP that season as well.

Slick Watts In 1975-76, the ultra-quick Seattle Supersonic guard led the NBA in assists with an 8.1 mark and in steals with a 3.1 figure. The bald backcourtman became one of only a handful of pros ever to accomplish such a feat.

Jerry West In 1965-66, the Los Angeles Laker ranked second in league scoring at 31.3 points; fourth in assists at 6.1; fourth in FT% with an 86.0 mark; and tenth in FG% at 47.3. He was an All NBA first team selection and an All Star, and he made more free throws in that single season (840) than anyone in pro basketball history—before or since. West also led his Lakers to a place in the NBA finals against Boston.

Table 5.3—ABA Regular Season MVP Winners: Per Game Comparative Stats

Player/MVP	Year	Games	Points	Rebs	Asst	FT%	FG%
Connie Hawkins	1968	70	26.8	13.5	4.6	76	52
Mel Daniels	1969	76	24.0	16.5	1.5	60	48
Spencer Haywood	1970	84	30.0	19.5	2.3	78	49
Mel Daniels	1971	82	21.0	18.0	2.2	68	51
Artis Gilmore	1972	84	23.8	17.8	2.7	65	60
Bill Cunningham	1973	84	24.1	12.0	6.3	79	49
Julius Erving	1974	84	27.4	10.7	5.2	77	51
George McGinnis	1975	79	29.8	14.3	6.3	72	45
Julius Erving	1975	84	27.9	10.9	5.5	80	51
Julius Erving	1976	84	29.3	11.0	5.0	80	51

Comments: How do these greatest ABA MVP seasons compare with the best from the NBA? Very favorably. For example, Erving, who captured no less than three MVP awards in the ABA, had a higher scoring average during those seasons than 90 percent of NBA winners in their award years.

Weaker competition? Perhaps. But it was still a professional league, with much of the talent, at times on par, skillwise, with NBA counterparts, and the seasonal numbers, across the board, were quite impressive. NBA talent *was* generally considered better, however.

Table 5.4 — NBA Regular Season MVP Winners: Per Game Comparative Stats

Player/MVP	Year	Games	Points	Rebs	Asst	FT%	FG%	Scoring Rank	Position
Bob Pettit	1956	72	25.7	16.2	2.6	74	43	1st	F/C
Bob Cousy	1957	64	20.6	4.8	7.5	82	38	8th	G
Bill Russell	1958	69	16.6	22.7	2.9	85	35	17th	C
Bob Pettit	1959	72	29.2	16.4	3.1	76	44	1st	F/C
Wilt Chamberlain	1960	72	37.6	27.0	2.3	58	46	1st	C
Bill Russell	1961	78	16.9	23.9	3.4	55	43	18th	C
Bill Russell	1962	76	18.9	23.6	4.5	60	46	17th	C
Bill Russell	1963	78	16.8	23.0	4.5	56	43	19th	C
Oscar Robertson	1964	79	31.4	9.9	11.0	85	48	2nd	G
Bill Russell	1965	78	14.1	24.1	5.3	57	44	*	C
Wilt Chamberlain	1966	79	33.5	24.6	5.2	51	54	1st	C
Wilt Chamberlain	1967	81	24.1	24.2	7.8	44	68	3rd	C
Wilt Chamberlain	1968	82	24.3	23.0	8.6	38	60	3rd	C
Wes Unseld	1969	82	13.8	18.2	2.6	61	48	*	C
Willis Reed	1970	81	21.7	13.9	2.0	76	51	15th	C
Kareem Abdul-Jabbar	1971	82	31.7	16.0	3.3	69	58	1st	C
Kareem Abdul-Jabbar	1972	81	34.8	16.6	4.6	69	57	1st	C
Dave Cowens	1973	82	20.5	16.2	4.1	78	45	17th	C
Kareem Abdul-Jabbar	1974	81	27.0	15.1	4.8	70	54	3rd	C
Bob McAdoo	1975	82	34.5	14.1	2.2	81	51	1st	F/C
Kareem Abdul-Jabbar	1976	78	31.1	16.9	5.3	70	53	2nd	C
Kareem Abdul-Jabbar	1977	82	26.2	13.3	3.9	70	58	3rd	C
Bill Walton	1978	58	18.9	13.2	5.0	72	52	*	C
Moses Malone	1979	82	24.8	17.6	1.8	74	54	5th	C
Kareem Abdul-Jabbar	1980	82	24.8	10.8	4.5	77	48	6th	C
Julius Erving	1981	82	24.6	8.0	4.4	79	52	7th	F
Moses Malone	1982	81	31.1	14.7	1.8	76	52	2nd	C
Moses Malone	1983	78	24.5	15.3	1.3	76	50	5th	C
Larry Bird	1984	79	24.2	10.1	6.6	89	49	7th	F
Larry Bird	1985	80	28.7	10.5	6.6	88	52	2nd	F
Larry Bird	1986	82	25.8	9.8	6.8	90	50	4th	F
Magic Johnson	1987	80	23.9	6.3	12.2	85	52	10th	G
Michael Jordan	1988	82	35.0	5.5	5.9	84	54	1st	G
Magic Johnson	1989	77	22.5	7.9	12.8	91	51	15th	G

Jerry West was the first recipient of the Playoff MVP Award in 1969. (Photo courtesy of Naismith Memorial Basketball Hall of Fame.)

Table 5.4—NBA Regular Season MVP Winners: Per Game Comparative Stats *(cont.)*

Player/MVP	Year	Games	Points	Rebs	Asst	FT%	FG%	Scoring Rank	Position
Magic Johnson	1990	79	22.3	6.6	11.5	89	48	19th	G
Michael Jordan	1991	82	31.5	6.0	5.5	85	54	1st	G

*Indicates player's scoring rank wasn't even in top 20 that year.

Notice the scoring range of some of these league MVP winners: from Chamberlain's high of 37.6 (1960) to Russell's (1965) and Unseld's (1969) lows of 14.1 ppg and 13.8 ppg, respectively—almost 25 points difference. Also, notice the even wider range of rebounding totals. Why? Simply because only four players in NBA history who played the guard position ever captured the elusive MVP. They are Cousy, Robertson, Johnson and Jordan, and guards don't rebound like the frontcourt players.

Notice too that when Russell and Chamberlain faded from the scene that rebounding totals plunged continuously, year after year—partly as a consequence of higher shooting percentages (FG%) as players' skills increased during the early 1970s (i.e. fewer missed shots equals fewer rebound attempts).

Only nine players in history have won the season MVP award more than once. They are: Kareem Abdul-Jabbar (six times), Bill Russell (five times), Wilt Chamberlain (four times), Julius Erving (four times), Larry Bird (three times), Moses Malone (three times), Bob Pettit (two times), Magic Johnson (three times) and Michael Jordan (two times).

The greatest MVP season in history would probably be either Chamberlain's 1960 campaign (his numbers were simply staggering) or else Robertson's 1964 season. Both players also captured the mid-season All Star game MVP award in those seasons. It is strange that the year Wilt averaged his mind boggling 50.4 ppg (1962) that he wasn't voted the league MVP (Russell was). Maybe this is due to his team's loss in the Eastern Conference Finals (Russell's Celtics won the team title that year).

Table 5.5—NBA Playoff MVP Award Winners

1969	Jerry West	Los Angeles Lakers
1970	Willis Reed	New York Knicks*
1971	Lew Alcindor	Milwaukee Bucks*
1972	Wilt Chamberlain	Los Angeles Lakers*
1973	Willis Reed	New York Knicks*
1974	John Havlicek	Boston Celtics
1975	Rick Barry	Golden State Warriors*
1976	Jo Jo White	Boston Celtics*
1977	Bill Walton	Portland Trailblazers*
1978	Wes Unseld	Washington Bullets*
1979	Dennis Johnson	Seattle Supersonics*
1980	Magic Johnson	Los Angeles Lakers*
1981	Cedric Maxwell	Boston Celtics*
1982	Magic Johnson	Los Angeles Lakers*
1983	Moses Malone	Philadelphia 76ers*
1984	Larry Bird	Boston Celtics*
1985	Kareem Abdul-Jabbar	Los Angeles Lakers*
1986	Larry Bird	Boston Celtics*
1987	Magic Johnson	Los Angeles Lakers*
1988	James Worthy	Los Angeles Lakers*

Table 5.5—NBA Playoff MVP Award Winners *(cont.)*

1989	Joe Dumars	Detroit Pistons*
1990	Isiah Thomas	Detroit Pistons*
1991	Michael Jordan	Chicago Bulls*

*Indicates team also won the NBA title that year. The award was first officially given in 1969.

Table 5.6—ABA All Star Game MVP Winners: Per Game Comparative Stats

Player	Year	Minutes	Points	Rebs	Asst	FT%	FG%	High Scorer
Larry Brown	1968	22	17	3	5	100	71	No
John Beasley	1969	29	19	14	2	100	67	No
Spencer Haywood	1970	39	23	19	2	75	53	Yes
Mel Daniels	1971	30	29	13	3	71	63	Yes
Dan Issel	1972	23	21	9	5	75	69	No
Warren Jabali	1973	31	16	4	7	33	55	No
Artis Gilmore	1974	27	18	13	1	67	67	No
Fred Lewis	1975	33	26	5	10	100	71	Yes
David Thompson	1976	34	29	8	2	85	50	Yes

Comments: Warren Jabali, a 6′2″ guard, changed his name from Warren Armstrong in the early 1970s after converting to the Muslim faith. He had averaged over 20 points per game in his first two ABA seasons (1969 and 1970).

Another name probably unfamiliar to most fans is John Beasley. He was in his second season when he captured the MVP award. He was a 6′9″ center for the Dallas Chaparrals that year and had posted a 19.3 ppg mark before being named to the squad.

Also, six-foot guard Fred Lewis was a veteran ABA all star and was averaging 22.2 per contest (before winning the MVP) for the 1975 season. He should not be confused with a former player of the same name, who starred, at 6′2″, for the Sheboygan Redskins and the Indianapolis Jets, among other teams, during the 1940s.

Larry Brown is the same person who coached in the pros and at Kansas University. The 5′9″ sparkplug was an ABA rookie when he captured the All Star MVP award.

Haywood also totaled seven blocked shots in the 1970 contest.

Table 5.7—NBA All Star Game MVP Winners: Per Game Stats

Player	Year	Minutes	Points	Rebs	Asst	FT%	FG%	High Scorer
Ed Macauley	1951	31	20	6	1	85.7	58.3	Yes
Paul Arizin	1952	32	26	6	0	100.0	69.2	Yes*
George Mikan	1953	40	22	16	3	100.0	34.6	Yes
Bob Cousy	1954	34	20	11	4	100.0	40.0	No
Bill Sharman	1955	18	15	4	2	100.0	50.0	No
Bob Pettit	1956	31	20	24	7	85.7	41.1	Yes
Bob Cousy	1957	28	10	5	7	100.0	28.5	No
Bob Pettit	1958	38	28	26	1	80.0	47.6	Yes
Elgin Baylor	1959	32	24	11	1	80.0	50.0	No
Wilt Chamberlain	1960	30	23	25	2	71.4	45.0	No
Oscar Robertson	1961	34	23	9	14	77.7	61.5	No
Bob Pettit	1962	37	25	27	2	100.0	50.0	No
Bill Russell	1963	37	19	24	5	75.0	57.1	No
Oscar Robertson	1964	42	26	14	8	60.0	43.4	Yes
Jerry Lucas	1965	35	25	10	1	100.0	63.1	No
Adrian Smith	1966	26	24	8	3	100.0	50.0	Yes
Rick Barry	1967	34	38	6	3	75.0	59.2	Yes
Hal Greer	1968	17	21	3	3	71.4	100.0	No
Oscar Robertson	1969	32	24	6	5	100.0	50.0	Yes
Willis Reed	1970	30	21	11	0	100.0	50.0	No
Len Wilkens	1971	20	21	1	1	100.0	72.7	Yes
Jerry West	1972	27	13	6	5	50.0	66.6	No
Dave Cowens	1973	30	15	13	1	100.0	46.6	No
Bob Lanier	1974	26	24	10	2	100.0	73.3	Yes
Walt Frazier	1975	35	30	5	2	90.9	58.8	Yes
Dave Bing	1976	26	16	3	4	100.0	63.6	No
Julius Erving	1977	30	30	12	3	100.0	60.0	Yes†
Randy Smith	1978	29	27	7	6	83.3	78.5	Yes
David Thompson	1979	34	25	5	2	42.8	64.7	No
George Gervin	1980	40	34	10	3	66.6	53.8	Yes
Nate Archibald	1981	25	9	5	9	33.3	57.1	No
Larry Bird	1982	28	19	12	5	62.5	58.3	No
Julius Erving	1983	28	25	6	3	100.0	57.8	Yes
Isiah Thomas	1984	39	21	5	15	100.0	52.9	No
Ralph Sampson	1985	29	24	10	1	66.6	66.6	Yes
Isiah Thomas	1986	36	30	1	10	88.8	57.8	Yes
Tom Chambers	1987	29	34	4	2	66.6	52.0	Yes
Michael Jordan	1988	29	40	8	3	100.0	73.9	Yes
Karl Malone	1989	26	28	9	3	66.6	70.5	Yes†
Magic Johnson	1990	25	22	6	4	000.0	60.0	Yes

Table 5.7—NBA All Star Game MVP Winners: Per Game Stats *(cont.)*

Player	Year	Minutes	Points	Rebs	Asst	FT%	FG%	High Scorer
Charles Barkley	1991	35	17	22	4	100.0	53.3	No
Magic Johnson	1992	29	25	5	9	100.0	75.0	No

*In 1952, Arizin tied for game high scorer with George Mikan of the West squad. Arizin's East team coasted to victory, however, 108–91.

†In 1977, Erving tied with McAdoo, and in 1989 Malone tied with Jordan for game highs.

With the exception of Adrian Smith (1966), Randy Smith (1978), David Thompson (1979), George Gervin (1980), Magic Johnson (1990 and 1992), and the handful of still active players on this list, every other MVP winner is already in the Naismith Hall of Fame. Thompson, Gervin and Johnson most certainly will be inducted when their respective eligibility allows.

Chamberlain's 42 points in the 1962 contest (an all time high) were not enough to win the MVP award. Pettit's West squad won the game by 20 points, and, understandably, he won the MVP even though he was not the West's high scorer.

Table 5.8—The Best NBA Draft Seasons

The following seasons have resulted in some of the greatest players of all time entering the NBA in the same year.

1956 Bill Russell, Tom Heinsohn, K. C. Jones, Willie Naulls, Sihugo Green, Richie Guerin and "Hot Rod" Hundley.

1960 Oscar Robertson, Jerry West, Satch Sanders, Darrell Imhoff and Lenny Wilkens.

1965 Rick Barry, Bill Bradley, Gail Goodrich, Billy Cunningham and Jerry Sloan, and Tom and Dick Van Arsdale.

1970 Pete Maravich, Calvin Murphy, Nate Archibald, Dan Issel, Bob Lanier, Dave Cowens, Geoff Petrie, Spencer Haywood, Rudy Tomjanovich, Rick Mount, Jim McMillan, and high-scoring Charlie Scott. This was probably the finest draft year in NBA history.

1977 Walter Davis, Bernard King, Norm Nixon, Jack Sikma, Marques Johnson, Cedric Maxwell, Tree Rollins, Ricky Green, Ray Williams and Otis Birdsong. While there was a lot of good talent in 1977, it wasn't nearly as great as the 1970 draft.

1979 Larry Bird, Magic Johnson, Bill Cartwright, Vinnie Johnson, Jim Paxson and Sidney Moncrief.

1984 Michael Jordan, Charles Barkley, Hakeem Olajuwon, Sam Bowie, Michael Cage, John Stockton and Alvin Robertson.

Table 5.9—First Picks in the Annual NBA Drafts

Player	Year
Cazzie Russell	1966
Jimmy Walker	1967
Elvin Hayes	1968
Kareem Abdul-Jabbar	1969
Bob Lanier	1970
Austin Carr	1971
Larue Martin	1972
Doug Collins	1973
Bill Walton	1974
David Thompson*	1975
John Lucas	1976
Kent Benson	1977
Mychal Thompson	1978
Magic Johnson	1979
Joe Barry Carroll	1980
Mark Aguirre	1981
James Worthy	1982
Ralph Sampson	1983
Hakeem Olajuwon	1984
Patrick Ewing	1985
Brad Daugherty	1986
David Robinson	1987
Danny Manning	1988
Pervis Ellison	1989
Derrick Coleman	1990
Larry Johnson	1991
Shaquille O'Neal	1992

*ABA Choice.

Table 5.10—Some First Round Draft Picks Not #1 Overall

Player	Pick	Year
Bill Russell	3rd	1956
Jerry West	2nd	1960
Earl Monroe	2nd	1967
Walt Frazier	5th	1967
Wes Unseld	2nd	1968
Pete Maravich	3rd	1970
Bob McAdoo	2nd	1972
Julius Erving	12th	1972
Larry Bird*	6th	1978
Kevin McHale	3rd	1980
Isiah Thomas	2nd	1981

David Robinson was the first pick in the 1987 draft.

Table 5.10 – Some First Round Draft Picks Not #1 Overall *(cont.)*

Player	Pick	Year
Dominique Wilkins	3rd	1982
Michael Jordan	3rd	1984
Charles Barkley	5th	1984

*He was only a junior.

Table 5.11—Basketball's Triple Crown Contenders*

Player (NBA)	Season	Season's End Statistical Rankings in Each Category (Top Ten Rank or Better)					
		Points	Rebs	Asst	FG%	FT%	Other
George Mikan	1950-51	1st	2nd	6th	3rd	—	—
Neil Johnston	1952-53	1st	2nd	—	1st	—	—
Dolph Schayes	1957-58	2nd	4th	10th	—	1st	—
Wilt Chamberlain	1959-60	1st	1st	—	6th	—	—
Wilt Chamberlain	1960-61	1st	1st	—	1st	—	—
Oscar Robertson	1960-61	3rd	—	1st	4th	9th	—
Oscar Robertson	1961-62	3rd	8th	1st	4th	—	—
Wilt Chamberlain	1961-62	1st	1st	—	2nd	—	—
Wilt Chamberlain	1962-63	1st	1st	—	1st	—	—
Wilt Chamberlain	1963-64	1st	2nd	5th	2nd	—	—
Oscar Robertson	1963-64	2nd	—	1st	1st	—	—
Wilt Chamberlain	1964-65	1st	2nd	—	1st	—	—
Oscar Robertson	1964-65	3rd	—	1st	9th	2nd	—
Wilt Chamberlain	1965-66	1st	1st	7th	1st	—	—
Wilt Chamberlain	1966-67	3rd	1st	3rd	1st	—	—
Wilt Chamberlain†	1967-68	3rd	1st	1st	1st	—	—
Nate Archibald	1972-73	1st	—	1st	—	11th (tied)	—
Bob McAdoo	1973-74	1st	3rd	—	1st	—	3rd/Blocks
Rick Barry	1974-75	2nd	—	6th	—	1st	1st/Steals
Kareem Abdul-Jabbar	1975-76	2nd	1st	—	5th	—	1st/Blocks
Larry Bird	1984-85	2nd	8th	—	—	6th	2nd/3-pt FG%
Connie Hawkins	1967-68	1st	2nd	4th	2nd	—	—
Artis Gilmore	1972-73	10th	1st	—	1st	—	—
Julius Erving	1973-74	1st	7th	5th	9th	—	3rd/Steals and 3rd/Blocks
George McGinnis	1974-75	1st	5th	3rd	—	—	2nd/Steals and 4th 3-pt FG%
Julius Erving	1975-76	1st	5th	7th	9th	10th	3rd/Steals

*Points, rebounds and assists.
†Wilt's 1967-68 season was the closest any player has ever come.

One final note on the best pro basketball seasons in history: While baseball has its "triple-crown" (that is, one player totaling the number one league ranking in home runs, RBIs and batting average), basketball has no such honor.

The basketball equivalent of the "triple-crown" would be for a single player to rank number one in scoring average, assists, and rebounds.

The problem is that while a guard can grab the assists and pour in the points, he usually falls far short in rebounds. Similarly, while a larger forward or center can rank up front in rebounds as well as points, his efforts in the assists category fall short.

Both of these predicaments are due to the nature of the position—unlike baseball where a single player has the opportunity, without position limitations, to capture all three categories.

However, in basketball, the closest anyone has ranked in a single pro (NBA/ABA) season in capturing the basketball "triple-crown" is Wilt Chamberlain (1968): first in assists and rebounds and third in scoring.

Table 5.12—Rookie of the Year Winners (ABA): Season Per Game Comparative Stats

Player	Year	Games	Points	Rebs	Asst	FT%	FG%
Mel Daniels	1968	78	22.2	15.8	1.4	58	41
War Armstrong	1969	71	21.5	9.7	3.5	68	45
Spencer Haywood	1970	84	30.0	19.5	2.3	78	49
Dan Issel	1971	83	29.9	13.2	2.0	81	49
(co-winners)							
Charlie Scott	1971	84	27.1	5.2	5.6	75	46
Artis Gilmore	1972	84	23.8	17.8	2.7	65	60
Brian Taylor	1973	63	15.3	3.2	2.8	74	51
Swen Nater	1974	79	13.6	12.6	1.5	69	55
Marvin Barnes	1975	77	24.0	15.6	3.2	67	50
David Thompson	1976	83	26.0	6.3	3.7	79	51

Notice the low per game assist averages, which is indicative of the position played by each winner. Except for Brian Taylor, Charlie Scott and jumping jack David Thompson, the seven others were all frontcourtmen (either forwards or centers).

Moreover, notice from both this chart and the MVP chart that Spencer Haywood captured both the Rookie of the Year and the MVP award during the same season (as did Artis Gilmore). For comparison, the only NBA stars to achieve such a feat were Wilt Chamberlain in 1960 and Wes Unseld in 1969. Two players in each league—only four in pro basketball history.

Table 5.13 — Rookie of the Year Winners (NBA): Season Per Game Stats

Player	Year Won	Games	Points	Rebs	Asst	FT%	FG%	Team
Don Meineke	1953	68	10.8	6.9	2.4	78	38	Ft. Wayne
Ray Felix	1954	72	17.6	13.3	1.1	64	42	Balt
Bob Pettit	1955	72	20.4	13.8	3.2	75	41	Milw
Maurice Stokes	1956	67	16.8	16.3	4.9	71	35	Roch
Tom Heinsohn	1957	72	16.2	9.9	1.6	79	40	Bost
Woody Sauldsberry	1958	71	12.8	10.3	0.82	62	36	Phil
Elgin Baylor	1959	70	24.9	15.0	4.1	78	41	Minn
Wilt Chamberlain	1960	72	37.6	27.0	2.3	58	46	Phil
Oscar Robertson	1961	71	30.5	10.1	9.7	82	47	Cin
Walt Bellamy	1962	79	31.6	19.0	2.7	64	53	Chic
Terry Dischinger	1963	57	25.5	8.0	3.1	77	51	Chic
Jerry Lucas	1964	79	17.7	17.4	2.6	78	53	Cin
Willis Reed	1965	80	19.5	14.7	1.7	74	43	NY
Rick Barry	1966	80	25.7	10.6	2.2	86	44	San. Fran.
Dave Bing	1967	80	20.0	4.5	4.1	74	44	Detr
Earl Monroe	1968	82	24.3	5.7	4.3	78	45	Balt
Wes Unseld	1969	82	13.8	18.2	2.6	61	48	Balt
Kareem Abdul-Jabbar	1970	82	28.8	14.5	4.1	65	52	Milw
Dave Cowens	1971	81	17.0	15.0	2.8	73	42	Bost
(co-winners)								
Geoff Petrie	1971	82	24.8	3.4	4.8	77	44	Port
Sidney Wicks	1972	82	24.5	11.5	4.3	71	43	Port
Bob McAdoo	1973	80	18.0	9.1	1.7	77	45	Buff
Ernie DiGregorio	1974	81	15.2	2.7	8.2	90	42	Buff
Keith Wilkes	1975	82	14.2	8.2	2.2	73	44	G. St.
Alvan Adams	1976	80	19.0	9.1	5.6	74	47	Phoe
Adrian Dantley	1977	77	20.3	7.6	1.9	82	52	Buff
Walter Davis	1978	81	24.2	6.0	3.4	83	53	Phoe
Phil Ford	1979	89	15.9	2.3	8.6	81	47	KC
Larry Bird	1980	82	21.3	10.4	4.5	84	47	Bost
Darrell Griffith	1981	81	20.6	3.6	2.4	72	46	Utah
Buck Williams	1982	82	15.5	12.3	1.3	62	58	NJ
Terry Cummings	1983	70	23.7	10.6	2.5	71	52	SD
Ralph Sampson	1984	82	21.0	11.1	2.0	66	52	Hou
Michael Jordan	1985	82	28.2	6.5	5.9	85	52	Chic
Patrick Ewing	1986	50	20.0	9.0	2.0	74	47	NY
Chuck Person	1987	82	18.8	8.3	3.6	75	47	Ind
Mark Jackson	1988	82	13.6	4.8	10.6	77	43	NY
Mitch Richmond	1989	79	22.0	5.9	4.2	81	47	G. St.
David Robinson	1990	82	24.3	12.0	2.0	73	53	SA
Derrick Coleman	1991	74	18.4	10.3	2.2	73	47	NJ

The lowest scoring average for a "ROY" winner was Don Meineke's 1953 mark of 10.8 ppg; the highest, Wilt's 37.6 ppg mark in 1960.

Tom Heinsohn was the Rookie of the Year and on an NBA Championship team (Boston) in 1957. (Photo courtesy of Naismith Memorial Basketball Hall of Fame.)

Back-to-back rookie of the year winners on the *same* team: Bellamy and Dischinger (Chicago, 1962 and 1963); Monroe and Unseld (Baltimore, 1968 and 1969); Petrie/co-winner and Wicks (Portland, 1971 and 1972); and McAdoo and DiGregorio (Buffalo, 1973 and 1974).

In 1985, Michael Jordan, with his 28.2 ppg mark, posted the fifth highest scoring average of any rookie ever. That year, "Air" also posted the third best FT% mark (85 percent) of any Rookie of the Year. The only two award winners ahead of Jordan in FT% were DiGregorio's 90 percent and Barry's 86 percent marks.

Table 5.14—Greatest Rookie Seasons in NBA History

Player	Year Won	Year-End Stat Category Rankings
Ray Felix	1954	Ranked 4th in scoring; 5th in FG%; 4th in rebounds
Bob Pettit	1955	Ranked 4th in scoring; 3rd in rebounds
Maurice Stokes	1956	Ranked 11th in scoring; 2nd in rebounds; 9th in assists
Elgin Baylor	1959	Ranked 4th in scoring; 3rd in rebounds; 9th in assists
Wilt Chamberlain	1960	Ranked 1st in scoring and rebounds; 6th in FG%
Oscar Robertson	1961	Ranked 3rd in scoring; 4th in FG%; 9th in FT%
Walt Bellamy	1962	Ranked 2nd in scoring; 1st in FG%; 3rd in rebounds
Jerry Lucas	1964	Ranked 1st in FG%; 3rd in rebounds
Willis Reed	1965	Ranked 7th in scoring; 5th in rebounds
Rick Barry	1966	Ranked 4th in scoring; 2nd in FT%; 10th in rebounds
Earl Monroe	1968	Ranked 4th in scoring
Wes Unseld	1969	Ranked 2nd in rebounds
Kareem Abdul-Jabbar	1970	Ranked 2nd in scoring; 3rd in rebounds; 7th in FG%
Ernie DiGregorio	1974	Ranked 1st in assists and FT%
Keith Wilkes	1975	Won NBA team title with Golden State Warriors
Phil Ford	1979	Ranked 4th in assists; 5th in steals
Larry Bird	1980	Ranked 3rd in 3-point FG%; 10th in rebounds
Buck Williams	1982	Ranked 3rd in FG%; 3rd in rebounds
Terry Cummings	1983	Ranked 10th in both scoring and rebounds
Ralph Sampson	1984	Ranked 3rd in blocked shots; 5th in rebounds
Michael Jordan	1985	Ranked 3rd in scoring; 4th in steals

The only three Rookies of the Year on NBA championship teams: Magic Johnson (Lakers/1980); Tom Heinsohn (Celtics/1957) and Wilkes (as per above).

Chapter 6

Scorers and Shooters

Table 6.1—The Top 100 NBA Career Scorers

Player	Total Points	Player	Total Points
1. Kareem Abdul-Jabbar	38,887	31. Earl Monroe	17,454
2. Wilt Chamberlain	31,419	32. Ron Boone	17,437
3. Julius Erving	30,026	33. Spencer Haywood	17,111
4. Moses Malone	27,500	34. George McGinnis	17,009
5. Dan Issel	27,482	35. Bob Cousy	16,960
6. Elvin Hayes	27,313	36. Nate Archibald	16,481
7. Oscar Robertson	26,710	37. Billy Cunningham	16,310
8. George Gervin	26,595	38. Paul Arizin	16,266
9. John Havlicek	26,395	39. Randy Smith	16,262
10. Rick Barry	25,279	40. Pete Maravich	15,948
11. Jerry West	25,192	41. Jack Twyman	15,840
12. Artis Gilmore	24,941	42. Walter Davis	15,666
13. Elgin Baylor	23,149	43. Robert Parish	15,583
14. Adrian Dantley	22,458	44. Walt Frazier	15,581
15. Alex English	23,417	45. Sam Jones	15,411
16. Hal Greer	21,586	46. Dick Barnett	15,358
17. Walt Bellamy	20,941	47. John Drew	15,291
18. Bob Pettit	20,880	48. Louie Dampier	15,279
19. Dolph Schayes	19,249	49. Dick Van Arsdale	15,079
20. Bob Lanier	19,248	50. Mike Mitchell	15,016
21. Gail Goodrich	19,181	51. Reggie Theus	15,106*
22. Chet Walker	18,831	52. Richie Guerin	14,659
23. Bob McAdoo	18,787	53. Jamaal Wilkes	14,644
24. Dave Bing	18,327	54. Bill Russell	14,522
25. World B. Free	17,955	55. Nate Thurmond	14,437
26. Calvin Murphy	17,949	56. Jack Sikma	15,119*
27. Lou Hudson	17,940	57. Jo Jo White	14,399
28. Larry Bird	17,783	58. Dennis Johnson	14,283
29. Len Wilkens	17,772	59. Tom Van Arsdale	14,232
30. Bailey Howell	17,770	60. Bernard King	14,104

Table 6.1—The Top 100 NBA Career Scorers *(cont.)*

Player	Total Points	Player	Total Points
61. Gus Williams	14,093	81. Jack Marin	12,541
62. Dave Debusschere	14,053	82. Otis Birdsong	12,507
63. Jerry Lucas	14,053	83. Mike Newlin	12,507 (tie)
64. Fred Brown	14,018	84. Johnny Kerr	12,480
65. Alvan Adams	13,910	85. Dominique Wilkins	12,458
66. Bob Love	13,895	86. Cazzie Russell	12,377
67. Marques Johnson	13,852	87. Maurice Lucas	12,339
68. Billy Cunningham	13,626**	88. Johnny Green	12,281
69. Dave Cowens	13,516	89. Magic Johnson	12,213
70. Cliff Hagan	13,447	90. Tom Heinsohn	12,194
71. Rudy Tomjanovich	13,383	91. Willis Reed	12,183
72. Kiki Vandeweghe	13,276	92. Len Robinson	11,988
73. Purvis Short	13,053	93. Clyde Lovellette	11,947
74. Jeff Mullins	13,017	94. Scott Wedman	11,916
75. Mark Aguirre	12,977	95. Archie Clark	11,819
76. Bob Boozer	12,964	96. Paul Silas	11,782
77. Paul Westphal	12,809	97. George Mikan	11,764
78. Sidney Wicks	12,803	98. Dick Snyder	11,755
79. Mickey Johnson	12,748	99. Norm Nixon	11,703
80. Bill Sharman	12,665	100. Isiah Thomas	11,692*

*Totals through 1992 season.
**Combined ABA/NBA career totals.

In 1960, Dolph Schayes was the first pro player to reach 15,000 career points. Only two players ever scored 3,000 points in one season, Wilt Chamberlain (1961, 1962 and 1963) and Michael Jordan (1987).

Table 6.2—The Scoring Champs in the Early Pro Leagues

Year	Player	Team	Points Per Game Average
The Philadelphia League			
1904	Schwer*	Jasper	13.3
1905	Jack Reynolds	Philadelphia	15.8
1906	Dark	St. Simeon	12.3
The Hudson River League			
1910	Tobey Matthews	Catskills	10.4
1911	Carl Mueller	Troy	6.3
1912	Streusand	Newburgh	12.7

Note: This league also was short-lived (three seasons).

Adolph Schayes is a Hall of Fame player as well as being named NBA Coach of the Year in 1966. (Photo courtesy of Naismith Memorial Basketball Hall of Fame.)

Year	Player	Team	Points Per Game Average
The Eastern League			
1910	Harry Hough	Trenton	17.3
1911	John Donohue	Jasper	13.8
1912	Harry Hough	Trenton	16.9
1913	Jack Adams	Camden	19.1
1914	W. Kummer	Camden	17.9
1915	Roy Steele	Camden	15.7
1916	Adams	Camden	16.7
1917	Joe Fogarty	Greystock	18.9
1918	John Beckman	Deneri	9.3
1920	James Campbell	Camden	7.4
1921	Nat Holman	Germantown	8.4
The New York State League			
1913	Jack Inglis	Troy	8.4
1914	Sugarman	Cahoes	8.5
1915	Jack Inglis	Troy	6.9
1917	Al Schuler	Utica	7.3
1920	Noll	Mohawk	8.1
1921	Barney Sedran	Albany	8.4
1922	Michael Johnson	Cahoes	7.1
1923	Bennie Borgman	Kingston	11.7
Note: No league play in 1916, 1918–19.			
Western Pennsylvania League			
1913	Anderegg	Southside	17.8
Note: League lasted only one season.			

Table 6.2—The Scoring Champs in the Early Pro Leagues *(cont.)*

Year	Player	Team	Points Per Game Average
The Pennsylvania State League			
1915	John Haston	Pittson	16.4
1916	Curlett	Wilkes-Barre	18.0
1917	Jack Inglis	Carbondale	10.0
1918	Leary	Plymouth-Hazelton	6.4
1920	John Beckman	Nanticoke	9.1
1921	John Beckman	Nanticoke	9.0

Note: No league play in 1919.

Year	Player	Team	Points Per Game Average
The Interstate League			
1916	Muller	Jersey City	7.8
1921	Dowd	Springfield	6.8

Note: Lasted only two seasons. See Chapter 7 for more on individual early pro leagues.

Year	Player	Team	Points Per Game Average
The Metropolitan League			
1922	Bernhard Borgman	Powers	12.1
1923	Bernhard Borgman	Powers	12.3
1924	Bernhard Borgman	Powers	10.7
1925	Bernhard Borgman	Powers	11.8

Note: In this short-lived league, Borgman was the Michael Jordan of his era, with four consecutive scoring titles. Moreover, he continued his dominance in the ABL. He starred in 2,500 pro games and entered the Hall of Fame (1961).

Year	Player	Team	Points Per Game Average
The American Basketball League (ABL)			
1929	Bernhard Borgman	Ft. Wayne	7.7
1930	Bernhard Borgman	Patterson	8.3
1931	Bernhard Borgman	Chicago	8.8
1934	Bernhard Borgman	Newark	10.0
1936	McDermott	Brooklyn	9.6
1937	Rabin	Kingston	13.2
1938	Rabin	Kingston	13.4
1939	Rabin	Jersey Reds	10.3
1940	McDermott	Baltimore	11.0
1941	Rosenberg	Philadelphia	8.9
1942	N. Frankel	Washington	9.4
1943	Juenger	Harrisburg	11.6
1944	Bloom	Trenton	10.5
1945	Juenger	Patterson	10.9
1947	Resnick	Troy	16.1
1948	Ostrowski	Wilkes-Barre	18.1
1949	Richard Holb	Patterson	20.4
1950	Morganhaller	Scranton	19.7
1951	Ike Walthur	Saratoga	18.6

Note: The ABL's statistics for the years 1932, 1933, 1935, and 1946 were unobtainable, as were many of the players' first names. Sadly, careless statistics were kept.

The American Basketball League (ABL) lasted from 1961 to 1963 the second time around. It was founded by Abe Saperstein (of Harlem Globetrotters' fame).

Year	Player	Team	Points Per Game Average
1961	Connie Hawkins	Pittsburgh	27.5
1963	Bill Bridges	Kansas City	29.2

*First names of some early pro players were unobtainable.

Table 6.3—Pro Basketball's Scoring Champs for the Last 54 Years

Player	League/Team	Scoring Average	Year
Leroy Edwards	NBL	16.2	1938
Leroy Edwards	NBL	11.9	1939
Leroy Edwards	NBL	12.9	1940
Ben Stephens	NBL	11.0	1941
Chuck Chuckovits	NBL	18.5	1942
Bobby McDermott	NBL	13.7	1943
Mel Riebe	NBL	17.9	1944
Mel Riebe	NBL	20.2	1945
Bob Carpenter	NBL	17.9	1946
George Mikan	NBL (Minn)	16.5	1947
Joe Fulks	BAA (Phil)	23.2	1947
George Mikan	NBL (Minn)	21.3	1948
Joe Fulks	BAA (Phil)	22.1	1948
George Mikan	BAA (Minn)	28.3	1949
Don Otten	NBL	14.0	1949
George Mikan	NBA (Minn)	27.7	1950
George Mikan	NBA (Minn)	28.4	1951
Paul Arizin	Philadelphia	25.4	1952
Neil Johnston	Philadelphia	22.3	1953
Neil Johnston	Philadelphia	24.4	1954
Neil Johnston	Philadelphia	22.7	1955
Bob Pettit	St. Louis	25.7	1956
Paul Arizin	Philadelphia	25.6	1957
George Yardley	Detroit	27.8	1958
Bob Pettit	St. Louis	29.2	1959
Wilt Chamberlain	Philadelphia	37.6	1960
Wilt Chamberlain	Philadelphia	38.4	1961
Wilt Chamberlain	Philadelphia	50.2	1962
Wilt Chamberlain	San Fran.	44.8	1963
Wilt Chamberlain	San Fran.	36.9	1964
Wilt Chamberlain	San Fran. & Philadelphia	34.7	1965
Wilt Chamberlain	Philadelphia	33.5	1966
Rick Barry	San Fran.	35.6	1967
Dave Bing	Detroit	27.1	1968
Elvin Hayes	San Diego	28.4	1969

Table 6.3 — Pro Basketball's Scoring Champs for the Last 54 Years *(cont.)*

Player	League/Team	Scoring Average	Year
Jerry West	Los Angeles	31.2	1970
Kareem Abdul-Jabbar	Milwaukee	31.7	1971
Kareem Abdul-Jabbar	Milwaukee	34.8	1972
Nate Archibald	KC/Omaha	34.0	1973
Bob McAdoo	Buffalo	30.6	1974
Bob McAdoo	Buffalo	34.5	1975
Bob McAdoo	Buffalo	31.1	1976
Pete Maravich	New Orleans	31.1	1977
George Gervin	San Antonio	27.2	1978
George Gervin	San Antonio	29.6	1979
George Gervin	San Antonio	33.1	1980
Adrian Dantley	Utah	30.7	1981
George Gervin	San Antonio	32.2	1982
Alex English	Denver	28.4	1983
Adrian Dantley	Utah	30.6	1984
Bernard King	New York	32.9	1985
Dominique Wilkins	Atlanta	30.3	1986
Michael Jordan	Chicago	37.1	1987
Michael Jordan	Chicago	35.0	1988
Michael Jordan	Chicago	32.5	1989
Michael Jordan	Chicago	33.6	1990
Michael Jordan	Chicago	31.5	1991

Table 6.4 — ABA Scoring Champions

Player	Scoring Average	Year
Connie Hawkins	26.8	1968
Rick Barry	34.0	1969
Spencer Haywood	30.0	1970
Dan Issel	29.9	1971
Charlie Scott	34.6	1972
Julius Erving	31.9	1973
Julius Erving	27.4	1974
George McGinnis	29.8	1975
Julius Erving	29.3	1976

Table 6.5 — ABA Shooting Champs

FG% Champ	Year	FG%
Trooper Washington	1968	52.3
Bill McGill	1969	55.2

Connie Hawkins was the ABA scoring champ in 1968. (Photo courtesy of Naismith Memorial Basketball Hall of Fame.)

FG% Champ	Year	FG%
Frank Card	1970	52.3
Zelmo Beatty	1971	55.5
Artis Gilmore	1972	59.8
Artis Gilmore	1973	55.0
Swen Nater	1974	55.2
Bobby Jones	1975	60.4

FT% Champ	Year	FT%
Charlie Beasley	1968	87.2
Rick Barry	1969	88.8

Table 6.5—ABA Shooting Champs *(cont.)*

FT% Champ	Year	FT%
Darel Carrier	1970	89.2
Rick Barry	1971	89.0
Rick Barry	1972	87.8
Bill Keller	1973	87.0
Jimmy Jones	1974	88.4
Mack Calvin	1975	89.6

Table 6.6—Regular Season Scoring Records

Most Field Goals Made 15,837 goals: Kareem Abdul-Jabbar, Los Angeles and Milwaukee

Most Free Throws Made 7,694 free throws: Oscar Robertson, Cincinnati and Milwaukee

Highest Field Goal Percentage 59.9 percent: Artis Gilmore

Highest Free Throw Percentage 90 percent: Rick Barry

Highest Scoring Average 32.6 points per game: Michael Jordan (11,263 points in 345 games)

Highest Three Point Field Goal Percentage 43.8 percent: Mark Price

Most Three Point Field Goals Made 472 three pointers: Dale Ellis

Most Field Goals Scored in a Single Game 36 goals: Wilt Chamberlain, Philadelphia, 1962

Most Free Throws Scored in a Single Game 28 free throws: Wilt Chamberlain, Philadelphia, 1962; and Adrian Dantley, Utah, 1984

Most Seasons Leading League in Scoring 7 seasons: Wilt Chamberlain

Most Points in a Single Season 4,029 points: Wilt Chamberlain, 1962

Highest Scoring Average in a Season 50.4 points per: Wilt Chamberlain (1962)

Most Points by a Rookie (Game) 58 points: Wilt Chamberlain, 1960; (Season) 2,707 points: Wilt Chamberlain

Highest Season Field Goal Percentage 72.7 percent: Wilt Chamberlain, 1973

Highest Season Free Throw Percentage 95.8 percent: Calvin Murphy, 1981

Highest Season Three-Point Field Goal Percentage 52.2 percent: John Sundvold, 1989

Table 6.7—Ten Greatest Single Playoff Game Scorers

Player	Team	Points Scored
Michael Jordan	Chicago, 1986	63
Elgin Baylor	Los Angeles, 1962	61
Wilt Chamberlain	Philadelphia, 1961	56
Rick Barry	San Francisco, 1967	55
Michael Jordan	Chicago, 1988	55
John Havlicek	Boston, 1973	54
Wilt Chamberlain	Philadelphia, 1960	53

Bill Sharman was an NBA champion free throw shooter. (Photo courtesy of Naismith Memorial Basketball Hall of Fame.)

Player	Team	Points Scored
Jerry West	Los Angeles, 1969	53
Jerry West	Los Angeles, 1965	52
Sam Jones	Boston, 1967	51

Table 6.8—Playoff Scoring Records

Most Field Goals in a Playoff Game 24 goals made on 42 attempts by Wilt Chamberlain (1960); on 36 attempts by John Havlicek (1973); and on 45 attempts by Michael Jordan (1988).

Table 6.8 — Playoff Scoring Records *(cont.)*

Most Free Throws Made 30 free throws: Bob Cousy, Boston, 1953 (4 overtimes)

Most Career Field Goals Made 2,288 goals: Kareem Abdul-Jabbar, Los Angeles and Milwaukee

Most Free Throws Made 1,213 free throws: Jerry West, Los Angeles

Most Three Point Field Goals Made 100 goals: Michael Cooper, Los Angeles

Highest Three Point Field Goal Percentage 53.2 percent: Bob Hansen, Utah

Highest Free Throw Percentage 93.2 percent: Calvin Murphy, Houston

Highest Field Goal Percentage 59.2 percent: Kurt Rambis, Los Angeles

Most Points NBA Finals Series: 284 points: Elgin Baylor, Los Angeles, 7 games, 1962

Highest Field Goal Percentage in NBA Finals 73.9 percent: Derrick Dickey, Golden State, 1975 (4 game series)

Highest Field Goal Percentage in NBA Finals 96.8 percent: Bill Sharman, Boston, 1958 (6 games)

Most Field Goals Made in NBA Finals 101 goals: Elgin Baylor, Los Angeles, 1962 (7 games)

Most Free Throws Made in NBA Finals 82 free throws: Elgin Baylor, Los Angeles, 1962 (7 games)

Most Points in a Single Game by a Rookie 42 points: Magic Johnson, Los Angeles, 1980 (NBA finals)

Highest Scoring Average in One Playoff/Finals Series 46.3 points per game: Jerry West, Los Angeles, 1965 (6 game series)

Table 6.9 — All Star Game Scoring Records

Most Points Career 251 points: Kareem Abdul-Jabbar

Most Points Single Game 42 points: Wilt Chamberlain, 1962

Highest Scoring Average 21.5 points: Michael Jordan

Most Field Goals Made in a Single Game 17: Wilt Chamberlain (1962); and 17: Michael Jordan (1988)

Most Free Throws Made Single Game 12 free throws: Elgin Baylor (1962); and 12: Oscar Robertson (1965)

Most Field Goals Made Career 105 goals: Kareem Abdul-Jabbar

Most Free Throws Made Career 78 free throws: Elgin Baylor

Most Three Point Field Goals Made in a Game 4 goals: Isiah Thomas

Table 6.10 — All Time Career Leaders in Scoring

Most Career Points	
Kareem Abdul-Jabbar	38,387
Wilt Chamberlain	31,419
Julius Erving	30,026

*Highest Per Game Scoring Average**	
Wilt Chamberlain	30.1
Elgin Baylor	27.4
Jerry West	27.0

Most Total Playoff Points

Kareem Abdul-Jabbar	5,762
Jerry West	4,457
John Havlicek	3,776

Highest Playoff Per Game Scoring Average

Michael Jordan	35.9
Jerry West	29.1
Hakeem Olajuwon	27.8

Highest All Star Game Scoring Average

Michael Jordan	21.5
Oscar Robertson	20.5
Bob Pettit	20.4

*Indicates that while Michael Jordan has a higher per game mark—32.6 points per game—the other three, Chamberlain, Baylor and West, have all played in at least twice the amount of games than the younger Jordan has—so they get the nod for highest average.

Table 6.11—The 10 Players to Win the Scoring Title as a Rookie

Player	League	Year	Points Per Game
Leroy Edwards	NBL	1937	16.2
Mel Riebe	NBL	1944	17.9
Bob Carpenter	NBL	1946	13.8
George Mikan	NBL	1947	16.8
Joe Fulks	BAA	1947	23.2
Wilt Chamberlain	NBA	1960	37.6
Connie Hawkins	ABA	1968	26.8
Elvin Hayes	NBA	1969	28.4
Spencer Haywood	ABA	1970	30.0
Dan Issel	ABA	1971	29.9

To win a league scoring title says a player is one of the best. To win it as a rookie, says he's a true superstar.

What follows are some other young pro prodigies. These players won the league scoring title in only their second pro seasons:

Table 6.12—The 11 Players to Win the Scoring Title in Their Second Season

Player	League	Year	Points Per Game
Max Zaslofsky	NBA	1948	21.0†
Paul Arizin*	NBA	1952	25.4

Elvin Hayes was the Rookie of the Year and led the league in scoring in 1969. (Photo courtesy of Naismith Memorial Basketball Hall of Fame.)

Table 6.12 – The 11 Players to Win the Scoring Title in Their Second Season *(cont.)*

Player	League	Year	Points Per Game
Neil Johnston*	NBA	1953	22.3
Bob Pettit*	NBA	1956	25.7
Rick Barry*	NBA	1967	35.6
Dave Bing	NBA	1968	27.1
Kareem Abdul-Jabbar*	NBA	1971	31.7
Charlie Scott	ABA	1972	34.6
Julius Erving*	ABA	1973	31.9
Bob McAdoo*	NBA	1974	30.6
George Gervin*	NBA	1978	27.2††

*Indicates player led league in scoring on more than one occasion.

†While Zaslofsky, had more total points (1,007) that season, Joe Fulks had a slightly higher average (22.1 to 21.0). The title was given to the player with the higher total.

††Gervin, a second year NBA player, had played in the ABA for four seasons.

Table 6.13 – Highest Rookie Scoring Averages in the ABA

Player	Points	Scoring Rank in League	Rookie Season
Spencer Haywood	30.0	1st	1970
Dan Issel	29.9	1st	1971

Player	Points	Scoring Rank in League	Rookie Season
Julius Erving	27.3	6th	1972
Charlie Scott	27.1	5th	1971
Connie Hawkins	26.8	1st	1968
David Thompson	26.0	6th	1976

Table 6.14—Highest Rookie Scoring Averages in the NBA

Player	Points	Scoring Rank in League	Rookie Season
Wilt Chamberlain	37.6	1st	1960
Walt Bellamy	31.6	2nd	1962
Oscar Robertson	30.5	3rd	1961
Kareem Abdul-Jabbar	28.8	2nd	1970
Michael Jordan	28.2	3rd	1985
Elvin Hayes	28.4	1st	1969
Rick Barry	25.7	4th	1966
Terry Dischinger	25.5	14th*	1963
Elgin Baylor	24.9	4th	1959
Geoff Petrie	24.8	7th	1971
Sidney Wicks	24.5	12th	1972
Earl Monroe	24.3	4th	1968
Bernard King	24.2	10th	1978
Walter Davis	24.2	9th	1978
Terry Cummings	23.7	10th	1983
Joe Fulks	23.7	1st	1946
Pete Maravich	23.2	8th	1971

*Dischinger only played 57 games that year.

Only three rookies in NBA history have averaged more than 30 points per game: they are Wilt Chamberlain at 37.6 in 1960; Walt Bellamy at 31.6 in 1962; and Oscar Robertson at 30.5 in 1961. Only Chamberlain led the league in scoring with his great mark. Bellamy was second, and Robertson was in third place in season-end league scoring rankings.

What follows are the rookie scoring averages of some all time greats as well as some surprising averages of many current greats.

Table 6.15—Rookie Scoring Averages of Notable ABA and NBA Players

Player	Scoring Average	Year
Nate Archibald*	16.0	1971
Paul Arizin	17.2	1951

Table 6.15 – Rookie Scoring Averages of Notable ABA and NBA Players *(cont.)*

Player	Scoring Average	Year
Charles Barkley*	14.0	1985
Marvin Barnes	24.8	1971 (ABA)
Dave Bing**	20.6	1967
Larry Bird	21.3	1980
Otis Birdsong	15.8	1978
Tyronne Bogues	5.0	1988
Manute Bol	3.7	1986
Bill Bradley***	8.0	1968
Fred Brown*	4.2	1972
Larry Brown†	13.4	1968 (ABA)
Mack Calvin	16.8	1972 (ABA)
Austin Carr***	21.2	1972
Maurice Cheeks	8.4	1979
Phil Chenier	12.3	1972
Doug Collins*†	8.7	1974
Michael Cooper	2.0	1979
Bob Cousy	15.6	1951
Dave Cowens	17.0	1971
Billy Cunningham*†	14.3	1966
Bob Dandridge	13.2	1970
Adrian Dantley**	20.3	1977
Darryl Dawkins	2.4	1976
John Drew	18.5	1975
Alex English**	5.2	1977
Patrick Ewing	20.0	1986
Walt Frazier*	9.0	1968
World B. Free*	8.3	1976
Tom Gola***	10.8	1958
Gail Goodrich*	7.8	1966
Hal Greer*	11.1	1959
John Havlicek	14.3	1963
Bailey Howell	17.8	1960
Lou Hudson*	18.4	1967
Dennis Johnson	9.2	1977
Magic Johnson	18.0	1980
Neil Johnston**	6.0	1952
Billy Knight*	17.1	1975 (ABA)
Bob Lanier*	15.6	1971
Jerry Lucas	17.7	1964
Bob McAdoo*	18.0	1973
Ed Macauley	16.1	1950
Xavier McDaniel	17.1	1986
Karl Malone	14.9	1986
Moses Malone	18.8	1975 (ABA)
George Mikan**	16.5	1952
Doug Moe†	24.2	1968 (ABA)

Player	Scoring Average	Year
Sidney Moncrief*	8.5	1980
Calvin Murphy	15.8	1971
Don Nelson†	6.8	1963
Robert Parish	9.1	1977
Bob Pettit	20.4	1955
Kevin Porter	6.0	1973
Willis Reed†	19.5	1965
Michael R. Richardson	6.5	1979
Pat Riley†	7.9	1968
Doc Rivers	9.3	1984
Anthony Roberts***	9.5	1978
Bill Russell	14.7	1957
Dolph Schayes	12.8	1949
Purvis Short*	10.6	1979
Gene Shue†	4.2	1955
Jack Sikma	10.7	1978
Paul Silas	4.6	1965
John Stockton	5.6	1985
Reggie Theus	16.3	1979
Isiah Thomas	17.0	1982
Waymond Tisdale***	14.7	1986
Rudy Tomjanovich*	5.3	1971
Kelly Tripucka	21.6	1982
Wes Unseld	13.8	1969
Kiki Vandeweghe*	11.5	1981
Bill Walton	12.8	1975
Spud Webb	7.8	1986
Jerry West**	17.6	1961
Paul Westphal*	4.1	1973
Jo Jo White	12.2	1970
Lenny Wilkens†	11.7	1961
Dominique Wilkins*	17.5	1983
Gerald Wilkins	12.5	1986
Freeman Williams***	10.4	1979
Bill Willoughby††	4.7	1976
James Worthy	13.4	1983
George Yardley**	9.0	1954

*Indicates he became a high pro scorer despite slow start.
**Indicates he went on to become a league scoring champ.
***Indicates he was a huge college scorer.
†Future NBA coach.
††Willoughby came right out of high school.

Table 6.16 — Highest Season Scoring Averages

Player	Average	Year
Wilt Chamberlain	50.4	1962
Wilt Chamberlain	44.8	1963
Wilt Chamberlain	38.4	1961
Wilt Chamberlain	37.6	1960
Michael Jordan	37.1	1986
Wilt Chamberlain	36.9	1964
Rick Barry	35.6	1967
Michael Jordan	35.0	1988
Kareem Abdul-Jabbar	34.8	1972
Wilt Chamberlain	34.7	1965
Charlie Scott	34.6	1972*
Bob McAdoo	34.5	1975
Nate Archibald	34.0	1973
Wilt Chamberlain	33.5	1966
George Gervin	33.1	1980
Bernard King	32.9	1985
George Gervin	32.3	1982
Julius Erving	31.9	1973*
Lew Alcindor	31.7	1971
Jerry West	31.2	1970
Pete Maravich	31.1	1977
Bob McAdoo	31.1	1976

*Indicates ABA seasons.

Table 6.17 — Highest Career Scoring Averages

Player	PPG Average
Michael Jordan	32.7
Wilt Chamberlain	30.1
Jerry West	27.0
Bob Pettit	26.4
Dominique Wilkins	26.0
Oscar Robertson	25.7
Adrian Dantley	25.5
Kareem Abdul-Jabbar	25.3
George Gervin	25.1
Larry Bird	25.0
Rick Barry	24.8
Julius Erving	24.2
Pete Maravich	24.2
Mark Aguirre	24.2
Kiki Vandeweghe	23.7
Moses Malone	22.8

Player	PPG Average
Bob McAdoo	22.1
Paul Arizin	22.8
Dan Issel	22.3

Table 6.18—Players Who Have Scored 50 or More Points in a Game

Player	Times	Player	Times
Wilt Chamberlain	121	Billy Cunningham	1***
Michael Jordan	21****	Mel Daniels	1*
Elgin Baylor	17	John Drew	1
Rick Barry	14	Clyde Drexler	1
Bernard King	6	Julius Erving	1*
Bob Pettit	6	Patrick Ewing	1
Larry Bird	5	Sleepy Floyd	1***
Bob McAdoo	5	Joe Fulks	1
Dominique Wilkins	5	Gail Goodrich	1
Adrian Dantley	4	Richie Guerin	1
George Gervin	4	John Havlicek	1***
Moses Malone	4	Elvin Hayes	1
Jerry West	3	Lionel Hollins	1
Kareem Abdul-Jabbar	2	Lou Hudson	1
Joe Barry Carroll	2	Neil Johnston	1
Tom Chambers	2	Sam Jones	1***
Dale Ellis	2	Larry Kennon	1
Alex English	2	George McGinnis	1*
Billy Knight	2	Kevin McHale	1
Geoff Petrie	2	Karl Malone	1
Oscar Robertson	2	Pete Maravich	1
Purvis Short	2	Vernon Maxwell	1
Phil Smith	2	George Mikan	1
Kiki Vandeweghe	2	Larry Miller	1*
Ray Williams	2	Earl Monroe	1
John Williamson	2	Calvin Murphy	1
George Yardley	2	Mike Newline	1
Michael Adams	1	Hakeem Olajuwon	1
Nate Archibald	1	Len Robinson	1
Zelmo Beatty	1*	Charles Smith	1
Dave Bing	1	David Thompson	1
Bill Bridges	1**	Kelly Tripucka	1
Fred Brown	1	Jack Twyman	1
Phil Chenier	1	Chet Walker	1
Bob Cousy	1***	Walt Wesley	1
Terry Cummings	1	Freeman Williams	1

*Indicates ABA game.

**Indicates ABL game.

***Indicates playoff competition (not regular season).

****Included playoff games as well

Table 6.19—The 20 Greatest Field Goal Shooters

Player	Career Percentages
James Donaldson	58.8
Artis Gilmore	58.2
Steve Johnson	58.0
Charles Barkley	57.7*
Darryl Dawkins	57.2
Kevin McHale	56.7
Jeff Ruland	56.4
Kareem Abdul-Jabbar	56.1
Bobby Jones	56.0
Larry Nance	55.9
James Worthy	55.8
Adrian Dantley	54.6
Wilt Chamberlain	54.0
Bernard King	53.5
Robert Parish	53.4
Cedric Maxwell	54.6
Calvin Natt	53.0
Kiki Vandeweghe	53.4
Magic Johnson	53.3
Buck Williams	55.2**

*He has played only 310 games.
**He has played only 561 games.

Table 6.20—The 20 Greatest Free Throw Shooters

Player	Career Percentages
Rick Barry	90.0
Calvin Murphy	89.2
Bill Sharman	88.4
Larry Bird	87.9
Mike Newlin	87.0
Kiki Vandeweghe	86.9
Jeff Malone	86.7
Mack Calvin	85.9
John Long	85.9
Fred Brown	85.8
Larry Siegfried	85.4
Dolph Schayes	84.4
George Gervin	84.4
Jack Sikma	84.4
Junior Bridgeman	84.4
Jack Marin	84.3
Brian Winters	84.2

Player	Career Percentages
Ricky Sobers	84.1
Walter Davis	84.1
Oscar Robertson	83.8

Table 6.21 — The Players to Shoot Over 90% from the FT Line in a Single Season

Year	Player	Percentages
1952	Bobby Wanzer	90.4*
1957	Bill Sharman	90.5*
1957	Dolph Schayes	90.4
1958	Dolph Schayes	90.4*
1959	Bill Sharman	93.2*
1961	Bill Sharman	92.1*
1967	Adrian Smith	90.3*
1973	Rick Barry	90.2*
1974	Ernie DiGregorio	90.2*
1975	Rick Barry	90.4*
1976	Rick Barry	92.3*
1976	Calvin Murphy	90.7
1977	Ernie DiGregorio	94.5*
1977	Rick Barry	91.6
1978	Rick Barry	92.4*
1978	Calvin Murphy	91.8
1979	Rick Barry	94.7*
1979	Calvin Murphy	92.8
1980	Rick Barry	93.5*
1981	Calvin Murphy	95.8*
1981	Ricky Sobers	93.5
1983	Calvin Murphy	92.0*
1985	Kyle Macy	90.7*
1987	Larry Bird	91.0*
1988	Jack Sikma	92.2*
1988	Larry Bird	91.6
1988	John Long	90.7
1988	Mike Gminski	90.6
1989	Magic Johnson	91.1*
1989	Jack Sikma	90.5
1989	Scott Skiles	90.3
1989	Mark Price	90.1
1990	Larry Bird	93.0*
1990	Eddie Johnson	91.7
1990	Walter Davis	91.2
1990	Joe Dumars	90.0
1991	Reggie Miller	91.8*
1991	Jeff Malone	91.7
1991	Ricky Pierce	91.3

Table 6.21—The Players to Shoot Over 90% from the FT Line in a Single Season *(cont.)*

Year	Player	Average Percentages
1991	Kelly Tripucka	91.0
1991	Magic Johnson	90.6
1991	Scott Skiles	90.2

*Indicates led league that year as well.

Close calls—Rick Barry hit for exactly 89.9 percent in 1974 to finish second, and Kyle Macy also posted exactly 89.9 percent in 1982 to win the title.

No one ever topped 90 percent in an ABA season; the closest player to do it was Mack Calvin in 1975 with Denver when he averaged a close 89.6 percent from the line. Twenty-three separate players are on this list.

Table 6.22—The Best Long Range Shooters

Player	3-Pointers Made
Louie Dampier	794
Billy Keller	506
Glen Combs	503
Larry Bird	455
George Lehman	409
Darrel Carrier	398
Darrell Griffith	341
Warren Jabali	322
Craig Hodges	321
Roger Brown	314
Dale Ellis	310
Michael Cooper	298
Danny Ainge	290
Mike Evans	231
Trent Tucker	227
World B. Free	213
Michael Adams	210
Mike McGee	205
Mark Aguirre	204
John Lucas	200
Byron Scott	183
Isiah Thomas	179
Rick Barry	176
Brad Davis	176
Ron Boone	153
Gerald Henderson	143
Julius Erving	134

Rick Barry is the only player ever to lead both the NBA (1967) and ABA (1969) in scoring. (Photo courtesy of Naismith Memorial Basketball Hall of Fame.)

Player	3-Pointers Made
Mike Dunleavy	123
George Gervin	122
Purvis Short	106
Kevin McKenna	103
Kiki Vandeweghe	100

Table 6.23—Most Points (60 or More) Scored in a Single Game

Player	Year	Points
Wilt Chamberlain	1962	100
Wilt Chamberlain	1961	78

Table 6.23 — Most Points (60 or More) Scored in a Single Game *(cont.)*

Player	Year	Points
Wilt Chamberlain	1962	73
David Thompson	1978	73
Wilt Chamberlain	1962	72
Elgin Baylor	1960	71
Wilt Chamberlain	1963	70
Michael Jordan	1990	69
Wilt Chamberlain	1967	68
Pete Maravich	1977	68
Wilt Chamberlain	1961, 1962, 1963	67
Wilt Chamberlain	1969	66
Wilt Chamberlain	1962, 1966	65
Elgin Baylor	1959	64
Rick Barry	1974	64
Michael Jordan	1993	64
Joe Fulks	1949	63
Elgin Baylor	1961	63
Michael Jordan	1986	63
Jerry West	1962	63
George Gervin	1978	63
Wilt Chamberlain	1962, 1964	63
Wilt Chamberlain	1962 (3 times), 1963, 1964, 1966	63
George Mikan	1952	61
Wilt Chamberlain	1961, 1962 (6 times)	61
Michael Jordan	1987 (2 times)	61
Karl Malone	1990	61
Tom Chambers	1990	60
Wilt Chamberlain	1961, 1969 (3 times)	60
Larry Bird	1985	60
Bernard King	1984	60

There have also been three 60-plus point games in the ABA league: Julius Erving (63 pts., 1974, with the NY Nets); Zelmo Beatty (also 63 pts., in 1972, with Utah); and all time ABA single game scoring record holder, Larry Miller, who dumped in 67 points in 1972 for the Carolina Cougars.

Notice too that through 1992, there have only been 15 NBA players in history to post over 60 in one contest; 18 total, if we count ABA players (which we should).

Table 6.24 — Most Points Scored in a Game for Each NBA Season (1973–1992)

1973-74		Fred Brown	58
Rick Barry	64	Bob McAdoo	52

Cazzie Russell	49
Gail Goodrich	49
Jim McMillan	48
John Brisker	47
Bob Lanier	45
Kareem Abdul-Jabbar	44
Charlie Scott	44
Lou Hudson	44
Walt Frazier	44

1975-76

Bob McAdoo	52
Phil Smith	51
Pete Maravich	49
Kareem Abdul-Jabbar	48
Phil Chenier	44
John Drew	42
Lou Hudson	42
Fred Brown	41
Bob Lanier	41
Rick Barry	41

1974-75

Rick Barry	55
Gail Goodrich	53
Kareem Abdul-Jabbar	52
Bob McAdoo	51
Calvin Murphy	45
Dick Van Arsdale	45
Bob Lanier	45
John Drew	44
Pete Maravich	47
Walt Frazier	44
Mike Price	43
Norm Van Lier	42

1976-77

Pete Maravich	68
Phil Smith	51
Paul Westphal	47
Alvan Adams	47
Elvin Hayes	47
Connie Hawkins	44
Bob McAdoo	43
Brian Winters	43
Ron Boone	43
Billy Knight	43

1977-78

David Thompson	73
George Gervin	63
Calvin Murphy	57
Rick Barry	55
John Williamson	50
Paul Westphal	48
John Drew	48
Bernard King	44
Kareem Abdul-Jabbar	43
Kevin Grevey	43
Larry Wright	43

1979-80

Mike Newlin	52
George Gervin	55
Freeman Williams	51
Adrian Dantley	50
Larry Kenon	51
Otis Birdsong	49
Paul Westphal	49
World B. Free	49
Dan Issel	47
Mike Mitchell	46
Moses Malone	45

1978-79

George Gervin	52
Len Robinson	51
John Drew	50
World B. Free	49
John Williamson	48
Maurice Lucas	46
Spencer Haywood	46
Moses Malone	45
David Thompson	44
Bob McAdoo	45
Paul Westphal	43

1980-81

Adrian Dantley	55
Billy Knight	52
Moses Malone	51
Bernard King	50
George Gervin	49
Rudy Tomjanovich	48
John Drew	47
J. B. Carroll	46
Purvis Short	45
Julius Erving	45
David Thompson	44

1981-82

Moses Malone	53

Table 6.24—Most Points Scored in a Game for Each NBA Season (1973–1992) *(cont.)*

Adrian Dantley	53
Ray Williams	52
George Gervin	50
Kelly Tripucka	49
Andrew Toney	46
Mike Mitchell	45
Bernard King	45
Jim Brewer	44
Mark Aguirre	42
Gus Williams	42
Brian Winters	42
1983-84	
Purvis Short	57
Kiki Vandeweghe	51
Kiki Vandeweghe	50
Bernard King	50
Adrian Dantley	47
Alex English	47
Isiah Thomas	47
Mike Mitchell	47
Mark Aguirre	46
Ricky Green	45
1982-83	
Adrian Dantley	57
Kelly Tripucka	56
Larry Bird	53
J. B. Carroll	52
Kiki Vandeweghe	49
Mike Woodson	48
George Gervin	47
Isiah Thomas	46
Reggie Theus	46
Alex English	45
Mark Aguirre	44
Julius Erving	44
1984-85	
Bernard King	60
Bernard King	55
Bernard King	52
Larry Bird	60
Purvis Short	59
Kevin McHale	56
Moses Malone	51
Mark Aguirre	49
Michael Jordan	49
Dominique Wilkins	48
1985-86	
Dominique Wilkins	57
Alex English	54
Larry Bird	50
Dominique Wilkins	49
Larry Bird	47
Adrian Dantley	47
Kareem Abdul-Jabbar	46
Rolando Blackman	46
Dominique Wilkins	46
George Gervin	45
1987-88	
Michael Jordan	59
Michael Jordan	52
Dominique Wilkins	51
Michael Jordan	50
Dominique Wilkins	50
Larry Bird	49
Michael Jordan	49
Dominique Wilkins	49
Dominique Wilkins	48
Dale Ellis	47
Charles Barkley	47
1986-87	
Michael Jordan	61
Michael Jordan	61
Dominique Wilkins	57
Moses Malone	50
Jeff Malone	48
Kiki Vandeweghe	48
Larry Bird	47
Alex English	46
Walter Davis	45
John Long	44
Hakeem Olajuwon	44
1988-89	
Michael Jordan	53
Michael Jordan	52
Alex English	51
Clyde Drexler	50
Michael Jordan	50
Chuck Person	47
Chris Mullin	47
Mitch Richmond	46
Patrick Ewing	45

1988-89
Danny Ainge 45
Ed Johnson 45

1989-90
Michael Jordan 69
Karl Malone 61
Tom Chambers 60
Dale Ellis 53
Terry Cummings 52
Patrick Ewing 51
Hakeem Olajuwon 52
Larry Bird 50
Dominique Wilkins 44
Reggie Miller 44

1990-91
Michael Adams 54
Charles Smith 52
Bernard King 52
Patrick Ewing 50
Cedric Maxwell 51
Michael Jordan 46
Dominique Wilkins 45
Larry Bird 45
Charles Barkley 45
Jeff Malone 43

Detailed individual offensive scoring highs were not tallied by the NBA prior to the 1973-74 season.

Table 6.25 — Most Total Points Scored in Playoff Games: The Top 75 Players

Player	Point Total	Player	Point Total
Kareem Abdul-Jabbar	5,742	Walt Frazier	1,927
Jerry West	4,457	Gus Williams	1,927
John Havlicek	3,776	Chet Walker	1,916
Elgin Baylor	3,623	Oscar Robertson	1,910
Wilt Chamberlain	3,607	Hal Greer	1,876
Larry Bird	3,559	Cliff Hagan	1,834
Julius Erving	3,088	Rick Barry	1,833
Dennis Johnson	3,047	Jamaal Wilkes	1,820
Magic Johnson	2,999	Maurice Cheeks	1,730
Sam Jones	2,909	Jo Jo White	1,720
Bill Russell	2,673	Bob McAdoo	1,718
Kevin McHale	2,603	Dave Cowens	1,684
Robert Parish	2,379	Byron Scott	1,671
James Worthy	2,356	Isiah Thomas	1,606
Bob Pettit	2,240	Alex English	1,602
Elvin Hayes	2,194	George Gervin	1,592
George Mikan	2,141	Don Nelson	1,577
Tom Heinsohn	2,058	Michael Cooper	1,558
Moses Malone	2,056	Adrian Dantley	1,553
Bob Cousy	2,018	Dick Barnett	1,539
Dolph Schayes	1,973	Dave DeBusschere	1,536
Bob Dandridge	1,967	Earl Monroe	1,471

Table 6.25—Most Total Points Scored in Playoff Games: The Top 75 Players *(cont.)*

Player	Point Total	Player	Point Total
Bobby Jones	1,453	Mark Aguirre	1,249
Sidney Moncrief	1,451	Bob Lanier	1,244
Gail Goodrich	1,450	Bill Bradley	1,222
Bill Sharman	1,446	Danny Ainge	1,211
Jack Sikma	1,429	Fred Brown	1,197
Bailey Howell	1,401	Jim McMillan	1,194
Willis Reed	1,385	Paul Arizin	1,186
Darryl Dawkins	1,375	Hakeem Olajuwon	1,185
Walter Davis	1,365	Bill Bridges	1,163
Rudy LaRusso	1,344	Marques Johnson	1,159
Paul Westphal	1,337	Maurice Lucas	1,151
Frank Ramsey	1,331	Dominique Wilkins	1,142
Michael Jordan	1,309	Tom Sanders	1,141
Lou Hudson	1,300	Vern Mikkelsen	1,125
Wes Unseld	1,260	Archie Clark	1,125
Andrew Toney	1,254		

All totals are through and including the 1992 NBA season.

Table 6.26—Most Field Goals Made in a Single Game

Wilt Chamberlain	36 (1962)
Wilt Chamberlain	31 (1961)
Wilt Chamberlain	30 (1967)
Rick Barry	30 (1974)
Wilt Chamberlain	29 (1962 [three times] and 1969 [four times])
Elgin Baylor	28 (1960)
Wilt Chamberlain	28 (1961, 1963, 1966 [three times])
David Thompson	28 (1978)
Joe Fulks	27 (1949)
Wilt Chamberlain	27 (1962)—seven times

Table 6.27—Most Free Throws Made in a Single Game

Wilt Chamberlain	28 (1962)
Adrian Dantley	28 (1984)
Adrian Dantley	27 (1983)
Michael Jordan	26 (1987)
Adrian Dantley	26 (1980)
Frank Selvy	24 (1954)
Dolph Schayes	23 (1952)
Nate Archibald	23 (1972 and 1975 [two times])
Pete Maravich	23 (1975)

Several players had 22: Larry Foust (1957); Richie Guerin (1961); Oscar Robertson (1964 [two times] and 1966 [once]; John Williamson (1978); World B. Free (1979); Bernard

King (1985); and Rolando Blackman (1986). Bob Cousy made 30 (1953) in a playoff game.

Table 6.28—All Time Top Scorers by Position

Player	Total Points	Avg.	High
	Guards		
Oscar Robertson	26,710	25.7	56
George Gervin	26,595	25.1	63
Jerry West	25,192	27.0	63
Hal Greer	21,586	19.2	45
Gail Goodrich	19,181	19.6	53
Dave Bing	18,327	20.3	54
World B. Free	17,955	20.3	49
Calvin Murphy	17,949	17.9	57
Len Wilkens	17,772	16.5	42
Earl Monroe	17,454	18.8	56
	Forwards		
Julius Erving	30,026	24.2	63
John Havlicek	26,395	20.8	54
Rick Barry	25,279	24.8	64
Elgin Baylor	23,149	27.4	71
Alex English	23,417	22.3	54
Adrian Dantley	22,458	25.5	57
Bob Pettit	20,880	26.4	57
Dolph Schayes	19,249	18.2	41
Chet Walker	18,831	18.2	56
Lou Hudson	17,940	20.2	57
	Centers		
Kareem Abdul-Jabbar	38,887	25.3	55
Wilt Chamberlain	31,419	30.1	100
Dan Issel	27,482	22.6	49
Elvin Hayes	27,313	21.0	54
Artis Gilmore	24,941	18.8	42
Moses Malone	27,500 +	22.8	53*
Walt Bellamy	20,941	20.1	44
Bob Lanier	19,248	20.1	48
Bob McAdoo	18,787	22.1	52
Bailey Howell	17,770	18.7	41

*Still active.

Table 6.29—Team Scoring Leaders Season by Season, 1947–1991

1947: Boston/Connie Simmons/10.3 points; Chicago/Max Zaslofsky/14.4; Cleveland/Ed Sadowski/16.5; Detroit/Stan Miasek/14.9; New York/Sid Hertzberg/

Table 6.29—Team Scoring Leaders Season by Season, 1947–1991 *(cont.)*

8.7 points; Philadelphia/Joe Fulks/23.2; Pittsburgh/Coulby Gunther/14.1; Providence/Ernie Calverly/14.3; St. Louis/John Logan/12.6; Toronto/Leo Mogus/13.0; and Washington/Bob Feerick/16.8

1948: Baltimore/Clarence Hermsen/12.0; Boston/Ed Sadowski/19.4; Chicago/Max Zaslofsky/21.0; New York/Carl Braun/14.3; Philadelphia/Joe Fulks/22.1; Providence/Ernie Calverly/11.9; St. Louis/John Logan/13.4; and Washington/Bob Feerick/16.1

1949: Baltimore/Connie Simmons/13.0; Boston/George Nostrand/9.8; Chicago/Max Zaslofsky/20.6; Ft. Wayne/Bruce Hale/10.5; Indianapolis/Carlisle Towery/10.0; Minneapolis/George Mikan/28.3; New York/Carl Braun/14.2; Philadelphia/Joe Fulks/26.0; Providence/Ken Sailors/15.8; Rochester/Arnie Risen/16.6; St. Louis/Bellus Smawley/15.5; and Washington/Bob Feerick/13.0

1950: Anderson/Frank Brian/17.8; Baltimore/Ed Sadowski/12.6; Boston/Sid Hertzberg/10.2; Chicago/Max Zaslofsky/16.4; Denver/Ken Sailors/17.3; Ft. Wayne/Fred Schaus/14.3; Indianapolis/Alex Groza/23.4; Minneapolis/George Mikan/27.4; New York/Carl Braun/15.4; Philadelphia/Joe Fulks/14.2; Rochester/Bob Davies/14.0; St. Louis/Ed Macauley/16.1; Sheboygan/Max Morris/12.6; Syracuse/Dolph Schayes/16.8; Tri-Cities/Dwight Eddleman/12.9; Waterloo/Rich Mehen/14.4; and Washington/Fred Scolari/13.0

1951: Baltimore/Red Rocha/13.1; Boston/Ed Macauley/20.4; Ft. Wayne/Fred Schaus/15.1; Indianapolis/Alex Groza/21.7; Minneapolis/George Mikan/28.4; New York/Vince Boryla/14.9; Philadelphia/Joe Fulks/18.7; Rochester/Arnie Risen/16.3; Syracuse/Dolph Schayes/17.0; Tri-Cities/Frank Brian/16.8; and Washington/Bill Sharman/12.2

1952: Baltimore/Fred Scolari/14.6; Boston/Bob Cousy/21.7; Ft. Wayne/Frank Brian/15.9; Indianapolis/Joe Grabowski/13.7; Milwaukee/Don Otten/12.0; Minneapolis/George Mikan/23.8; New York/Max Zaslofsky/14.1; Philadelphia/Paul Arizin/25.4; Rochester/Bob Davies/16.2; and Syracuse/Dolph Schayes/13.8

1953: Baltimore/Don Barksdale/13.8; Boston/Bob Cousy/19.8; Ft. Wayne/Larry Foust/14.3; Indianapolis/Leo Barnhorst/13.6; Milwaukee/Jack Nichols/15.8; Minneapolis/George Mikan/20.6; New York/Carl Braun/14.0; Philadelphia/Neil Johnston/22.3; Rochester/Bob Davies/15.6; and Syracuse/Dolph Schayes/17.8

1954: Baltimore/Ray Felix/17.6; Boston/Bob Cousy/19.2; Ft. Wayne/Larry Foust/15.1; Milwaukee/Don Sunderlage/11.2; Minneapolis/George Mikan/18.1; New York/Carl Braun/14.8; Philadelphia/Neil Johnston/24.4; Rochester/Bob Wanzer/13.3; and Syracuse/Dolph Schayes/17.1

1955: Baltimore/Rollen Hans/5.6; Boston/Bob Cousy/21.2; Ft. Wayne/Larry Foust/17.0; Milwaukee/Bob Pettit/20.4; Minneapolis/Vern Mikkelsen/19.4; New York/Carl Braun/15.1; Philadelphia/Neil Johnston/22.7; Rochester/Bob Wanzer/13.1; and Syracuse/Dolph Schayes/18.5

1956: Boston/Bill Sharman/19.9; Ft. Wayne/George Yardley/17.4; Minneapolis/Clyde Lovellette/21.5; New York/Carl Braun/15.4; Philadelphia/Paul Arizin/24.2; Rochester/Maurice Stokes/16.8; St. Louis/Bob Pettit/25.7; and Syracuse/Dolph Schayes/20.4

George Mikan was the Minneapolis Lakers scoring leader *and* league scoring leader for three seasons, 1949–1951. (Photo courtesy of Naismith Memorial Basketball Hall of Fame.)

1957: Boston/Bill Sharman/21.1; Ft. Wayne/George Yardley/21.5; Minneapolis/Clyde Lovellette/20.8; New York/Harry Gallatin/15.0; Philadelphia/Paul Arizin/25.6; Rochester/Jack Twyman/16.3; St. Louis/Bob Pettit/24.7; and Syracuse/Dolph Schayes/22.5

1958: Boston/Bill Sharman/22.3; Cincinnati/Clyde Lovellette/23.4; Detroit/George Yardley/27.8; Minneapolis/Vern Mikkelsen/17.3; New York/Kenny Sears/18.6; Philadelphia/Paul Arizin/20.7; St. Louis/Bob Pettit/24.6; and Syracuse/Dolph Schayes/24.9

1959: Boston/Bill Sharman/20.4; Cincinnati/Jack Twyman/25.8; Detroit/Gene Shue/17.6; Minneapolis/Elgin Baylor/24.9; New York/Kenny Sears/21.0; Philadelphia/Paul Arizin/26.4; St. Louis/Bob Pettit/29.2; and Syracuse/Dolph Schayes/21.3

Table 6.29—Team Scoring Leaders Season by Season, 1947–1991 *(cont.)*

1960: Boston/Tom Heinsohn/21.7 points; Cincinnati/Jack Twyman/31.2; Detroit/Gene Shue/22.8; Minneapolis/Elgin Baylor/29.6; New York/Richie Guerin/21.8; Philadelphia/Wilt Chamberlain/37.6; St. Louis/Bob Pettit/26.1; and Syracuse/Dolph Schayes/22.5

1961: Boston/Tom Heinsohn/21.3; Cincinnati/Oscar Robertson/30.5; Detroit/Bailey Howell/23.6; Los Angeles/Elgin Baylor/34.8; New York/Willie Naulls/23.4; Philadelphia/Wilt Chamberlain/38.4; St. Louis/Bob Pettit/27.9; and Syracuse/Dolph Schayes/23.6

1962: Boston/Tom Heinsohn/22.1; Chicago/Walt Bellamy/31.6; Cincinnati/Oscar Robertson/30.8; Detroit/Bailey Howell/19.9; Los Angeles/Jerry West/30.8; New York/Richie Guerin/29.5; Philadelphia/Wilt Chamberlain/50.4; St. Louis/Bob Pettit/31.1; and Syracuse/Hal Greer/22.8

1963: Boston/Sam Jones/19.7; Chicago/Walt Bellamy/27.9; Cincinnati/Oscar Robertson/28.3; Detroit/Bailey Howell/22.7; Los Angeles/Elgin Baylor/34.0; New York/Richie Guerin/21.5; St. Louis/Bob Pettit/28.4; San Francisco/Wilt Chamberlain/44.8; and Syracuse/Hal Greer/19.5

1964: Baltimore/Walt Bellamy/27.0; Boston/John Havlicek/19.9; Cincinnati/Oscar Robertson/31.4; Detroit/Bailey Howell/21.6; Los Angeles/Jerry West/28.7; New York/Len Chappell/17.1; Philadelphia/Hal Greer/23.3; St. Louis/Bob Pettit/27.4; and San Francisco/Wilt Chamberlain/36.9

1965: Baltimore/Walt Bellamy/24.8; Boston/Sam Jones/25.9; Cincinnati/Oscar Robertson/30.4; Detroit/Terry Dischinger/18.2; Los Angeles/Jerry West/31.0; New York/Willis Reed/19.5; Philadelphia/Wilt Chamberlain/30.1; St. Louis/Bob Pettit/22.5; and San Francisco/Wilt Chamberlain/38.9 (Wilt was traded halfway into this 1964-65 season so he played for both clubs.)

1966: Baltimore/Don Ohl/20.6; Boston/Sam Jones/23.5; Cincinnati/Oscar Robertson/31.3; Detroit/Eddie Miles/19.6; Los Angeles/Jerry West/31.3; New York/Walt Bellamy/23.8; Philadelphia/Wilt Chamberlain/33.5; St. Louis/Zelmo Beatty/20.7; and San Francisco/Rick Barry/25.7

1967: Baltimore/Gus Johnson/20.7; Boston/John Havlicek/21.4; Chicago/Guy Rodgers/18.0; Cincinnati/Oscar Robertson/30.5; Detroit/Dave Bing/20.0; Los Angeles/Jerry West/28.7; New York/Willis Reed/20.9; Philadelphia/Wilt Chamberlain/24.1; St. Louis/Lou Hudson/18.4; and San Francisco/Rick Barry/35.6

1968: Baltimore/Earl Monroe/24.3; Boston/John Havlicek/20.7; Chicago/Bob Boozer/21.5; Cincinnati/Oscar Robertson/29.2; Detroit/Dave Bing/27.1; Los Angeles/Elgin Baylor/26.0; New York/Willis Reed/20.8; Philadelphia/Wilt Chamberlain/24.3; St. Louis/Zelmo Beatty/21.1; San Diego/Don Kojis/19.7; San Francisco/Rudy LaRusso/21.8; and Seattle/Walt Hazzard/23.9

1969: Atlanta/Lou Hudson/21.9; Baltimore/Earl Monroe/25.8; Boston/John Havlicek/21.6; Chicago/Bob Boozer/21.7; Cincinnati/Oscar Robertson/24.7; Detroit/Dave Bing/23.4; Los Angeles/Elgin Baylor/24.8; Milwaukee/Flynn Robinson/20.0; New York/Willis Reed/21.1; Philadelphia/Billy Cunningham/24.8; Phoenix Suns/Gail Goodrich/23.8; San Diego/Elvin Hayes/28.4; San Francisco/Jeff Mullins/22.8; and Seattle/Bob Rule/24.0

1970: Atlanta/Lou Hudson/25.4; Baltimore/Earl Monroe/23.4; Boston/John Havlicek/24.2; Chicago/Chet Walker/21.5; Cincinnati/Oscar Robertson/25.3; Detroit/Dave Bing/22.9; Los Angeles/Jerry West/31.2; Milwaukee/Kareem Abdul-Jabbar/28.8; New York/Willis Reed/21.7; Philadelphia/Billy Cunningham/26.1; Phoenix/Connie Hawkins/24.6; San Diego/Elvin Hayes/27.5; San Francisco/Jeff Mullins/22.1; and Seattle/Bob Rule/24.6

1971: Atlanta/Lou Hudson/26.8; Baltimore/Earl Monroe/21.4; Boston/John Havlicek/28.9; Buffalo/Bob Kauffman/20.4; Chicago/Bob Love/25.2; Cincinnati/Tom Van Arsdale/27.9; Cleveland/Walt Wesley/17.7; Detroit/Dave Bing/27.0; Los Angeles/Jerry West/16.9; Milwaukee/Kareem Abdul-Jabbar/31.7; New York/Walt Frazier/21.7; Philadelphia/Billy Cunningham/23.0; Phoenix/Dick Van Arsdale/21.9; Portland/Geoff Petrie/24.8; San Diego/Elvin Hayes/28.7; San Francisco/Jeff Mullins/20.8; and Seattle/Bob Rule/29.8

1972: Atlanta/Lou Hudson/24.7; Baltimore/Archie Clark/25.2; Boston/John Havlicek/27.5; Buffalo/Bob Kauffman/18.9; Chicago/Bob Love/25.8; Cincinnati/Nate Archibald/28.2; Cleveland/Austin Carr/21.2; Detroit/Bob Lanier/25.7; Golden State/Jeff Mullins/21.5; Houston/Elvin Hayes/25.2; Los Angeles/Gail Goodrich/25.9; Milwaukee/Kareem Abdul-Jabbar/34.8; New York/Walt Frazier/23.2; Philadelphia/Billy Cunningham/23.3; Phoenix/Connie Hawkins/21.0; Portland/Sidney Wicks/24.5; and Seattle/Spencer Haywood/26.2

1973: Atlanta/Lou Hudson/27.1; Baltimore/Elvin Hayes/21.2; Boston/John Havlicek/23.8; Buffalo/Elmore Smith/18.3; Chicago/Bob Love/23.1; Cleveland/Austin Carr/20.5; Detroit/Bob Lanier/23.8; Golden State/Rick Barry/22.3; Houston/Rudy Tomjanovich/19.3; Kansas City/Nate Archibald/34.0; Los Angeles/Gail Goodrich/23.9; Milwaukee/Kareem Abdul-Jabbar/30.2; New York/Walt Frazier/21.1; Philadelphia/Fred Carter/20.0; Phoenix/Charlie Scott/25.3; Portland/Geoff Petrie/24.9; and Seattle/Spencer Haywood/29.2

1974: Atlanta/Pete Maravich/27.7; Boston/John Havlicek/22.6; Buffalo/Bob McAdoo/30.6; Capital Bullets/Phil Chenier/21.9; Chicago/Bob Love/21.8; Cleveland/Austin Carr/21.9; Detroit/Bob Lanier/22.5; Golden State/Rick Barry/25.1; Houston/Rudy Tomjanovich/24.5; Kansas City-Omaha/Jimmy Walker/19.2; Los Angeles/Gail Goodrich/25.3; Milwaukee/Kareem Abdul-Jabbar/27.0; New York/Walt Frazier/20.5; Philadelphia/Fred Carter/21.4; Phoenix/Charlie Scott/25.4; Portland/Geoff Petrie/24.3; and Seattle/Spencer Haywood/23.5

1975: Atlanta/Lou Hudson/22.0; Boston/Dave Cowens/20.4; Buffalo/Bob McAdoo/34.5; Chicago/Bob Love/22.0; Cleveland/Randy Smith/15.9; Detroit/Bob Lanier/24.0; Golden State/Rick Barry/30.6; Houston/Rudy Tomjanovich/20.7; Kansas City-Omaha/Nate Archibald/26.5; Los Angeles/Gail Goodrich/22.6; Milwaukee/Kareem Abdul-Jabbar/30.0; New Orleans/Pete Maravich/21.5; New York/Walt Frazier/21.5; Philadelphia/Fred Carter/21.9; Phoenix/Charlie Scott/24.3; Portland/Sidney Wicks/21.7; Seattle/Spencer Haywood/22.4; and Washington/Elvin Hayes/23.0

1976: Atlanta/John Drew/21.6; Boston/Dave Cowens/19.0; Buffalo/Bob McAdoo/31.1; Chicago/Bob Love/19.1; Cleveland/Jim Chones/15.8; Detroit/Bob Lanier/21.3; Golden State/Rick Barry/21.0; Houston/Calvin Murphy/21.0; Kansas City/Nate Archibald/24.8; Los Angeles/Kareem Abdul-Jabbar/27.7; Milwaukee/Bob Dandridge/21.5; New Orleans/Pete Maravich/25.9; New York/Earl Monroe/20.7; Philadelphia/George McGinnis/23.0; Phoenix/Paul Westphal/20.5; Portland/Sidney Wicks/19.1; Seattle/Fred Brown/23.1; and Washington/Phil Chenier/19.9

Table 6.29 — Team Scoring Leaders Season by Season, 1947–1991 *(cont.)*

1977: Atlanta/John Drew/24.2 points; Boston/Jo Jo White/19.6; Buffalo/Bob McAdoo/23.7; Chicago Bulls/Artis Gilmore/18.6; Cleveland/Campy Russell/16.5; Denver/David Thompson/25.9; Detroit/Bob Lanier/25.3; Golden State/Rick Barry/21.8; Houston/Rudy Tomjanovich/21.6; Indiana/Billy Knight/26.6; Kansas City/Ron Boone/22.2; Los Angeles/Kareem Abdul-Jabbar/26.2; Milwaukee/Bob Dandridge/20.8; New Orleans/Pete Maravich/31.1; New York/Bob McAdoo/25.8 (he played for two teams); NY Nets/John Williamson/20.8; Philadelphia/Julius Erving/21.6; Phoenix/Paul Westphal/21.3; Portland/Maurice Lucas/20.2; San Antonio/George Gervin/23.1; Seattle/Fred Brown/17.2; and Washington/Elvin Hayes/23.7

1978: Atlanta/John Drew/23.2; Boston/Dave Cowens/18.6; Buffalo/Randy Smith/24.6; Chicago/Artis Gilmore/22.9; Cleveland/Campy Russell/19.4; Denver/David Thompson/27.2; Detroit/Bob Lanier/24.5; Golden State/Rick Barry/23.1; Houston/Calvin Murphy/25.6; Indiana/Adrian Dantley/26.5; Kansas City/Scott Wedman/17.7; Los Angeles/Kareem Abdul-Jabbar/25.8; Milwaukee/Brian Winters/19.9; NJ Nets/Bernard King/24.2; New Orleans/Pete Maravich/27.0; New York/Bob McAdoo/26.5; Philadelphia/Julius Erving/20.6; Phoenix/Paul Westphal/25.2; Portland/Bill Walton/18.9; San Antonio/George Gervin/27.2; Seattle/Gus Williams/18.1; and Washington/Elvin Hayes/19.7

1979: Atlanta/John Drew/22.7; Boston/Bob McAdoo/20.6; Chicago/Artis Gilmore/23.7; Cleveland/Campy Russell/21.9; Denver Nuggets/David Thompson/24.0; Detroit/Bob Lanier/23.6; Golden State/Phil Smith/19.9; Houston/Moses Malone/24.8; Indiana/Johnny Davis/18.3; Kansas City/Otis Birdsong/21.7; Los Angeles/Kareem Abdul-Jabbar/23.8; Milwaukee/Marques Johnson/25.6; NJ Nets/John Williamson/22.2; New Orleans/Truck Robinson/24.2; New York/Bob McAdoo/26.9; Philadelphia/Julius Erving/23.1; Phoenix/Paul Westphal/24.0; Portland/Maurice Lucas/20.4; San Antonio/George Gervin/29.6; San Diego/World B. Free/28.8; Seattle/Gus Williams/19.2; and Washington/Elvin Hayes/21.8

1980: Atlanta/John Drew/19.5; Boston/Larry Bird/21.3; Chicago/Reggie Theus/20.2; Cleveland/Mike Mitchell/22.2; Denver/Dan Issel/23.8; Detroit/Bob Lanier/21.7; Golden State/Purvis Short/17.0; Houston/Moses Malone/25.8; Indiana/M. Johnson/19.1; Kansas City/Otis Birdsong/22.7; Los Angeles/Kareem Abdul-Jabbar/24.8; Milwaukee/Marques Johnson/21.7; NJ Nets/Mike Newlin/20.9; New York/Bill Cartwright/21.7; Philadelphia/Julius Erving/26.9; Phoenix/Paul Westphal/21.9; Portland/Calvin Natt/19.9; San Antonio/George Gervin/33.1; San Diego/World B. Free/30.2; Seattle/Gus Williams/22.1; Utah/Adrian Dantley/28.0; and Washington/Elvin Hayes/23.0

1981: Atlanta/John Drew/21.7; Boston/Larry Bird/21.2; Chicago/Reggie Theus/18.9; Cleveland/Mike Mitchell/24.5; Dallas/Jim Spanarkel/14.4; Denver/David Thompson/25.5; Detroit/John Long/17.7; Golden State/World B. Free/24.1; Houston/Moses Malone/27.8; Indiana/Bobby Knight/17.5; Kansas City/Otis Birdsong/24.6; Los Angeles/Kareem Abdul-Jabbar/26.2; Milwaukee/Marques Johnson/20.3; NY Nets/Mike Newlin/21.4; New York/Bill Cartwright/20.1; Philadelphia/Julius Erving/24.6; Phoenix/Truck Robinson/18.8; Portland/Jim Paxson/17.1; San Antonio Spurs/George Gervin/27.1; San Diego/Freeman Williams/19.3; Seattle/Jack Sikma/18.7; Utah/Adrian Dantley/30.7; and Washington/Elvin Hayes/17.8

1982: Atlanta/Dan Roundfield/18.6; Boston/Larry Bird/22.9; Chicago/Artis Gilmore/18.5; Cleveland/Mike Mitchell/19.6; Dallas/Jay Vincent/21.4; Denver/Alex

English/25.4; Detroit/John Long/21.9; Golden State/Bernard King/23.2; Houston/Moses Malone/31.1; Indiana/Johnny Davis/17.0; Kansas City/Cliff Robinson/20.2; Los Angeles/Kareem Abdul-Jabbar/23.9; Milwaukee/Sidney Moncrief/19.8; NJ Nets/Ray Williams/20.4; New York/Michael Ray Richardson/17.9; Philadelphia/Julius Erving/24.4; Phoenix/Dennis Johnson/19.5; Portland/Thompson/20.8; San Antonio/George Gervin/32.3; San Diego/Tom Chambers/17.2; Seattle/Gus Williams/23.4; Utah/Adrian Dantley/30.3; and Washington/Greg Ballard/18.8

1983: Atlanta/Dan Roundfield/19.0; Boston/Larry Bird/23.6; Chicago/Reggie Theus/23.8; Cleveland/World B. Free/23.9; Dallas/Mark Aguirre/24.4; Denver/Alex English/28.4; Detroit/Kelly Tripucka/26.5; Golden State/Joe Barry Carroll/24.1; Houston/Allan Leavall/14.8; Indiana/Clark Kellog/20.1; Kansas City/Larry Drew/20.1; Los Angeles/Kareem Abdul-Jabbar/21.8; Milwaukee/Sidney Moncrief/22.5; NJ Nets/Albert King/17.0; New York/Bernard King/21.9; Philadelphia/Moses Malone/24.5; Phoenix/Walter Davis/19.0; Portland/Jim Paxson/21.7; San Antonio/George Gervin/26.2; San Diego/Terry Cummings/23.7; Seattle/Gus Williams/20.0; Utah/Adrian Dantley/30.7; and Washington/Jeff Ruland/19.4

1984: Atlanta/Dominique Wilkins/21.6; Boston/Larry Bird/24.2; Chicago/Orlando Woolridge/19.3; Cleveland/World B. Free/22.3; Dallas/Mark Aguirre/29.5; Denver/Kiki Vandeweghe/29.4; Detroit/Isiah Thomas/21.3; Golden State/Purvis Short/22.8; Houston/Ralph Sampson/21.0; Indiana/Clark Kellog/19.1; Kansas City/Eddie Johnson/21.9; Los Angeles/Kareem Abdul-Jabbar/21.5; Milwaukee/Sidney Moncrief/20.9; NJ Nets/Otis Birdsong/19.8; New York/Bernard King/26.3; Philadelphia/Moses Malone/22.7; Phoenix/Walter Davis/20.0; Portland/Jim Paxson/21.3; San Antonio/George Gervin/25.9; San Diego/Terry Cummings/22.9; Seattle/Jack Sikma/19.1; Utah/Adrian Dantley/30.6; and Washington/Jeff Ruland/22.2

1985: Atlanta/Dominique Wilkins/27.4; Boston/Larry Bird/28.7; Chicago/Michael Jordan/28.2; Cleveland/World B. Free/22.5; Dallas/Mark Aguirre/25.7; Denver/Alex English/27.9; Detroit/Isiah Thomas/21.2; Golden State/Purvis Short/28.0; Houston/Ralph Sampson/22.1; Indiana/Clark Kellog/18.6; Kansas City/Eddie Johnson/22.9; LA Clippers/Derek Smith/22.1; LA Lakers/Kareem Abdul-Jabbar/22.0; Milwaukee/Terry Cummings/23.6; NJ Nets/Otis Birdsong/20.6; New York/Bernard King/32.9; Philadelphia/Moses Malone/24.6; Phoenix/Larry Nance/19.9; Portland/Kiki Vandeweghe/22.4; San Antonio/Mike Mitchell/22.2; Seattle/Tom Chambers/21.5; Utah/Adrian Dantley/26.6; and Washington/Gus Williams/20.0

1986: Atlanta/Dominique Wilkins/30.3; Boston/Larry Bird/25.8; Chicago/Michael Jordan/22.7; Cleveland/World B. Free/23.4; Dallas/Mark Aguirre/22.6; Denver/Alex English/29.8; Detroit/Isiah Thomas/20.9; Golden State/Purvis Short/25.5; Houston/Hakeem Olajuwon/23.5; Indiana/Herb Williams/19.9; LA Clippers/Derek Smith/23.5; LA Lakers/Kareem Abdul-Jabbar/23.4; Milwaukee/Sidney Moncrief/20.2; NJ Nets/Mike Gminski/16.5; New York/Pat Ewing/20.0; Philadelphia/Moses Malone/23.8; Phoenix/Walter Davis/21.8; Portland/Kiki Vandeweghe/24.8; Sacramento/Johnson/18.7; San Antonio/Mike Mitchell/23.4; Seattle/Tom Chambers/18.5; Utah/Adrian Dantley/29.8; and Washington/Moses Malone/22.4

1987: Atlanta/Dominique Wilkins/29.0; Boston/Larry Bird/28.1; Chicago/Michael Jordan/37.1; Cleveland/Ron Harper/22.9; Dallas/Mark Aguirre/25.7; Denver/Alex English/28.6; Detroit/Adrian Dantley/21.5; Golden State/Joe Barry Carroll/21.2; Houston/Hakeem Olajuwon/23.4; Indiana/Chuck Person/18.8; LA Clippers/Mike

Table 6.29—Team Scoring Leaders Season by Season, 1947–1991 *(cont.)*

Woodson/17.1; LA Lakers/Magic Johnson/23.9; Milwaukee/Terry Cummings/20.8; NJ Nets/Orlando Woolridge/20.7; New York/Bernard King/22.7; Philadelphia/Charles Barkley/23.0; Phoenix/Walter Davis/23.6; Portland/Kiki Vandeweghe/26.9; Sacramento/Reggie Theus/20.3; San Antonio/Alvin Robertson/17.7; Seattle/Dale Ellis/24.9; Utah/Karl Malone/21.7; and Washington/Moses Malone/24.1

1988: Atlanta/Dominique Wilkins/30.7; Boston/Larry Bird/29.9; Chicago/Michael Jordan/35.0; Cleveland/Larry Nance/19.1; Dallas/Mark Aguirre/25.1; Denver/Alex English/25.0; Detroit/Adrian Dantley/20.0; Golden State/Sleepy Floyd/21.2; Houston/Hakeem Olajuwon/22.8; Indiana/Chuck Person/17.0; LA Clippers/Mike Woodson/18.0; LA Lakers/Byron Scott/21.7; Milwaukee/Terry Cummings/21.3; NJ Nets/Buck Williams/18.3; New York/Pat Ewing/20.2; Philadelphia/Charles Barkley/28.3; Phoenix/Larry Nance/21.1; Portland/Clyde Drexler/27.0; Sacramento/Reggie Theus/21.6; San Antonio/Alin Robertson/19.6; Seattle/Dale Ellis/25.8; Utah/Karl Malone/27.7; Washington/Jeff Malone/20.5

1989: Atlanta/Dominique Wilkins/26.2; Boston/Kevin McHale/22.5; Charlotte/Kelly Tripucka/22.6; Chicago/Michael Jordan/32.5; Cleveland/Brad Daugherty/18.9; Dallas/Mark Aguirre/21.7; Denver/Alex English/26.5; Detroit/Mark Aguirre/18.9; Golden State/Chris Mullin/26.5; Houston/Hakeem Olajuwon/24.8; Indiana/Chuck Person/21.6; LA Clippers/Kenny Norman/18.1; LA Lakers/Magic Johnson/22.5; Miami/Kevin Edwards/13.8; Milwaukee/Terry Cummings/22.9; NJ Nets/Roy Hinson/16.0; New York/Pat Ewing/22.7; Philadelphia/Charles Barkley/25.8; Phoenix/Tom Chambers/25.7; Portland/Clyde Drexler/27.2; Sacramento/Danny Ainge/20.3; San Antonio/W. Anderson/18.6; Seattle/Dale Ellis/27.5; Utah/Karl Malone/29.1; Washington/Moses Malone/21.7

1990: Atlanta/Dominique Wilkins/26.7; Boston/Larry Bird/24.3; Charlotte/Rex Chapman/17.5; Chicago/Michael Jordan/33.6; Cleveland/Ron Harper/22.0; Dallas/Rolando Blackman/19.4; Denver/Lafayette Lever/18.3; Detroit/Isiah Thomas/18.4; Golden State/Chris Mullin/25.1; Houston/Hakeem Olajuwon/24.3; Indiana/Reggie Miller/24.3; LA Clippers/Ron Harper/22.8 (he played with both Cleveland and LA Clippers that season); LA Lakers/Magic Johnson/22.3; Miami/Ron Seikaly/16.6; Milwaukee/Ricky Pierce/23.0; Minnesota/Ricky Campbell/23.2; NJ Nets/Dennis Hopson/15.8; NY Knicks/Patrick Ewing/28.6; Orlando/Terry Catledge/19.4; Philadelphia/Charles Barkley/25.2; Phoenix/Tom Chambers/27.2; Portland/Clyde Drexler/23.3; Sacramento/Waymond Tisdale/22.3; San Antonio/David Robinson/24.3; Seattle/Dale Ellis/23.5; Utah/Karl Malone/31.0; and Washington/Jeff Malone/24.3

1991: Atlanta/Dominique Wilkins/25.9; Boston/Larry Bird/19.4; Charlotte/Armon Gilliam/19.8; Chicago/Michael Jordan/31.5; Cleveland/Brad Daugherty/21.6; Dallas/Roy Tarpley/20.4; Denver/Michael Adams/26.5; Detroit/Joe Dumars/20.4; Golden State/Chris Mullin/25.7; Houston/Hakeem Olajuwon/21.2; Indiana/Reggie Miller/22.6; LA Clippers/Reggie Smith/20.0; LA Lakers/James Worthy/21.4; Miami/Sherman Douglas/18.5; Milwaukee/Ricky Pierce/22.5; Minnesota/Ricky Campbell/21.8; NJ Nets/Reggie Theus/18.6; NY Knicks/Patrick Ewing/26.6; Orlando/Scott Skiles/17.2; Philadelphia/Charles Barkley/27.6; Phoenix/Kevin Johnson/22.2; Portland/Clyde Drexler/21.5; Sacramento/Kenny Carr/20.1; San Antonio/David Robinson/25.6; Seattle/Xavier McDaniel/21.8; Utah/Karl Malone/29.0; and Washington/Bernard King/28.4

Chapter 7

Team and League Records

Table 7.1—Chronology of Professional Basketball Leagues

National Basketball League (NBL) First ever. Began in 1898 and lasted through 1903 until it was reformed again in 1937. The NBL merged with the BAA in 1949 to form the current NBA.

Philadelphia League Began in 1904 and became known as the **Eastern League** in 1909.

Central League Started in 1906 out of Pennsylvania.

Hudson River League Started in 1909 in New York.

New York State League Began in 1911.

West Pennsylvania League Began in 1912.

Pennsylvania State League Began in 1914.

Inter-State League Began in 1915.

Metropolitan League Began in 1921.

American Basketball League (ABL) Began in 1926.

Harlem Globetrotters Began in 1927.

Basketball Association of America (BAA) Began in 1946.

Eastern League Began in 1946 as a minor league.

National Basketball Association (NBA) Began in 1949 as the NBL and BAA merged.

American Basketball League The second coming of the ABL began in 1961 and folded before the middle of the next year.

American Basketball Association (ABA) Began in 1967; lasted through 1976.

Continental Basketball Association Began in 1980. The CBA is an extension of the Eastern League as a minor league.

American Basketball League (ABL)

The ABL had two different eras; the first was when an eight team league was started in 1926 by two men. Both George Preston Marshall (a businessman who owned a laundry) and Joe Carr (who would become the league's president) decided a competitive league was needed to match the various local leagues (see chronology).

The teams of this first ABL included: Washington, Rochester, Philadelphia, New York, Ft. Wayne, Chicago, Baltimore and Cleveland. The names of the teams included the Celtics (from NY), the Rosenblums (from Cleveland), the Sphas (from Philadelphia), to mention a few. The Sphas (South Philadelphia Hebrew Association) were the dominant team of the league, winning seven championships.

In 1930, during the depression, the ABL went bust, only to regroup again in 1933. It continued—in the background, however—through the 1950s and was renamed the Eastern League. The newer NBA overshadowed it.

The second ABL was formed in 1961 by Abe Saperstein (who later formed the Harlem Globetrotters) but due to undercapitalization, the league lasted only one and one-half seasons. Some great NBA stars played in the second ABL including Connie Hawkins, Dick Barnett, and Bill Bridges, while Saperstein played the commissioner role, as well as the banker role.

Teams of the second ABL era included: the Chicago Majors, Kansas City Steers, Hawaii Chiefs, as well as five other franchises located in Los Angeles (and later Long Beach), San Francisco (and later Oakland), Washington, Cleveland and Pittsburgh (the Pipers).

The eight team league featured scoring champ Hawkins, who poured in 27.5 a game in the first year, 1962, and Bridges, a 6′6″ forward who would later play in the NBA, leading the league in scoring in 1963—at 29.2 per game—as well as in rebounding for both of its seasons. He also scored a whopping 55 points in a single ABL game and won a team championship with Kansas City in 1963—the league's second and final season.

Table 7.2—ABL Team Champions

1961—Cleveland
1962—Kansas City Steers
1963—Kansas City Steers

Continental Basketball Association (CBA)

This minor pro league picked up where the Eastern League left off. It officially began in 1980.* In 1989 there were 12 teams in the league. They play only a 54 game season schedule from November 17 to March 12, with the league championships in April.

Attendance is well over one million spectators a year. The all time league

**Note:* The CBA has been ongoing (unofficially) since 1945, however.

leading scorer is Tico Brown. Many famous NBA players started in the CBA before they made it to the NBA.

The Continental Basketball Association is the current minor league equivalent to baseball's minors. The CBA has sent many stars up to the pros as they acquired more experience and fundamentals after their college careers were over. Conversely, many players have also "dropped" down to the CBA after having played in the NBA. Former NBA players now in the CBA include: George Gervin, Marvin Webster, Kenny Natt, Freeman Williams, Fred Cofield and Quintin Dailey. They are there now either because of age, retirement from the NBA, injuries or personal problems. They play a competitive schedule of 54 season games and are well coached and prepared for an NBA team to offer them a contract.

Many CBA players have moved up to the NBA, including: Michael Adams, Terry Teagle, Manute Bol, Tyrone Bogues, Rod Higgins, Tony Campbell, Brad Davis and Eddie Lee Wilkins of the NY Knicks.

Bill Musselman, the CBA's all time best coach—with four league championships—has paved the way for other coaches to try to earn an NBA coaching spot. Phil Jackson, now with the Chicago Bulls, worked, too, in the CBA. Henry Bibby, the former great pro, is a coach in the CBA as is Cazzie Russell.

Eastern League

It was originally formed in 1910 as an early pro league, but lasted only through 1922. When one speaks of the Eastern League, however, they usually are referring to the minor pro league that is the training ground for players, coaches and officials. It was started in 1947 and the official name is the Eastern Professional Basketball League. It lasted through the 1970s before it was replaced by the CBA.

Teams of the Eastern League included: Allentown Jets; Wilkes-Barre Barons; Williamsport Billies; Pottsville Packers; Sunbury Mercuries; Scranton Miners; Easton Madisons; Camden Bullets; Hamden Bics; and the Wilmington Blue Bombers.

The Early Pro Teams

The Buffalo Germans (1895–1925) They had a 792–86 win/lose record in the NBL and captured 111 consecutive games in one brilliant streak.

The Cleveland Rosenblums (1920s) They were among the most dominant teams in the ABL.

The Harlem Globetrotters Formed in 1926 and continuing strongly through the present day, they've won an astonishing 15,000 plus games with only one defeat. That defeat came accidentally on January 5, 1971, when the opposing team, the Washington Generals—which was supposed to lose—sank an errant basket. Abe Saperstein, the founder and coach, assembled such talented players as Goose Tatum, Marques Haynes, Nat "Sweetwater" Clifton, Charles Cooper, Curly Neal, Meadlowlark Lemon, Bob Karstens, Wilt Chamberlain and Connie Hawkins.

The New York Celtics (1914–1917) A short lived pro team with two main stars: John Witte and future original Celtic, Pete Barry. They ran out of funds to support themselves.

The New York Jewels (1920s) A brilliantly talented squad in the ABL, they challenged the Rosenblums for league dominance before the Great Depression.

The New York Rens (Renaissance Big 5) (1922–1947) Their awesome record was 2,318 wins with only 381 losses, mainly in the New York State League.

The Original Celtics (1914–1936) While there are no official records of exact games won/lost, the Celtics won 90 percent of their games during these years, mainly playing in the NY State League.

The Philadelphia Sphas (1918–1934) They captured 11 titles in the West Pennsylvania League—among others—and the Eastern League.

The Troy Trojans (1990s) They won five league titles in both the NY State League and the Hudson River League. This squad helped popularize such concepts as the "fast-break," the bounce pass, and individual free throw shots after every personal foul.

Table 7.3—The Early Leagues: Year by Year Team Champions

Year	Team	Season Record	League
		The Early Pros	
1899	Trenton	17–2	NBL
1900	Trenton	16–5	NBL
1901	New York	22–9	NBL
1902	Bristol	27–13	NBL
1903	Camden	21–7	NBL
1904	Jasper	24–4	Philadelphia
1905	Conshohocken	31–8	Philadelphia
1906	Deneri	24–6	Philadelphia
1910	Troy	24–4	Hudson River
1911	Troy	29–10	Hudson River
1912	Kingston	14–8	Hudson River
1913	Southside	24–5	Western Pennsylvania

Year	Team	Season Record
	The Eastern League	
1910	Trenton	20–10
1911	Deneri	28–12
1912	Trenton	29–11
1913	Reading	30–10
1914	Jasper	23–17
1915	Camden	25–15
1916	Greystock	27–13
1917	Jasper	14–6
1918	Jasper	4–2 (shortened year)
1920	Camden	15–5
1921	Reading	15–5
1922	Trenton	24–3 (last year of the league)

Note: There was no league play in 1919 due to World War I.

Year	Team	Season Record
	The New York State League	
1912	Troy	36–12
1913	Troy	35–13
1914	Utica	46–17
1915	Troy	19–8
1917	Schenectady	15–7
1920	Troy	27–5
1921	Albany	22–6
1922	Gloversville	20–9
1923	Kingston	20–4

Note: No play in the years 1916, 1918–19.

Year	Team	Season Record
	The Pennsylvania State League	
1915	Pittston	18–2
1916	Wilkes-Barre	29–13
1917	Carbondale	33–7
1918	Pittston	22–6
1920	Scranton	18–6
1921	Kingston	14–10

Note: No play in 1919.

Year	Team	Season Record
	The Metropolitan League	
1922	Brooklyn	12–8
1923	Patterson	20–11
1924	Brooklyn	13–7
1925	Brooklyn	14–5
1926	Yonkers	15–6
	The American League	
1927	New York	19–1
1928	New York	40–9
1930	Rochester	19–11

Table 7.3—The Early Leagues: Year by Year Team Champions *(cont.)*

Year	Team	Season Record
1931	Brooklyn	14–7
1934	Trenton	22–6
1935	NY Jewels	16–6
1936	Philadelphia Hebrews	14–5
1937	Jersey Reds	14–4
1938	Jersey Reds	16–6
1939	Kingston Colonials	28–7
1940	Philadelphia Hebrews	20–13
1941	Brooklyn Celtics	11–4
1943	Trenton	11–2
1944	Wilmington Bombers	12–4
1945	Philadelphia Sphas	22–8
1946	Baltimore Bullets	21–13
1947	Baltimore Bullets	31–3
1948	Wilkes-Barre	26–8
1949	Wilkes-Barre	29–12
1950	Scranton Miners	27–11
1951	Scranton Miners	26–8
1952	Scranton Miners	24–11

Note: No league play in 1929, 1932–33.

	The National Basketball League	
1938	Firestone	14–4
1939	Firestone	24–3
1940	Firestone	18–9
1941	Oshkosh	18–6
1942	Oshkosh	20–4
1943	Ft. Wayne	17–5
1944	Ft. Wayne	18–4
1945	Ft. Wayne	22–5
1946	Ft. Wayne	26–8
1947	Rochester	31–13
1948	Rochester	44–16
1949	Anderson	49–15

Table 7.4—Teams of the Basketball Association of America (BAA), 1946–49

Baltimore Bullets
Boston Celtics
Chicago Stags
Cleveland Rebels
Detroit Falcons
Ft. Wayne Zollner Pistons
Indianapolis Jets
Minneapolis Lakers
New York Knickerbockers
Philadelphia Warriors
Pittsburgh Ironmen
Providence Steamrollers

Rochester Royals	Toronto Huskies
St. Louis Bombers	Washington Capitols

*Best Teams: Washington Capitols and Rochester Royals. In the three seasons of its existence, the BAA had 60 game seasons and 8 to 12 teams in the league each year.

Table 7.5—Teams of the National Basketball League (NBL), 1937–49

Anderson	Denver	Pittsburgh
Akron Firestone	Detroit	Rochester
Akron Goodyear	Flint	Syracuse
Buffalo	Ft. Wayne	Tri Cities
Chicago	Hammond	Toledo
Cleveland	Indianapolis	Warren
Cincinnati	Kankakee	Waterloo
Columbus	Minneapolis	Youngstown
Dayton	Oshkosh	

Note: Most NBL teams had no second name. Leagues were made up of between 8 to 12 teams each year. The total number of games played per season varied from 13 to 30, all the way up to 64 games in the final season, 1948-49. This was due to travel problems and restrictions of different teams. Some teams played 60, 62 or 64 games in the final season. Best Teams: Minneapolis Lakers and the Rochester Royals, who, by the way, continued their dominance the following season, 1949-50, when the NBA was first formed.

Table 7.6—The Basketball Association of America and the National Basketball League: Won/Lost Records

Team	All Time Won/Lost Record
The Basketball Association of America (BAA)	
Baltimore Bullets	29–31
Boston Celtics	67–101
Cleveland Rebels	30–30
Chicago Stags	105–64
Detroit Falcons	20–40
Ft. Wayne Pistons	22–38
Indianapolis Jets	18–42
Minneapolis Lakers	44–16
New York Knickerbockers	91–77
Pittsburgh Ironmen	15–45
Philadelphia Warriors	55–53
Providence Steamrollers	28–32
Rochester Royals	45–15
St. Louis Bombers	58–50
Toronto Huskies	22–38
Washington Capitols	115–53

As one can obviously see, many of the teams in the short-lived BAA were losers. That is why it was so short-lived (only three seasons, 1946–1949). Even the future dominant team of the NBA, the Boston Celtics, were struggling. Only a few of the BAA's teams entered the NBA in the early 1950s. The best of the bunch were the Lakers and the Royals, who dominated most of the 1950s in pro ball.

Team	All Time Won/Lost Record
The National Basketball League (NBL)	
Akron Firestone	69–27
Akron Goodyear	67–55
Anderson	115–53
Buffalo	3–6
Chicago	98–108
Cincinnati	3–7
Cleveland	34–61
Columbus	1–12
Dayton	2–11
Denver	18–44
Detroit	35–79
Flint	8–52
Ft. Wayne Pistons	179–78
Hammond	34–84
Indianapolis	99–126
Kankakee	3–11
Minneapolis	43–17
Oshkosh All-Stars	208–170
Pittsburgh	28–42
Rochester	99–39
Sheboygan	199–182
Syracuse	85–82
Toledo	46–85
Tri Cities	85–83
Warren	30–32
Waterloo	30–32
Whitting	12–3
Youngstown	25–52

Table 7.7 — The American Basketball Association and the National Basketball Association: Won/Lost Records

Team	Regular Season	Playoffs
The American Basketball Association (ABA)		
Anaheim Amigos	25–53	0–0
Carolina Cougars	215–205	7–9

Team	Regular Season	Playoffs
Dallas Chaparrals	202–206	9–16
Denver Nuggets	413–331	27–35
Denver Rockets	288–288	14–22
Floridians	73–95	2–8
Houston Mavericks	52–104	0–3
Indiana Pacers	427–317	69–50
Kentucky Colonels	448–296	55–46
Los Angeles Stars	76–86	10–7
Memphis Sounds	139–291	1–8
Minnesota Muskies	50–28	4–6
Minnesota Pipers	36–42	3–4
New Jersey Americans	36–42	0–0
New Orleans Buccaneers	136–104	14–14
New York Nets	338–328	37–32
Oakland Oaks	82–74	12–4
Pittsburgh Condors	61–107	0–0
Pittsburgh Pipers	83–79	11–4
San Antonio Spurs	146–106	8–12
San Diego Conquistadors	101–73	2–8
San Diego Sails	3–8	0–0
Spirits of St. Louis	67–101	5–5
Texas Chaparrals	30–54	0–4
Utah Stars	265–171	36–27
Virginia Squires	200–303	15–18
Washington Capitols	44–40	3–4

The National Basketball Association

Team	Regular Season	Playoffs
Anderson Packers	37–27	4–4
Atlanta Hawks	1522–1536	96–113
Baltimore Bullets	161–303	9–7
Boston Celtics	2073–1158	257–167
Chicago Bulls	855–948	27–57
Chicago Stags	145–92	7–13
Cleveland Cavaliers	573–903	10–17
Cleveland Rebels	30–30	1–2
Dallas Mavericks	320–336	21–24
Denver Nuggets	531–453	33–44
Detroit Falcons	20–40	0–0
Detroit Pistons	1429–1691	72–87
Golden State Warriors	1553–1673	90–100
Houston Rockets	780–942	47–51
Indiana Pacers	394–590	1–5
Indianapolis Jets	18–42	0–0
Los Angeles Clippers	537–939	9–13
Los Angeles Lakers	1898–1223	265–176
Milwaukee Bucks	992–648	81–72
New Jersey Nets	403–581	5–18

Table 7.7—The American Basketball Association and the National Basketball Association: Won/Lost Records *(cont.)*

Team	Regular Season	Playoffs
New York Knickerbockers	1573–1654	98–98
Philadelphia 76ers	1764–1292	167–140
Phoenix Suns	811–829	40–48
Pittsburgh Ironmen	15–45	0–0
Portland Trail Blazers	725–751	31–36
Providence Steamrollers	46–122	0–0
Sacramento Kings	1496–1625	45–69
St. Louis Bombers	122–115	4–8
San Antonio Spurs	510–474	25–38
Sheboygan Redskins	22–40	1–2
Seattle SuperSonics	838–884	52–51
Toronto Huskies	22–38	0–0
Utah Jazz	487–661	18–23
Washington Bullets	1102–1101	69–94
Washington Capitols	157–114	8–11
Waterloo Hawks	19–43	0–0

Note: All NBA team totals are through the 1992 season.

Table 7.8—Years of Existence of ABA Teams

Team	Years	Team	Years
Anaheim Amigos	1967–68	Minnesota Pipers	1968–76
Carolina Cougars	1969–74	New Jersey Americans	1967–68
Dallas Chaparrals	1967–73	New York Nets	1968–76*
Denver Nuggets	1975–76*	Oakland Oaks	1967–69
Denver Rockets	1967–74	Pittsburgh Condors	1970–72
Houston Mavericks	1967–79	Pittsburgh Pipers	1967–70
Indiana Pacers	1967–76	San Antonio Spurs	1973–76
Kentucky Colonels	1967–76	San Diego Conquistadors	1972–75
Los Angeles Stars	1968–70	San Diego Sails	1975–76**
Memphis Tams	1973–74	Spirits of St. Louis	1974–76
Memphis Pros	1970–72	Texas Chaparrals	1970–71
Memphis Sounds	1974–75	Utah Stars	1970–76
Miami Floridians	1968–72	Virginia Squires	1971–76
Minnesota Muskies	1967–68	Washington Capitols	1969–70

*Team also played in the NBA.

**Team only played 11 games in 1976 year.

Table 7.9—Years of Existence of NBA Teams

Team	Years
Anderson Packers	1949–50
Atlanta Hawks	1969–Present
Baltimore Bullets	1947–55 and 1964–73
Boston Celtics	1946–Present

Buffalo Braves	1970–78
Capitol Bullets	1973–74
Chicago Bulls	1966–Present
Chicago Packers	1961–62
Chicago Stags	1946–50
Chicago Zephyrs	1963–64
Cincinnati Royals	1958–72
Cleveland Cavaliers	1970–Present
Cleveland Rebels	1946–47
Dallas Mavericks	1980–Present
Denver Nuggets	1949–50 and 1967–Present
Detroit Falcons	1946–47
Detroit Pistons	1958–Present
Ft. Wayne Pistons	1948–58
Golden State Warriors	1971–Present
Houston Rockets	1972–Present
Indiana Pacers	1967–Present
Indianapolis Jets	1948–49
Indianapolis Olympians	1949–53
Kansas City–Omaha Kings	1973–85
Los Angeles Clippers	1985–Present
Los Angeles Lakers	1961–Present
Milwaukee Bucks	1968–Present
Minneapolis Lakers	1948–61
New Jersey Nets	1978–Present
New York Knicks	1946–Present
New York Nets	1967–77
New Orleans Jazz	1974–79
Philadelphia Warriors	1946–63
Philadelphia 76ers	1964–Present
Pittsburgh Ironmen	1946–47
Phoenix Suns	1968–Present
Portland Trail Blazers	1970–Present
Rochester Royals	1948–57
San Antonio Spurs	1976–Present
Sacramento Kings	1986–Present
San Diego Clippers	1979–84
San Diego Rockets	1967–72
San Francisco Warriors	1963–70
Seattle SuperSonics	1967–Present
Sheboygan Redskins	1949–50
St. Louis Bombers	1946–50
St. Louis Hawks	1956–69
Syracuse Nationals	1949–63
Toronto Huskies	1946–47
Tri Cities Blackhawks	1949–52
Utah Jazz	1980–Present
Washington Bullets	1974–Present
Washington Capitols	1946–51
Waterloo Hawks	1949–50

Table 7.10 – NBA Teams by Conferences and Divisions

Central Division	Atlantic Division
Eastern Conference	
Atlanta Hawks	Boston Celtics
Chicago Bulls	Charlotte Hornets
Cleveland Cavaliers	New Jersey Nets
Detroit Pistons	New York Knicks
Indiana Pacers	Orlando Magic
Milwaukee Bucks	Philadelphia 76ers
Minnesota Timberwolves	Washington Bullets

Western Conference

Midwest Division	Pacific Division
Dallas Mavericks	Golden State Warriors
Denver Nuggets	Los Angeles Clippers
Houston Rockets	Los Angeles Lakers
Miami Heat	Phoenix Suns
San Antonio Spurs	Portland Trail Blazers
Utah Jazz	Sacramento Kings
	Seattle SuperSonics

Table 7.11 – Best Season by Season Records (NBA)

Team	Year	Won/Lost Record
Chicago Stags	1947	38–22
Baltimore Bullets	1948	28–20
Minneapolis Lakers	1949	44–16
Syracuse Nationals	1950	51–13
Rochester Royals	1951	41–27
Minneapolis Lakers	1952	40–26
Minneapolis Lakers	1953	48–22
Minneapolis Lakers	1954	46–26
Ft. Wayne Pistons	1955	43–29
Philadelphia Warriors	1956	45–27
Boston Celtics	1957	44–28
Boston Celtics	1958	49–23
Boston Celtics	1959	52–20
Boston Celtics	1960	59–16
Boston Celtics	1961	57–22
Boston Celtics	1962	60–20
Boston Celtics	1963	58–22
Boston Celtics	1964	59–21
Boston Celtics	1965	62–18
Boston Celtics	1966	54–26

Team	Year	Won/Lost Record
Philadelphia 76ers	1967	68–13
Boston Celtics	1968	54–28
Los Angeles Lakers	1969	55–27
New York Knicks	1970	60–22
Milwaukee Bucks	1971	66–16
Los Angeles Lakers	1972	69–13
Los Angeles Lakers	1973	60–22
Milwaukee Bucks	1974	59–23
Washington Bullets	1975	60–22
Boston Celtics	1976	54–28
Philadelphia 76ers	1977	50–32
Seattle Supersonics	1978	47–35
Washington Bullets	1979	54–28
Los Angeles Lakers	1980	60–22
Boston Celtics	1981	62–20
Philadelphia 76ers	1982	58–24
Philadelphia 76ers	1983	65–17
Boston Celtics	1984	62–20
Boston Celtics	1985	63–19
Boston Celtics	1986	67–15
Los Angeles Lakers	1987	65–17
Los Angeles Lakers	1988	62–20
Detroit Pistons	1989	63–19
Los Angeles Lakers	1990	63–19
Chicago Bulls	1991	62–20
Chicago Bulls	1992	66–16

Table 7.12—ABA Teams to Win 60 or More Games in a Single Season

1969	Oakland Oaks	60–18*
1972	Kentucky Colonels	68–16
1972	Utah Stars	60–24
1975	Denver Nuggets	65–19
1976	Denver Nuggets	60–24

*Indicates won ABA Championship as well.

ABA teams began playing a 78 game schedule in 1968 then moved to 84 in 1970, two more than in NBA.

Table 7.13—NBA Teams to Win 60 or More Games in a Single Season

Year	Team	Won/Lost Record
1962	Boston Celtics	60–20*
1965	Boston Celtics	62–18*

Table 7.13—NBA Teams to Win 60 or More Games in a Single Season *(cont.)*

Year	Team	Won/Lost Record
1967	Philadelphia 76ers	68–13*
1967	Boston Celtics	60–21
1968	Philadelphia 76ers	62–20
1970	New York Knicks	60–22*
1971	Milwaukee Bucks	66–16*
1972	Milwaukee Bucks	63–19
1972	Los Angeles Lakers	69–13*
1973	Boston Celtics	68–14
1973	Milwaukee Bucks	60–22
1973	Los Angeles Lakers	60–22
1975	Washington Bullets	60–22
1975	Boston Celtics	60–22
1980	Los Angeles Lakers	60–22*
1980	Boston Celtics	61–21
1981	Boston Celtics	62–20*
1981	Philadelphia 76ers	62–20
1983	Philadelphia 76ers	65–17*
1983	Boston Celtics	63–19
1984	Boston Celtics	62–20*
1985	Boston Celtics	63–19
1985	Los Angeles Lakers	62–20*
1986	Los Angeles Lakers	62–20
1986	Boston Celtics	67–15*
1987	Los Angeles Lakers	65–17*
1988	Los Angeles Lakers	62–20*
1989	Detroit Pistons	63–19*
1990	Los Angeles Lakers	63–19
1991	Chicago Bulls	62–20*
1992	Chicago Bulls	66–16*

*Indicates won NBA Championship as well.

Table 7.14—ABA Champions

1968	Pittsburgh Pipers	1973	Indiana Pacers
1969	Oakland Oaks	1974	New York Nets
1970	Indiana Pacers	1975	Kentucky Colonels
1971	Utah Stars	1976	New York Nets
1972	Indiana Pacers		

Table 7.15—NBA Champions

1947	Philadelphia	1949	Minneapolis
1948	Baltimore	1950	Minneapolis

1951	Rochester	1972	Los Angeles
1952	Minneapolis	1973	New York
1953	Minneapolis	1974	Boston
1954	Minneapolis	1975	Golden State
1955	Syracuse	1976	Boston
1956	Philadelphia	1977	Portland
1957	Boston	1978	Washington
1958	St. Louis	1979	Seattle
1959	Boston	1980	Los Angeles
1960	Boston	1981	Boston
1961	Boston	1982	Los Angeles
1962	Boston	1983	Philadelphia
1963	Boston	1984	Boston
1964	Boston	1985	Los Angeles
1965	Boston	1986	Boston
1966	Boston	1987	Los Angeles
1967	Philadelphia	1988	Los Angeles
1968	Boston	1989	Detroit
1969	Boston	1990	Detroit
1970	New York	1991	Chicago
1971	Milwaukee	1992	Chicago

Table 7.16—ABA's All Star Game Selectees

1967-68
Mel Daniels, Minnesota
Connie Hawkins, Pittsburgh
Larry Jones, Denver
Doug Moe, New Orleans
Charles Williams, Pittsburgh

1968-69
Rick Barry, Oakland
Mel Daniels, Indiana
Connie Hawkins, Minnesota
James Jones, New Orleans
Larry Jones, Denver

1969-70
Rick Barry, Washington
Mel Daniels, Indiana
Spencer Haywood, Denver*
Larry Jones, Denver
Bob Verga, Carolina

1970-71
Rick Barry, New York
Roger Brown, Indiana
Mack Calvin, Floridians
Mel Daniels, Indiana*
Charlie Scott, Virginia

1971-72
Rick Barry, New York
Don Freeman, Dallas
Artis Gilmore, Kentucky
Dan Issel, Kentucky*
Bill Melchionni, New York

1972-73
Billy Cunningham, Carolina
Julius Erving, Virginia
Artis Gilmore, Kentucky
Warren Jabali, Denver*
James Jones, Utah

1973-74
Mack Calvin, Carolina
Julius Erving, New York
Artis Gilmore, Kentucky*
James Jones, Utah
George McGinnis, Indiana

1974-75
Ron Boone, Utah

Table 7.16—ABA's All Star Game Selectees *(cont.)*

Mack Calvin, Denver
Julius Erving, New York
Artis Gilmore, Kentucky
George McGinnis, Indiana
Artis Gilmore, Kentucky
Billy Knight, Indiana
James Silas, San Antonio
Ralph Simpson, Denver

1975-76
Julius Erving, New York
*Most valuable player.

Table 7.17—NBA's All NBA Team Members (First Team)

1946-47
Bob Feerick, Washington
Joe Fulks, Philadelphia
Bones McKinney, Washington
Stan Miasek, Detroit
Max Zaslofsky, Chicago

1947-48
Howie Dallmar, Philadelphia
Bob Feerick, Washington
Joe Fulks, Philadelphia
Ed Sadowski, Boston
Max Zaslofsky, Chicago

1948-49
Bob Davies, Rochester
Joe Fulks, Philadelphia
George Mikan, Minneapolis
Jim Pollard, Minneapolis
Max Zaslofsky, Chicago

1949-50
Bob Davies, Rochester
Alex Groza, Indianapolis
George Mikan, Minneapolis
Jim Pollard, Minneapolis
Max Zaslofsky, Chicago

1950-51
Ralph Beard, Indianapolis
Bob Davies, Rochester
Alex Groza, Indianapolis
Ed Macauley, Boston
George Mikan, Minneapolis

1951-52
Paul Arizin, Philadelphia
Bob Cousy, Boston
Bob Davies, Rochester
Ed Macauley, Boston
George Mikan, Minneapolis
Dolph Schayes, Syracuse

1952-53
Bob Cousy, Boston
Neil Johnston, Philadelphia
Ed Macauley, Boston
George Mikan, Minneapolis
Dolph Schayes, Syracuse

1953-54
Bob Cousy, Boston
Harry Gallatin, New York
Neil Johnston, Philadelphia
George Mikan, Minneapolis
Dolph Schayes, Syracuse

1954-55
Bob Cousy, Boston
Larry Foust, Ft. Wayne
Neil Johnston, Philadelphia
Bob Pettit, Milwaukee
Dolph Schayes, Syracuse

1955-56
Paul Arizin, Philadelphia
Bob Cousy, Boston
Neil Johnston, Philadelphia
Bob Pettit, St. Louis
Bill Sharman, Boston

1956-57
Paul Arizin, Philadelphia
Bob Cousy, Boston

Bob Pettit, St. Louis
Dolph Schayes, Syracuse
Bill Sharman, Boston

1957-58
Bob Cousy, Boston
Bob Pettit, St. Louis
Dolph Schayes, Syracuse
Bill Sharman, Boston
George Yardley, Detroit

1958-59
Elgin Baylor, Minneapolis
Bob Cousy, Boston
Bob Pettit, St. Louis
Bill Russell, Boston
Bill Sharman, Boston

1959-60
Elgin Baylor, Minneapolis
Wilt Chamberlain, Philadelphia
Bob Cousy, Boston
Bob Pettit, St. Louis
Gene Shue, Detroit

1960-61
Elgin Baylor, Los Angeles
Wilt Chamberlain, Philadelphia
Bob Cousy, Boston
Bob Pettit, St. Louis
Oscar Robertson, Cincinnati

1961-62
Elgin Baylor, Los Angeles
Wilt Chamberlain, Philadelphia
Bob Pettit, St. Louis
Oscar Robertson, Cincinnati
Jerry West, Los Angeles

1962-63
Elgin Baylor, Los Angeles
Bob Pettit, St. Louis
Oscar Robertson, Cincinnati
Bill Russell, Boston
Jerry West, Los Angeles

1963-64
Elgin Baylor, Los Angeles
Wilt Chamberlain, San Francisco
Bob Pettit, St. Louis
Oscar Robertson, Cincinnati
Jerry West, Los Angeles

1964-65
Elgin Baylor, Los Angeles
Jerry Lucas, Cincinnati
Oscar Robertson, Cincinnati
Bill Russell, Boston
Jerry West, Los Angeles

1965-66
Rick Barry, San Francisco
Wilt Chamberlain, Philadelphia
Jerry Lucas, Cincinnati
Oscar Robertson, Cincinnati
Jerry West, Los Angeles

1966-67
Rick Barry, San Francisco
Elgin Baylor, Los Angeles
Wilt Chamberlain, Philadelphia
Oscar Robertson, Cincinnati
Jerry West, Los Angeles

1967-68
Elgin Baylor, Los Angeles
Dave Bing, Detroit
Wilt Chamberlain, Philadelphia
Jerry Lucas, Cincinnati
Oscar Robertson, Cincinnati

1968-69
Elgin Baylor, Los Angeles
Billy Cunningham, Philadelphia
Earl Monroe, Baltimore
Oscar Robertson, Cincinnati
Wes Unseld, Baltimore

1969-70
Billy Cunningham, Philadelphia
Walt Frazier, New York
Connie Hawkins, Phoenix
Willis Reed, New York
Jerry West, Los Angeles

1970-71
Lew Alcindor, Milwaukee
Dave Bing, Detroit
Billy Cunningham, Philadelphia
John Havlicek, Boston
Jerry West, Los Angeles

1971-72
Kareem Abdul-Jabbar, Milwaukee

Table 7.17—NBA's All NBA Team Members (First Team) *(cont.)*

Walt Frazier, New York
John Havlicek, Boston
Spencer Haywood, Seattle
Jerry West, Los Angeles

1972-73
Kareem Abdul-Jabbar, Milwaukee
Nate Archibald, Kansas City-Omaha
John Havlicek, Boston
Spencer Haywood, Seattle
Jerry West, Los Angeles

1973-74
Kareem Abdul-Jabbar, Milwaukee
Rick Barry, Golden State
Walt Frazier, New York
Gail Goodrich, Los Angeles
John Havlicek, Boston

1974-75
Nate Archibald, Kansas City-Omaha
Rick Barry, Golden State
Walt Frazier, New York
Elvin Hayes, Washington
Bob McAdoo, Buffalo

1975-76
Kareem Abdul-Jabbar, Los Angeles
Nate Archibald, Kansas City
Rick Barry, Golden State
George McGinnis, Philadelphia
Pete Maravich, New Orleans

1976-77
Kareem Abdul-Jabbar, Los Angeles
Elvin Hayes, Washington
Pete Maravich, New Orleans
David Thompson, Denver
Paul Westphal, Phoenix

1977-78
Julius Erving, Philadelphia
George Gervin, San Antonio
Leonard Robinson, New Orleans
David Thompson, Denver
Bill Walton, Portland

1978-79
George Gervin, San Antonio
Elvin Hayes, Washington
Marques Johnson, Milwaukee
Moses Malone, Houston
Paul Westphal, Phoenix

1979-80
Kareem Abdul-Jabbar, Los Angeles
Larry Bird, Boston
Julius Erving, Philadelphia
George Gervin, San Antonio
Paul Westphal, Phoenix

1980-81
Kareem Abdul-Jabbar, Los Angeles
Larry Bird, Boston
Julius Erving, Philadelphia
George Gervin, San Antonio
Dennis Johnson, Phoenix

1981-82
Larry Bird, Boston
Julius Erving, Philadelphia
George Gervin, San Antonio
Moses Malone, Houston
Gus Williams, Seattle

1982-83
Larry Bird, Boston
Julius Erving, Philadelphia
Magic Johnson, Los Angeles
Moses Malone, Philadelphia
Sidney Moncrief, Milwaukee

1983-84
Kareem Abdul-Jabbar, Los Angeles
Larry Bird, Boston
Magic Johnson, Los Angeles
Bernard King, New York
Isiah Thomas, Detroit

1984-85
Larry Bird, Boston
Magic Johnson, Los Angeles
Bernard King, New York
Moses Malone, Philadelphia
Isiah Thomas, Detroit

1985-86
Kareem Abdul-Jabbar, Los Angeles

Larry Bird, Boston
Magic Johnson, Los Angeles
Isiah Thomas, Detroit
Dominique Wilkins, Atlanta

1986-87
Larry Bird, Boston
Magic Johnson, Los Angeles
Michael Jordan, Chicago
Kevin McHale, Boston
Hakeem Olajuwon, Houston

1987-88
Charles Barkley, Philadelphia
Larry Bird, Boston
Magic Johnson, Los Angeles
Michael Jordan, Chicago
Hakeem Olajuwon, Houston

1988-89
Charles Barkley, Philadelphia
Magic Johnson, Los Angeles
Michael Jordan, Chicago
Karl Malone, Utah
Hakeem Olajuwon, Houston

1989-90
Charles Barkley, Philadelphia
Patrick Ewing, New York
Magic Johnson, Los Angeles
Michael Jordan, Chicago
Karl Malone, Utah

1990-91
Charles Barkley, Philadelphia
Patrick Ewing, New York
Magic Johnson, Los Angeles
Michael Jordan, Chicago
Karl Malone, Utah

In addition to the All NBA teams listed, here are the rosters/selectees for the annual mid-season NBA All Star Game. The players are selected for each season's contest (10 for the West and 10 for the East squads) by the league coaches, players and fan voting totals. (Once in a while, 11 or 12 players per team are selected.)

Table 7.18—NBA All Star Game Selectees

1951
East Joe Fulks, Paul Arizin, Dolph Schayes, Vince Boryla, Ed Macauley,* Harry Gallatin, Bob Cousy, Red Rocha, Dick McGuire and Andy Phillip
West Alex Groza, Dike Eddleman, Jim Pollard, Vern Mikkelsen, George Mikan, Larry Foust, Bob Davies, Frank Brian, Ralph Beard and Fred Schaus

1952
East Paul Arizin,* Joe Fulks, Red Rocha, Max Zaslofsky, Ed Macauley, Harry Gallatin, Bob Cousy, Dick McGuire, Andy Phillip, Fred Scolari and Dolph Schayes
West Vern Mikkelsen, Dike Eddleman, Jim Pollard, Leo Barnhorst, George Mikan, Arnie Risen, Bob Davies, Paul Walther, Bobby Wanzer, Frank Brian and Larry Foust

1953
East Harry Gallatin, Don Barksdale, Dolph Schayes, Carl Braun, Ed Macauley, Neil Johnston, Bob Cousy, Paul Seymour, Bill Sharman, Billy Gabor and Fred Scolari

Table 7.18—NBA All Star Game Selectees *(cont.)*

West Mel Hutchins, Leo Barnhorst, Vern Mikkelsen, Larry Foust, George Mikan,* Arnie Risen, Andy Phillip, Bob Davies, Bob Wanzer and Slater Martin

1954

East Dolph Schayes, Carl Braun, Ed Macauley, Harry Gallatin, Ray Felix, Neil Johnston, Bob Cousy,* Bill Sharman, Dick McGuire and Paul Seymour

West Mel Hutchins, Don Sunderlage, Jim Pollard, Larry Foust, George Mikan, Arnie Risen, Bob Davies, Slater Martin, Bobby Wanzer and Andy Phillip

1955

East Harry Gallatin, Paul Arizin, Dolph Schayes, Carl Braun, Ed Macauley, Neil Johnston, Bob Cousy, Dick McGuire, Paul Seymour and Bill Sharman*

West Jim Pollard, Bob Pettit, George Yardley, Jack Coleman, Larry Foust, Vern Mikkelsen, Andy Phillip, Slater Martin, Bobby Wanzer, Frank Selvy and Arnie Risen

1956

East Bob Cousy, Paul Arizin, Neil Johnston, Bill Sharman, Dolph Schayes, Jack George, Ed Macauley, Dick McGuire, Johnny Kerr, Harry Gallatin and Carl Braun

West Bob Pettit,* Maurice Stokes, George Yardley, Clyde Lovellette, Slater Martin, Mel Hutchins, Larry Foust, Bobby Wanzer, Vern Mikkelsen and Robert Harrison

1957

East Paul Arizin, Harry Gallatin, Tom Heinsohn, Dolph Schayes, Neil Johnston, Nat Clifton, Bob Cousy,* Jack George, Bill Sharman and Carl Braun

West George Yardley, Ed Macauley, Bob Pettit, Jack Twyman, Mel Hutchins, Vern Mikkelsen, Slater Martin, Maurice Stokes, Richie Regan and Dick Garmaker

1958

East Ken Sears, Dolph Schayes, Willie Naulls, Paul Arizin, Bill Russell, Neil Johnston, Bob Cousy, Richie Guerin, Bill Sharman and Larry Costello

West Cliff Hagan, Dick McGuire, Dick Garmaker, Gene Shue, Slater Martin, Larry Foust, Bob Pettit,* Jack Twyman, Maurice Stokes and George Yardley

1959

East Richie Guerin, Bob Cousy, Larry Costello, Bill Sharman, Johnny Kerr, Bill Russell, Woody Sauldsberry, Paul Arizin, Dolph Schayes and Ken Sears

West Dick Garmaker, Slater Martin, Dick McGuire, Gene Shue, Larry Foust, Bob Pettit, Jack Twyman, Elgin Baylor,* George Yardley and Cliff Hagan

1960

East Paul Arizin, Larry Costello, Richie Guerin, Bill Sharman, Bob Cousy, Willie Naulls, Wilt Chamberlain,* Tom Gola, Bill Russell, George Yardley and Dolph Schayes

West Dick Garmaker, Elgin Baylor, Rod Hundley, Gene Shue, Clyde Lovellette, Walter Dukes, Chuck Noble, Jack Twyman, Cliff Hagan and Bob Pettit

1961

East Hal Greer, Tom Gola, Richie Guerin, Larry Costello, Bob Cousy, Bill Russell, Wilt Chamberlain, Willie Naulls, Dolph Schayes, Paul Arizin and Tom Heinsohn

West Rod Hundley, Jerry West, Oscar Robertson,* Gene Shue, Walter Dukes, Wayne Embry, Clyde Lovellette, Cliff Hagan, Bob Pettit, Bailey Howell and Elgin Baylor

1962

East Larry Costello, Tom Gola, Sam Jones, Richie Guerin, Hal Greer, Bob Cousy, Bill Russell, Wilt Chamberlain, Willie Naulls, John Green, Tom Heinsohn, Paul Arizin and Dolph Schayes

West Rudy LaRusso, Gene Shue, Jerry West, Frank Selvy, Oscar Robertson, Wayne Embry, Walt Bellamy, Jack Twyman, Bailey Howell, Cliff Hagan, Elgin Baylor and Bob Pettit*

1963

East Wayne Embry, Richie Guerin, Hal Greer, Bob Cousy, Tom Gola, Oscar Robertson, Johnny Kerr, Bill Russell,* John Green, Tom Heinsohn, Lee Shaffer and Jack Twyman

West Guy Rodgers, Terry Dischinger, Elgin Baylor, Len Wilkens, Doh Ohl, Jerry West, Wilt Chamberlain, Bailey Howell, Bob Pettit, Tom Meschery, Rudy LaRusso and Walt Bellamy

1964

East Sam Jones, Hal Greer, Chet Walker, Oscar Robertson,* Wayne Embry, Bill Russell, Tom Gola, Tom Heinsohn, Len Chappell and Jerry Lucas

West Lenny Wilkens, Guy Rodgers, Don Ohl, Jerry West, Wilt Chamberlain, Walt Bellamy, Bailey Howell, Elgin Baylor, Terry Dischinger and Bob Pettit

1965

East Tom Heinsohn, Larry Costello, Sam Jones, Hal Greer, Oscar Robertson, Wayne Embry, Bill Russell, Willis Reed, Lucious Jackson, Jerry Lucas* and John Green

West Terry Dischinger, Lenny Wilkens, Don Ohl, Jerry West, Walt Bellamy, Wilt Chamberlain, Nate Thurmond, Bob Pettit, Gus Johnson and Elgin Baylor

1966

East Adrian Smith,* Oscar Robertson, Hal Greer, Sam Jones, Bill Russell, Wilt Chamberlain, Willis Reed, John Havlicek, Chet Walker and Jerry Lucas

West Don Ohl, Jerry West, Eddie Miles, Guy Rodgers, Zelmo Beatty, Nate Thurmond, Rudy LaRusso, Bailey Howell, Dave DeBusschere and Rick Barry

1967

East Oscar Robertson, Don Ohl, Hal Greer, Bill Russell, Wilt Chamberlain, Jerry Lucas, Chet Walker, Willis Reed, John Havlicek and Bailey Howell

West Len Wilkens, Jerry West, Jerry Sloan, Guy Rodgers, Darrall Imhoff, Nate Thurmond, Dave DeBusschere, Elgin Baylor, Bill Bridges and Rick Barry*

1968

East Hal Greer,* Sam Jones, Oscar Robertson, Dick Barnett, Dave Bing, Bill Russell, Wilt Chamberlain, John Havlicek, Dave DeBusschere, Willis Reed, Gus Johnson and Jerry Lucas

West Jim King, Walt Hazzard, Len Wilkens, Archie Clark, Jerry West, Clyde Lee, Zelmo Beatty, Rudy LaRusso, Bill Bridges, Elgin Baylor, Don Kojis and Bob Boozer

Table 7.18—NBA All Star Game Selectees *(cont.)*

1969

East Billy Cunningham, Wes Unseld, Earl Monroe, John Havlicek, Dave DeBusschere, Willis Reed, Hal Greer, Lew Alcindor, Oscar Robertson* and Walt Frazier

West Elgin Baylor, Jerry West, Nate Thurmond, Len Wilkens, Wilt Chamberlain, Bob Rule, Jeff Mullins, Chet Walker, Bill Bridges and Dick Van Arsdale

1970

East Flynn Robinson, Jimmy Walker, Walt Frazier, Hal Greer, Oscar Robertson, Lew Alcindor, Willis Reed,* Tom Van Arsdale, Gus Johnson, John Havlicek, Dave DeBusschere and Billy Cunningham

West Nate Thurmond, Lenny Wilkens, Dick Van Arsdale, Lou Hudson, Jeff Mullins, Jerry West, Bob Rule, Elvin Hayes, Chet Walker, Joe Caldwell, Connie Hawkins, Bill Bridges and Elgin Baylor

1971

East Jo Jo White, Tom Van Arsdale, Wes Unseld, Willis Reed, Earl Monroe, Bob Kauffman, John Johnson, Gus Johnson, Lou Hudson, John Havlicek, Johnny Green, Walt Frazier, Dave DeBusschere and Billy Cunningham

West Lenny Wilkens,* Jerry West, Chet Walker, Dick Van Arsdale, Oscar Robertson, Geoff Petrie, Jeff Mullins, Jerry Lucas, Bob Love, Elvin Hayes, Connie Hawkins, Wilt Chamberlain, Dave Bing and Lew Alcindor

1972

East Butch Beard, Archie Clark, Dave Cowens, Billy Cunningham, Dave DeBusschere, Walt Frazier, John Havlicek, Lou Hudson, John Johnson, Bob Kauffman, Jack Marin, Wes Unseld, Jo Jo White and Tom Van Arsdale

West Sidney Wicks, Jerry West,* Jimmy Walker, Paul Silas, Cazzie Russell, Oscar Robertson, Bob Love, Bob Lanier, Spencer Haywood, Elvin Hayes, Connie Hawkins, Gail Goodrich, Wilt Chamberlain and Kareem Abdul-Jabbar

1973

East John Block, Bill Bradley, Dave Cowens,* Dave DeBusschere, Walt Frazier, John Havlicek, Elvin Hayes, Lou Hudson, Bob Kauffman, Pete Maravich, Jack Marin, Wes Unseld, Jo Jo White and Len Wilkens

West Sidney Wicks, Jerry West, Chet Walker, Nate Thurmond, Charlie Scott, Bob Love, Bob Lanier, Spencer Haywood, Connie Hawkins, Gail Goodrich, Bob Dandridge, Wilt Chamberlain, Dave Bing, Rick Barry, Nate Archibald and Kareem Abdul-Jabbar

1974

East John Havlicek, Kareem Abdul-Jabbar, Walt Frazier, Bob McAdoo, Elvin Hayes, Paul Silas, Jo Jo White, Dave Cowens, Wes Unseld, Earl Monroe, Rudy Tomjanovich, Ernie DiGregorio, Pete Maravich and Lou Hudson

West Elmore Smith, Rick Barry, Gail Goodrich, Spencer Haywood, Dave Bing, Norm Van Lier, Sidney Wicks, Bob Lanier,* Bob Dandridge, Rudy Tomjanovich, Geoff Petrie and Jeff Mullins

1975

East Paul Silas, Jo Jo White, Steve Mix, Dave Cowens, Phil Chenier, Wes Unseld,

Rudy Tomjanovich, Earl Monroe, Walt Frazier,* Bob McAdoo, Elvin Hayes and John Havlicek

West Jim Price, Sam Lacey, Bob Dandridge, Dave Bing, Charlie Scott, Bob Lanier, Sidney Wicks, Gail Goodrich, Nate Archibald, Kareem Abdul-Jabbar, Spencer Haywood and Rick Barry

1976

East Randy Smith, Doug Collins, Jo Jo White, John Drew, Rudy Tomjanovich, George McGinnis, Dave Cowens, Dave Bing,* Walt Frazier, Bob McAdoo, Elvin Hayes and John Havlicek

West Phil Smith, Fred Brown, Norm Van Lier, Scott Wedman, Curtis Rowe, Jamaal Wilkes, Alvan Adams, Brian Winters, Bob Dandridge, Nate Archibald, Kareem Abdul-Jabbar and Rick Barry

1977

East George Gervin, Phil Chenier, Rudy Tomjanovich, Elvin Hayes, Jo Jo White, Earl Monroe, John Havlicek, Pete Maravich, Doug Collins, Bob McAdoo, George McGinnis and Julius Erving*

West Maurice Lucas, Bob Lanier, Billy Knight, Phil Smith, Don Buse, Rick Barry, Kareem Abdul-Jabbar, Norm Van Lier, Paul Westphal, Dan Issel, David Thompson and Bobby Jones

1978

East Moses Malone, Elvin Hayes, Bob McAdoo, Randy Smith,* Len Robinson, Doug Collins, John Havlicek, George Gervin, Dave Cowens, Larry Kenon and Julius Erving

West Bob Lanier, Brian Winters, Bobby Jones, Lionel Hollins, Artis Gilmore, Walter Davis, Paul Westphal, David Thompson, Bill Walton and Maurice Lucas

1979

East Doug Collins, Campy Russell, Calvin Murphy, Bob Lanier, Larry Kenon, Elvin Hayes, Bob Dandridge, George Gervin, Pete Maravich, Moses Malone, Rudy Tomjanovich and Julius Erving

West Jack Sikma, Maurice Lucas, Dennis Johnson, Artis Gilmore, Walter Davis, Otis Birdsong, Paul Westphal, David Thompson,* Kareem Abdul-Jabbar, George McGinnis and Marques Johnson

1980

East Larry Bird, Bill Cartwright, Michael Ray Richardson, Elvin Hayes, Nate Archibald, Dan Roundfield, Eddie Johnson, George Gervin,* Moses Malone, Julius Erving and John Drew

West Otis Birdsong, Kermit Washington, Paul Westphal, Jack Sikma, Walter Davis, Dennis Johnson, Magic Johnson, Lloyd Free, Kareem Abdul-Jabbar, Marques Johnson and Adrian Dantley

1981

East Julius Erving, Robert Parish, Nate Archibald,* Larry Bird, Michael Ray Richardson, John Drew, Mike Mitchell, Ray Williams and Reggie Theus

West Kareem Abdul-Jabbar, George Gervin, Dennis Johnson, Marques Johnson, Adrian Dantley, Moses Malone, Otis Birdsong, David Thompson, Alex English, Jack Sikma and Truck (Len) Robinson

Table 7.18—NBA All Star Game Selectees ***(cont.)***

1982

East Larry Bird,* Julius Erving, Robert Parish, Nate Archibald, Maurice Cheeks, Buck Williams, Kelly Tripucka, Isiah Thomas, Reggie Theus, Artis Gilmore and Walter Davis

West Gus Williams, Moses Malone, George Gervin, Alex English, Bernard King, Magic Johnson, Sidney Moncrief, Norm Nixon, Adrian Dantley, Kareem Abdul-Jabbar, Dennis Johnson and Jack Sikma

1983

East Larry Bird, Julius Erving,* Moses Malone, Buck Williams, Isiah Thomas, Andrew Toney, Kelly Tripucka, Reggie Theus, Marques Johnson, Bernard King, Maurice Cheeks and Jim Paxson

West Magic Johnson, Maurice Lucas, Sidney Moncrief, Kareem Abdul-Jabbar, George Gervin, Alex English, Kiki Vandeweghe, Jack Sikma, Mark Aguirre, Terry Cummings, Darrel Griffith and Dan Roundfield

1984

East Julius Erving, Robert Parish, Isiah Thomas,* Larry Bird, Bernard King, Andrew Toney, Dominique Wilkins, Kelly Tripucka, Jeff Ruland, Buck Williams, Moses Malone and Kevin McHale

West Adrian Dantley, Jim Paxson, Sidney Moncrief, Magic Johnson, Kareem Abdul-Jabbar, Mark Aguirre, Kiki Vandeweghe, Alex English, Terry Cummings, Rolando Blackman, Jack Sikma, Ricky Green and Ralph Sampson

1985

East Isiah Thomas, Jeff Ruland, Michael Ray Richardson, Robert Parish, Sidney Moncrief, Moses Malone, Bernard King, Michael Jordan, Dennis Johnson, Julius Erving, Terry Cummings and Larry Bird

West Jack Sikma, Ralph Sampson,* Hakeem Olajuwon, Norm Nixon, Calvin Natt, Larry Nance, Magic Johnson, George Gervin, Alex English, Adrian Dantley, Rolando Blackman, Kareem Abdul-Jabbar and Norm Nixon

1986

East Buck Williams, Dominique Wilkins, Isiah Thomas,* Robert Parish, Sidney Moncrief, Kevin McHale, Moses Malone, Jeff Malone, Patrick Ewing, Julius Erving, Maurice Cheeks and Larry Bird

West James Worthy, Ralph Sampson, Hakeem Olajuwon, Alvin Robertson, Marques Johnson, Magic Johnson, Artis Gilmore, Alex English, Clyde Drexler, Adrian Dantley, Rolando Blackman and Kareem Abdul-Jabbar

1987

East Kevin McHale, Michael Jordan, Larry Bird, Isiah Thomas, Dominique Wilkins, Moses Malone, Doc Rivers, Charles Barkley, Danny Ainge and Maurice Cheeks

West Hakeem Olajuwon, Alvin Robertson, Walter Davis, Tom Chambers,* Alex English, Karl Malone, Magic Johnson, Clyde Drexler, Mark Aguirre and Lafayette Lever

1988

East Maurice Cheeks, Brad Daugherty, Danny Ainge, Charles Barkley, Kevin

McHale, Doc Rivers, Patrick Ewing, Michael Jordan,* Isiah Thomas, Moses Malone, Dominique Wilkins and Larry Bird

West James Donaldson, James Worthy, Clyde Drexler, Xavier McDaniel, Alvin Robertson, Kareem Abdul-Jabbar, Mark Aguirre, Lafayette Lever, Magic Johnson, Hakeem Olajuwon, Karl Malone and Alex English

1989

East Michael Jordan, Kevin McHale, Brad Daugherty, Mark Jackson, Mark Price, Larry Nance, Terry Cummings, Patrick Ewing, Isiah Thomas, Moses Malone, Dominique Wilkins and Charles Barkley

West Kevin Duckworth, Mark Eaton, James Worthy, Chris Mullin, Tom Chambers, Clyde Drexler, Kareem Abdul-Jabbar, John Stockton, Dale Ellis, Hakeem Olajuwon, Karl Malone* and Alex English

1990

East Charles Barkley, Larry Bird, Patrick Ewing, Michael Jordan, Isiah Thomas, Kevin McHale, Joe Dumars, Robert Parish, Reggie Miller, Dominique Wilkins, Dennis Rodman and Scottie Pippen

West A. C. Green, James Worthy, Hakeem Olajuwon, Magic Johnson,* John Stockton, Tom Chambers, Clyde Drexler, David Robinson, Chris Mullin, Kevin Johnson, Rolando Blackman and Lafayette Lever

1991

East Bernard King, Charles Barkley,* Patrick Ewing, Joe Dumars, Michael Jordan, Alvin Robertson, Dominique Wilkins, Robert Parish, Kevin McHale, Ricky Pierce, Brad Daugherty and Hersey Hawkins

West Karl Malone, Chris Mullin, David Robinson, Magic Johnson, Kevin Duckworth, Clyde Drexler, James Worthy, Terry Porter, Tom Chambers, John Stockton and Tim Hardaway

1992

East Scottie Pippen, Charles Barkley, Patrick Ewing, Isiah Thomas, Michael Jordan, Mark Price, Brad Daugherty, Joe Dumars, Dennis Rodman, Kevin Willis, Michael Adams, Reggie Lewis

West Karl Malone, Chris Mullin, David Robinson, Clyde Drexler, Magic Johnson,* Tim Hardaway, Jeff Hornacek, Otis Thorpe, James Worthy, John Stockton, Dan Majerle and Derek Mutombo

*Most valuable player.

Table 7.19—NBA All Defensive Teams (First Team)

1969
Dave DeBusschere, New York
Walt Frazier, New York
Bill Russell, Boston
Jerry Sloan, Chicago
Nate Thurmond, San Francisco

1970
Dave DeBusschere, New York
Walt Frazier, New York
Gus Johnson, Baltimore
Willis Reed, New York
Jerry West, Los Angeles

1971
Dave DeBusschere, New York
Walt Frazier, New York
Gus Johnson, Baltimore
Nate Thurmond, San Francisco
Jerry West, Los Angeles

Table 7.19—NBA All Defensive Teams (First Team) *(cont.)*

1972
Wilt Chamberlain, Los Angeles
Dave DeBusschere, New York
Walt Frazier, New York
John Havlicek, Boston
Jerry Sloan, Chicago
Jerry West, Los Angeles

1973
Wilt Chamberlain, Los Angeles
Dave DeBusschere, New York
Walt Frazier, New York
John Havlicek, Boston
Jerry West, Los Angeles

1974
Kareem Abdul-Jabbar, Milwaukee
Dave DeBusschere, New York
Walt Frazier, New York
John Havlicek, Boston
Jerry Sloan, Chicago
Norm Van Lier, Chicago

1975
Kareem Abdul-Jabbar, Milwaukee
Walt Frazier, New York
John Havlicek, Boston
Paul Silas, Boston
Jerry Sloan, Chicago

1976
Dave Cowens, Boston
John Havlicek, Boston
Paul Silas, Boston
Norm Van Lier, Chicago
Don Watts, Seattle

1977
Don Buse, Indiana
E. C. Coleman, New Orleans
Bobby Jones, Denver
Norm Van Lier, Chicago
Bill Walton, Portland

1978
Don Buse, Phoenix
Lionel Hollins, Portland
Bobby Jones, Denver
Maurice Lucas, Portland
Bill Walton, Portland

1979
Kareem Abdul-Jabbar, Los Angeles
Don Buse, Phoenix
Bobby Dandridge, Washington
Dennis Johnson, Seattle
Bobby Jones, Philadelphia

1980
Kareem Abdul-Jabbar, Los Angeles
Don Buse, Phoenix
Dennis Johnson, Seattle
Bobby Jones, Philadelphia
Michael Ray Richardson, New York
Dan Roundfield, Atlanta

1981
Kareem Abdul-Jabbar, Los Angeles
Dennis Johnson, Phoenix
Bobby Jones, Philadelphia
Caldwell Jones, Philadelphia
Michael Ray Richardson, New York

1982
Michael Cooper, Los Angeles
Dennis Johnson, Phoenix
Bobby Jones, Philadelphia
Caldwell Jones, Philadelphia
Dan Roundfield, Atlanta

1983
Maurice Cheeks, Philadelphia
Dennis Johnson, Phoenix
Bobby Jones, Philadelphia
Moses Malone, Philadelphia
Sidney Moncrief, Milwaukee
Dan Roundfield, Atlanta

1984
Maurice Cheeks, Philadelphia
Michael Cooper, Los Angeles
Bobby Jones, Philadelphia
Sidney Moncrief, Milwaukee
Wayne Rollins, Atlanta

1985
Maurice Cheeks, Philadelphia
Michael Cooper, Los Angeles
Mark Eaton, Utah
Sidney Moncrief, Milwaukee
Paul Pressey, Milwaukee

1986
Maurice Cheeks, Philadelphia
Mark Eaton, Utah
Kevin McHale, Boston
Sidney Moncrief, Milwaukee
Paul Pressey, Milwaukee

1987
Michael Cooper, Los Angeles
Dennis Johnson, Boston
Kevin McHale, Boston
Hakeem Olajuwon, Houston
Alvin Robertson, San Antonio

1988
Michael Cooper, Los Angeles
Michael Jordan, Chicago
Rodney McCray, Houston
Kevin McHale
Hakeem Olajuwon, Houston

1989
Joe Dumars, Detroit
Mark Eaton, Utah
Michael Jordan, Chicago
Larry Nance, Cleveland
Dennis Rodman, Detroit

1990
Michael Jordan, Chicago
Alvin Robertson, Milwaukee
David Robinson, San Antonio
Dennis Rodman, Detroit
Buck Williams, Portland

1991
Michael Jordan, Chicago
Alvin Robertson, Milwaukee
David Robinson, San Antonio
Dennis Rodman, Detroit
Buck Williams, Portland

Table 7.20—NBA Career Team Leaders Through 1992

Team	Most Points	Most Rebounds	Most Assists
Atlanta Hawks	B. Pettit 20,880	B. Pettit 12,851	L. Wilkens 3,048
Boston Celtics	J. Havlicek 26,395	B. Russell 21,620	B. Cousy 6,945
Charlotte Hornets	R. Chapman 1,267	E. Cureton 488	T. Bogues 620
Chicago Bulls	M. Jordan 13,840	T. Boerwinkle 5,745	N. Van Lier 3,676
Cleveland Cavaliers	A. Carr 10,625	J. Chones 3,790	J. Bagley 2,311
Dallas Mavericks	M. Aguirre 12,977	M. Aguirre 3,009	B. Davis 3,744
Denver Nuggets	A. English 23,417	D. Issel 6,630	A. English 4,021
Detroit Pistons	B. Lanier 15,488	B. Lanier 8,033	I. Thomas 6,220
Golden State Warriors	W. Chamberlain 17,783	N. Thurmond 12,771	G. Rodgers 4,845
Houston Rockets	C. Murphy 17,949	E. Hayes 6,974	C. Murphy 4,402

Table 7.20—NBA Career Team Leaders Through 1992

Team	Most Points	Most Rebounds	Most Assists
Indiana Pacers	B. Knight 10,780	M. Daniels 7,622	D. Buse 2,747
LA Clippers	R. Smith 12,735	B. McAdoo 4,299	R. Smith 3,498
LA Lakers	J. West 25,192	E. Baylor 11,463	M. Johnson 8,025
Miami Heat	K. Edwards 1,094	B. Thompson 572	R. Sparrow 429
Milwaukee Bucks	K. Abdul-Jabbar 14,211	K. Abdul-Jabbar 7,161	P. Pressey 2,589
New Jersey Nets	B. Williams 10,440	B. Williams 7,576	B. Melchionni 2,251
New York Knicks	W. Frazier 14,617	W. Reed 8,414	W. Frazier 4,719
Philadelphia 76ers	H. Greer 21,586	D. Schayes 11,256	M. Cheeks 5,023
Phoenix Suns	W. Davis 15,660	A. Adams 6,937	A. Adams 4,012
Portland Trail Blazers	J. Paxson 10,003	M. Thompson 4,878	G. Petrie 2,057
Sacramento Kings	O. Robertson 22,009	J. Lucas 8,831	O. Robertson 7,721
San Antonio Spurs	G. Gervin 23,603	G. Gervin 4,841	J. Moore 3,663
Seattle Supersonics	F. Brown 14,018	J. Sikma 7,729	F. Brown 3,160
Utah Jazz	A. Dantley 13,545	M. Eaton 4,073	R. Green 4,159
Washington Bullets	E. Hayes 15,551	W. Unseld 13,769	W. Unseld 3,822

Comments: Teams are listed as they are currently named. So for example, the Sacramento Kings used to be named the Cincinnati Royals, thus Oscar Robertson is the club's all-time career scorer. Moreover, the career totals in the various categories for a team leader are for his tenure with that team only—not for all of the other teams that he played for. Thus, while Oscar Robertson amassed a team leading 22,009 points for Sacramento, his career total (listed in another section of this encyclopedia) is 26,710 points.

Table 7.21—All Time Team Records, ABA and NBA

ABA

Most Wins 448 wins: Kentucky Colonels, 60.2 percent
Most League Titles 3 (1970, 1972 and 1973): Indiana Pacers

Most Playoff Wins 69 wins: Indiana Pacers

Team with Most League "Most Valuable Players" Representing Them New York Nets—1 (Julius Erving, three times); and Indiana Pacers—2 (George McGinnis and Mel Daniels)

Team with Most "Coach of the Year" Selections Denver Nuggets: 2 (Larry Brown [twice] and Joe Belmont)

All Star Games: East Squads—5 wins, West Squads—3 wins

Most Points in All Star Game by One Team 151 points: 1975 West Squad

Most Points by Both Teams 282 total points: 1976 All Star Game, East (144), West (138)

NBA

Most Championships 16 championships: Boston Celtics

Most Games Won Regular Season 2,115 games: Boston Celtics

Fewest Points Allowed Regular Season 89.7 points: Syracuse

Most Assists 31.4 assists: Los Angeles Lakers, 1984-85 season

Most Rebounds 71.5 rebounds: Boston Celtics, 1959-60 (75 games)

Highest Point Total (Per Game) 126.5 points: Denver Nuggets, 1981-82 season (82 games)

Highest Winning Percentage/Season 84.1 percent: Los Angeles Lakers, 1971-72 (69–13)

Most Consecutive Games Won/Season 33 games: Los Angeles Lakers, 1971-72. November 5, 1971–January 7, 1972

Most Playoff Games Won 276 games: Los Angeles Lakers

Best Playoff Series Record 75.3 percent: Boston Celtics (career), 61 wins and 20 losses

Best Playoff Home Record 75.8 percent: Los Angeles Lakers, 182 wins and 58 losses

Best Playoff Road Record 45.5 percent: Los Angeles Lakers, 94 wins and 122 losses

Most Points Scored in an NBA Finals Game 148 points: Boston Celtics versus Los Angeles Lakers, May 27, 1985

Most Points Scored for Both Teams in an NBA Finals Game 276 total points: Philadelphia (141 points) versus San Francisco (135 points) on April 14, 1967 (overtime)

Most Points in a Playoff Game 156 points: Milwaukee versus Philadelphia on March 30, 1970

Highest Won/Lost Percentage in a Playoff Series 92.3 percent: Philadelphia 76ers, 1983, 12 wins and 1 loss

NBA Team with Most "Rookies of the Year" Representing Them Baltimore Bullets—3 (Ray Felix, Earl Monroe and Wes Unseld); Chicago Bulls—3 (Walt Bellamy, Terry Dischinger and Michael Jordan); New York Knickerbockers—3 (Willis Reed, Patrick Ewing and Mark Jackson); Boston Celtics—3 (Tom Heinsohn, Dave Cowens and Larry Bird)

NBA Team with Most League "Most Valuable Players" Representing Them Boston Celtics—4 (Bob Cousy, Bill Russell, Dave Cowens and Larry Bird); Los Angeles Lakers—2 (Kareem Abdul-Jabbar and Magic Johnson); Philadelphia 76ers—3 (Wilt Chamberlain, Julius Erving and Moses Malone)

NBA Team with Most "Coach of the Year" Selections Representing Them Boston Celtics—3 (Red Auerbach, Tom Heinsohn and Bill Fitch)

NBA Team with Most League Scoring Champs Representing Them Philadelphia—11 seasons, 4 players (Joe Fulks, Paul Arizin (twice), Neil Johnston (three times), and Wilt Chamberlain (five times)

Chapter 8

Record Holders and Award Winners

Table 8.1—ABA Records

Most Games 728 games: Louie Dampier.
Most Points 13,726 points: Louie Dampier.
Most Minutes 27,770 minutes: Louie Dampier.
Most Assists 4,084 assists: Louie Dampier.
Most Rebounds 9,494 rebounds: Mel Daniels.
Most Points in a Single Game 67 points: Larry Miller.
Most Assists in a Single Game 23 assists: Larry Brown.
Most Rebounds in a Single Game 40 rebounds: Artis Gilmore.
Highest Scoring Average 34.6 average: Charlie Scott.

Table 8.2—ABA Blocked Shots and Steals Champ

	Blocked Shots		*Steals*
1973	Artis Gilmore	1973	Billy Cunningham
1974	Caldwell Jones	1974	Ted McLain
1975	Artis Gilmore	1975	Brian Taylor
1976	Billy Paultz		

Note: For ABA FG% and FT% champs *see* Chapter 6, ABA Shooting Champs.

Table 8.3—NBA Records

Single Game

Most Minutes Played 64 minutes: Norm Nixon, Los Angeles at Cleveland, January 29, 1980; and Eric Floyd, Golden State at New Jersey, February 1, 1987. Both were in four overtimes.

Most Points 100 points: Wilt Chamberlain, Philadelphia at New York, March 2, 1962.

Table 8.3 – NBA Records *(cont.)*

Most Rebounds 55 rebounds: Wilt Chamberlain, Philadelphia at Boston, November 24, 1960.

Most Assists 29 assists: Kevin Porter, New Jersey at Houston, February 24, 1978.

Most FT Attempts 34 attempts: Wilt Chamberlain, Philadelphia at St. Louis, February 22, 1962.

Most FTs Made 28 FTs: Wilt Chamberlain, Philadelphia at New York, March 2, 1962; and Adrian Dantley, Utah at Houston, January 4, 1984.

Most FG Attempts 63 attempts: Wilt Chamberlain, Philadelphia at New York, March 2, 1962.

Most FGs Made 36 FGs: Wilt Chamberlain, Philadelphia at New York, March 2, 1962.

Most Personal Fouls 8 fouls: Don Otten, Tri-Cities at Sheboygan, November 24, 1949.

Most Three Pointers Made 8 three pointers: Rick Barry, Houston at Utah, February 9, 1980; John Roche, Denver at Seattle, January 9, 1982; and Michael Adams, Denver at Milwaukee, January 21, 1989.

Most Blocked Shots 17 shots: Elmore Smith, Los Angeles at Portland, October 28, 1973.

Most Steals 11 steals: Larry Kenon, San Antonio at Kansas City, December 26, 1976.

Most Turnovers 14 turnovers: John Drew, Atlanta at New Jersey, March 1, 1978.

Most Points by a Rookie 58 points: Wilt Chamberlain, Philadelphia at Detroit, January 25, 1960.

Most Assists by a Rookie 25 assists: Ernie DiGregorio, Buffalo at Portland, January 1, 1974.

Most Rebounds by a Rookie 45 rebounds: Wilt Chamberlain, Philadelphia at Syracuse, February 6, 1960.

Most Points Scored by One Team 186 points: Detroit Pistons versus Denver Nuggets, December 13, 1983.

Most Points Scored by Both Teams 370 points: Detroit Pistons versus Denver Nuggets, December 13, 1983. Final score: Detroit 186, Denver 184.

Least Amount of Points Scored by One Team 18 points: Fort Wayne Pistons versus Minneapolis Lakers, November 22, 1950.

Least Amount Scored by Both Teams 37 points: Fort Wayne Pistons versus Minneapolis Lakers, November 22, 1950. Final score: Fort Wayne 19, Minneapolis 18.

Table 8.4 – Playoff Records

Most Minutes in Single Series 345 minutes: Kareem Abdul-Jabbar, 7 games, 1974.

Most Rebounds in Single Series 220 rebounds: Wilt Chamberlain, 7 games, 1965.

Most Assists in Single Series 115 assists: John Stockton, 7 games, 1988.

Most Steals in Single Series 28 steals: John Stockton, 7 games, 1988.

Most Blocked Shots in Single Series 28 shots: Elvin Hayes, 7 games, 1976.

Most Minutes in a Game 67 minutes: Red Rocha, Syracuse, 1953; and Dolph Schayes, Syracuse, 1953 (same game, four overtimes).

Most Rebounds in a Game 41 rebounds: Wilt Chamberlain, Philadelphia, 1967.

Most Assists in a Game 24 assists: Magic Johnson (twice), Los Angeles, 1984 and 1988.

Isiah Thomas is the record holder for most steals in an All Star game.

Most Blocked Shots in a Game 10 shots: Mark Eaton, Utah, 1985.
Most Seasons Played 18 seasons: Kareem Abdul-Jabbar.
Most Games Played 237 games: Kareem Abdul-Jabbar.
Most Minutes (Career) 8,851 minutes: Kareem Abdul-Jabbar.
Most Rebounds (Career) 4,104 rebounds: Bill Russell.
Most Assists (Career) 1,965 assists: Magic Johnson.
Most Steals (Career) 324 steals: Magic Johnson.
Most Blocked Shots (Career) 476 shots: Kareem Abdul-Jabbar.
Most Personal Fouls (Career) 797 fouls: Kareem Abdul-Jabbar.

Note: For all time playoff scoring records *see* Chapter 6, Scorers and Shooters.

Table 8.5 — All Star Game Records

Most Games Played 18 games: Kareem Abdul-Jabbar.
Most Rebounds Collected 197 rebounds: Wilt Chamberlain.
Most Assists 111 assists: Magic Johnson.
Most Steals 23 steals: Isiah Thomas.
Most Blocked Shots 31 shots: Kareem Abdul-Jabbar.
Most Minutes in a Single Game 42 minutes: Oscar Robertson, 1964; Bill Russell, 1964; Jerry West, 1964; and Nate Thurmond, 1967.
Most Rebounds in a Single Game 27 rebounds: Bob Pettit, 1962.
Most Assists in a Single Game 22 assists: Magic Johnson.
Most MVP Awards Won 4 awards: Bob Pettit.

Note: For All Star Game scoring records *see* Chapter 6, Scorers and Shooters.

Table 8.6 — All Time Career Leaders

Most Minutes Played	
Kareem Abdul-Jabbar	57,446
Elvin Hayes	50,000
Wilt Chamberlain	47,859

Most Rebounds	
Wilt Chamberlain	23,924
Bill Russell	21,620
Kareem Abdul-Jabbar	17,440

Most Assists	
Magic Johnson	10,000†
Oscar Robertson	9,887
Lenny Wilkens	7,211

Most Steals	
Julius Erving	2,272
Maurice Cheeks	1,849
Gus Williams	1,638

Most Blocked Shots	
Kareem Abdul-Jabbar	3,189
Artis Gilmore	3,178
Wayne Rollins	2,283

Best FG%	
James Donaldson	58.8
Artis Gilmore	58.2
Steve Johnson	58.0

Best FT%	
Rick Barry	89.3
Calvin Murphy	89.2
Bill Sharman	88.4

Best Three Point FG%	
Trent Tucker	42.3
Danny Ainge	38.9
Craig Hodges	38.4

Most Games Played	
Kareem Abdul-Jabbar	1,560
Artis Gilmore	1,329
Elvin Hayes	1,303

Most Seasons Played	
Kareem Abdul-Jabbar	20
Artis Gilmore	17
Julius Erving, Elvin Hayes, John Havlicek, Dolph Schayes, Paul Silas and Moses Malone	16

Table 8.7—Top Performers in the NBA Each Season: Scoring, Rebounding and Assist Champs

	Scoring	Rebounding	Assist
1947	Joe Fulks	None	Ernie Calverly
1948	Max Zaslofsky	None	Howie Dallmar
1949	George Mikan	None	Bob Davies
1950	George Mikan	None	Dick McGuire
1951	George Mikan	Dolph Schayes	Andy Phillip
1952	Paul Arizin	Mel Hutchins	Andy Phillip
1953	Neil Johnston	George Mikan	Bob Cousy
1954	Neil Johnston	Harry Gallatin	Bob Cousy
1955	Neil Johnston	Neil Johnston	Bob Cousy
1956	Bob Pettit	Bob Pettit	Bob Cousy
1957	Paul Arizin	Maurice Stokes	Bob Cousy
1958	George Yardley	Bill Russell	Bob Cousy
1959	Bob Pettit	Bill Russell	Bob Cousy
1960	Wilt Chamberlain	Wilt Chamberlain	Bob Cousy
1961	Wilt Chamberlain	Wilt Chamberlain	Oscar Robertson
1962	Wilt Chamberlain	Wilt Chamberlain	Oscar Robertson
1963	Wilt Chamberlain	Wilt Chamberlain	Guy Rodgers
1964	Wilt Chamberlain	Bill Russell	Oscar Robertson
1965	Wilt Chamberlain	Bill Russell	Oscar Robertson
1966	Wilt Chamberlain	Wilt Chamberlain	Oscar Robertson
1967	Rick Barry	Wilt Chamberlain	Guy Rodgers
1968	Dave Bing	Wilt Chamberlain	Wilt Chamberlain
1969	Elvin Hayes	Wilt Chamberlain	Oscar Robertson
1970	Jerry West	Elvin Hayes	Lenny Wilkens
1971	Lew Alcindor	Wilt Chamberlain	Norm Van Lier
1972	Kareem Abdul-Jabbar	Wilt Chamberlain	Jerry West
1973	Nate Archibald	Wilt Chamberlain	Nate Archibald
1974	Bob McAdoo	Elvin Hayes	Ernie DiGregorio
1975	Bob McAdoo	Wes Unseld	Kevin Porter
1976	Bob McAdoo	Kareem Abdul-Jabbar	Slick Watts
1977	Pete Maravich	Bill Walton	Don Buse
1978	George Gervin	Truck Robinson	Kevin Porter
1979	George Gervin	Moses Malone	Kevin Porter
1980	George Gervin	Swen Nater	Michael R. Richardson
1981	Adrian Dantley	Moses Malone	Kevin Porter
1982	George Gervin	Moses Malone	Johnny Moore
1983	Alex English	Moses Malone	Magic Johnson
1984	Adrian Dantley	Moses Malone	Magic Johnson
1985	Bernard King	Moses Malone	Isiah Thomas
1986	Dominique Wilkins	Bill Laimbeer	Magic Johnson
1987	Michael Jordan	Charles Barkley	Magic Johnson
1988	Michael Jordan	Michael Cage	John Stockton
1989	Michael Jordan	Hakeem Olajuwon	John Stockton
1990	Michael Jordan	Hakeem Olajuwon	John Stockton
1991	Michael Jordan	David Robinson	John Stockton
1992	Michael Jordan	Dennis Rodman	John Stockton

Bob Pettit was the 1956 scoring and rebounding champ. (Photo courtesy of Naismith Memorial Basketball Hall of Fame.)

Table 8.8 – Rebounds: All Time Career Leaders

Player	Rebounds	Player	Rebounds
Wilt Chamberlain	23,924	Paul Silas	12,357
Bill Russell	21,620	Elgin Baylor	11,463
Kareem Abdul-Jabbar	17,625	Dolph Schayes	11,256
Artis Gilmore	16,330*	Dan Issel	11,133*
Elvin Hayes	16,279	Bill Bridges	11,054
Moses Malone	16,000	Julius Erving	10,525*
Nate Thurmond	14,464	Dave Cowens	10,444
Walt Bellamy	14,241	Johnny Kerr	10,092
Wes Unseld	13,679	Jack Sikma	10,005
Jerry Lucas	12,942	Robert Parish	10,003
Bob Pettit	12,849		

*Denotes both ABA and NBA totals. Totals are through 1992 for the still active players (Moses Malone and Robert Parish).

Table 8.9 – Assists: All Time Career Leaders

Player	Assists	Player	Assists
Magic Johnson	10,000-plus	Guy Rodgers	6,917
Oscar Robertson	9,887	Nate Archibald	6,476
Lenny Wilkens	7,211	Jerry West	6,238
Bob Cousy	6,955	John Havlicek	6,114

Norm Nixon	6,047*	Gail Goodrich	4,805
John Lucas	5,956	Wilt Chamberlain	4,643
Maurice Cheeks	5,700*	Dennis Johnson	4,600*
Isiah Thomas	5,600*	Gus Williams	4,597
Kareem Abdul-Jabbar	5,600	Hal Greer	4,540
Dave Bing	5,397	Randy Smith	4,487
Kevin Porter	5,314	Calvin Murphy	4,402
Reggie Theus	5,300*	Larry Bird	4,367
John Stockton	5,286*	Richie Guerin	4,211
Julius Erving	5,176**	Bill Russell	4,100
Walt Frazier	5,040	Jo Jo White	4,095
Rick Barry	4,952**	Alvan Adams	4,012

*Indicates player is still active.
**Indicates both NBA and ABA.

Table 8.10 — Blocked Shots: All Time Career Leaders

Artis Gilmore	3,178	Terry Tyler	1,303
Kareem Abdul-Jabbar	3,104	Kevin McHale	1,172
Wayne Rollins	2,283	Bob McAdoo	1,147
Caldwell Jones	2,185	Wayne Cooper	1,141
George Johnson	2,082	Bob Lanier	1,100
Mark Eaton	2,076	Alton Lister	1,064
Julius Erving	1,941	Bill Walton	1,034
Elvin Hayes	1,771	Darryl Dawkins	1,022
Robert Parish	1,664	Herb Williams	1,014
Moses Malone	1,539	Larry Nance	1,003

Table 8.11 — Most Games Played: All Time Career Leaders

Kareem Abdul-Jabbar	1,560	George Gervin	1,057
Artis Gilmore	1,329	Don Nelson	1,053
Elvin Hayes	1,303	Leroy Ellis	1,048
Moses Malone	1,300*	Wilt Chamberlain	1,045
John Havlicek	1,270	Walt Bellamy	1,043
Paul Silas	1,254	Ron Boone	1,041
Julius Erving	1,243	Oscar Robertson	1,040
Dan Issel	1,218	Chet Walker	1,032
Caldwell Jones	1,155	Gail Goodrich	1,031
Hal Greer	1,122	Rick Barry	1,020
Lenny Wilkens	1,077	Sam Lacey	1,002
Dolph Schayes	1,059	Calvin Murphy	1,002
Johnny Green	1,057		

*Still active.

Table 8.12—Most All Star Games Played: All Time Career Leaders

Kareem Abdul-Jabbar	18	Rick Barry	12
Julius Erving	16	Elvin Hayes	12
Moses Malone	15	Bill Russell	12
Bob Cousy	13	Artis Gilmore	11
Wilt Chamberlain	13	Bob Pettit	11
John Havlicek	13	Elgin Baylor	11
Oscar Robertson	12	Dolph Schayes	11
Jerry West	12	Hal Greer	10
George Gervin	12	Paul Arizin	10

Table 8.13—Top 20 Coaches with the Most Career Victories

Red Auerbach	938	Al Attles	557
Jack Ramsay	864	Alex Hannum	471
Dick Motta	808	Pat Riley	470*
Gene Shue	784	K. C. Jones	463
Bill Fitch	762	Billy Cunningham	454
Red Holzman	696	Larry Costello	430
Lenny Wilkens	683*	Tom Heinsohn	427
John Macleod	670	John Kundla	423
Cotton Fitzsimmons	643	Hubie Brown	341
Don Nelson	600*	Kevin Loughery	341
Doug Moe	576*	Bill Russell	341

*Still active. Nelson's and Moe's totals are thru 1992.

Table 8.14—Coaches with the Most NBA Championships

	Team	Year	Number
Red Auerbach	Boston	1957, 1959–66	9
John Kundla	Minneapolis	1949–50, 1952–54	5
Pat Riley	Los Angeles	1982, 1985, 1987–88	4
K. C. Jones	Boston	1984, 1986	2
Alex Hannum	St. Louis / Philadelphia	1958 / 1967	2
Tom Heinsohn	Boston	1974, 1976	2
Red Holzman	New York	1970, 1973	2
Bill Russell	Boston	1968–69	2

Table 8.15—ABA Coach of the Year

	Team	Year
Vince Cazetta	Pittsburgh Pipers	1968
Alex Hannum	Oakland Oaks	1969

	Team	Year
Joe Belmont and Bill Sharman	Denver Nuggets and Los Angeles Stars	1970
Al Bianchi	Virginia Squires	1971
Tom Nissalke	Dallas Chaparrals	1972
Larry Brown	Carolina Cougars	1973
Babe McCarthy and Joe Mullaney	Kentucky Colonels and Utah Stars	1974
Larry Brown	Denver Nuggets	1975
Larry Brown	Denver Nuggets	1976

Table 8.16 – NBA Coach of the Year

	Team	Year
Harry Gallatin	St. Louis Hawks	1963
Alex Hannum	San Francisco Warriors	1964
Red Auerbach	Boston Celtics	1965
Dolph Schayes	Philadelphia 76ers	1966
Johnny Kerr	Chicago Bulls	1967
Richie Guerin	St. Louis Hawks	1968
Gene Shue	Baltimore Bullets	1969
Red Holzman	New York Knicks	1970
Dick Motta	Chicago Bulls	1971
Bill Sharman	Los Angeles Lakers	1972
Tom Heinsohn	Boston Celtics	1973
Ray Scott	Detroit Pistons	1974
Phil Johnson	Kansas City–Omaha Kings	1975
Bill Fitch	Cleveland Cavaliers	1976
Tom Nissalke	Houston Rockets	1977
Hubie Brown	Atlanta Hawks	1978
Cotton Fitzsimmons	Kansas City Kings	1979
Bill Fitch	Boston Celtics	1980
Jack McKinney	Indiana Pacers	1981
Gene Shue	Washington Bullets	1982
Don Nelson	Milwaukee Bucks	1983
Frank Layden	Utah Jazz	1984
Don Nelson	Milwaukee Bucks	1985
Mike Fratello	Atlanta Hawks	1986
Mike Schuller	Portland Trail Blazers	1987
Doug Moe	Denver Nuggets	1988
Cotton Fitzsimmons	Phoenix Suns	1989
		1990
		1991
		1992

Appendix A

Addresses

Atlanta Hawks One CNN Center, South Tower, Suite 405, Atlanta, GA 30303
Basketball Hall of Fame P.O. Box 179, 1150 West Columbus Avenue, Springfield, MA 01101-0179
Charlotte Hornets 2 First Union Plaza, Suite 200, Charlotte, NC 28282
Chicago Bulls 980 North Michigan Avenue, Suite 1600, Chicago, IL 60611
Cleveland Cavaliers The Coliseum, 2923 Streetsboro Road, Richfield, OH 44286
Dallas Mavericks Reunion Arena, 777 Sports Street, Dallas, TX 75207
Denver Nuggets 1635 Clay Street, P.O. Box 4658, Denver, CO 80204
Detroit Pistons Palace of Auburn Hills, 3777 Lapeer Road, Auburn Hills, MI 48057
Golden State Warriors Oakland Coliseum Avenue, Oakland, CA 94621
Houston Rockets 10 Greenway Plaza East, Houston, TX 77277
Indiana Pacers 300 East Market Street, Indianapolis, IN 46204
Los Angeles Clippers Los Angeles Sports Arena, 3939 South Figueros Street, Los Angeles, CA 90037
Los Angeles Lakers The Forum, 3900 West Manchester Boulevard, Inglewood, CA 90306
Miami Heat Miami Arena, Miami, FL 33136
Milwaukee Bucks 1001 North Fourth Street, Milwaukee, WI 53203
Minnesota Timberwolves 730 Hennepin Avenue, Suite 500, Minneapolis, MN 55403
National Basketball Association Olympic Tower, 645 Fifth Avenue, New York, NY 10022
National Basketball Association Properties Olympic Tower, 645 Fifth Avenue, New York, NY 10022
NBA Gifts and Athletic Supplies 10812 Alder Circle, Suite 1826, Dallas, TX 75238
NBA Entertainment, Inc. 38 East 32nd Street, 4th Floor, New York, NY 10016
NBA Videos and the Official Consumer Catalog Suite NBA 1840, 10812 Alder Circle, Dallas, TX 75238
New Jersey Nets Meadowlands Arena, East Rutherford, NJ 07073
New York Knicks Madison Square Garden, Four Pennsylvania Plaza, New York, NY 10001
Orlando Magic 390 North Orange Avenue, Suite 275, Orlando, FL 32802
Philadelphia 76ers Veterans Stadium, Philadelphia, PA 19417
Phoenix Suns 2910 North Central, Phoenix, AZ 85012
Portland Trail Blazers Lloyd Building, 700 Northeast Multnomah Street, Portland, OR 97232
Sacramento Kings One Sports Parkway, Sacramento, CA 95834

San Antonio Spurs 600 East Market Street, San Antonio, TX 78205
Seattle SuperSonics 190 Queen Ann Avenue North, Seattle, WA 98109
Utah Jazz 5 Triad Center, Suite 500, Salt Lake City, UT 84180
Washington Bullets Capital Centre, Landover, MD 20785

Appendix B
Birthdays

The following alphabetized reference of player and contributor birthdays is not intended to be all-inclusive, but, instead, simply representative of the more popular names in pro basketball's history. However every single Hall of Famer associated with the NBA is included, whether player, coach or contributor (commissioner, referee, league founder, instructor, or any person closely associated with the game).

Abdul-Jabbar, Kareem (player)
April 16, 1947
Adams, Alvan (player)
July 19, 1954
Albeck, Stan (coach)
May 17, 1931
Allen, Lucious (player)
September 26, 1947
Allen, Phog (coach)
October 9, 1885
Archibald, Nate (player)
April 18, 1948
Arizin, Paul (player)
April 9, 1928
Attles, Al (coach)
November 7, 1936
Auerbach, Red (coach)
September 20, 1917
Barnett, Dick (player)
October 2, 1936
Barnhorst, Leo (contributor)
May 17, 1924
Barry, Rick (player)
March 28, 1944
Baylor, Elgin (player)
September 16, 1934
Beard, Butch (player)
May 4, 1947
Beard, Ralph (player)
December 2, 1927
Beasley, Charles (player)
September 23, 1945
Beasley, John (player)
February 5, 1945
Beatty, Zelmo (player)
October 25, 1939
Beckman, John (contributor)
October 22, 1895
Bee, Clair (coach)
March 2, 1896
Bellamy, Walt (player)
July 24, 1939
Benson, Kent (player)
December 27, 1954
Bianchi, Al (player/coach)
March 26, 1932
Bibby, Henry (player/coach)
November 24, 1949
Bickerstaff, Bernie (coach)
February 11, 1944
Bing, Dave (player)
November 24, 1943
Birdsong, Otis (player)
December 9, 1955
Blood, Ernest (contributor)
1872

Boerwinkle, Tom (player)
August 23, 1945
Boone, Ron (player)
September 6, 1946
Boozer, Bob (player)
April 26, 1937
Borgman, Bennie (player)
November 21, 1894
Boryla, Vince (player/coach)
March 11, 1927
Bradley, Bill (player)
July 28, 1943
Braun, Carl (player)
September 25, 1927
Brian, Frank (player)
May 1, 1923
Bridges, Bill (player)
April 4, 1939
Brisker, John (player)
June 15, 1947
Brown, Fred (player)
May 22, 1942
Brown, Hubie (coach)
September 25, 1933
Brown, Larry (player/coach)
September 14, 1940
Brown, Roger (player)
May 22, 1942
Brown, Walter (contributor)
February 10, 1905
Buckner, Quinn (player/announcer)
August 20, 1950
Bunn, John (contributor)
September 26, 1898
Burleson, Tom (player)
February 24, 1952
Buse, Don (player)
August 10, 1950
Caldwell, Joe (player)
November 1, 1941
Calvin, Mack (player)
July 27, 1949
Cann, Howard (coach)
October 11, 1895
Carlson, Doc (coach/contributor)
July 4, 1894
Carnevale, Ben (coach)
October 30, 1915
Carr, Austin (player)
March 10, 1948
Carr, M. L. (player)
January 9, 1951
Carrier, Darel (player)
October 26, 1940
Carter, Fred (player)
February 14, 1945
Cervi, Al (player/coach)
February 12, 1917
Chamberlain, Wilt (player)
August 21, 1936
Chaney, Don (player/coach)
March 22, 1946
Chappell, Len (player)
January 31, 1941
Chenier, Phil (player)
October 30, 1950
Clark, Archie (player)
January 5, 1944
Cleamons, Jim (player)
September 13, 1949
Clifton, Nat (player)
October 13, 1922
Coleman, Jack (contributor)
May 23, 1924
Collins, Doug (player/coach)
July 28, 1951
Combs, Glen (player)
October 30, 1946
Conlin, Ed (contributor)
September 2, 1933
Costello, Larry (player)
July 2, 1931
Counts, Mel (player)
October 16, 1941
Cousy, Bob (player/coach)
August 9, 1928
Cowens, Dave (player)
October 25, 1948
Cunningham, Billy (player/coach)
June 3, 1943
Dallmar, Howie (player)
May 24, 1922
Dampier, Louie (player)
November 20, 1944
Dandridge, Bob (player)
November 15, 1947
Daniels, Mel (player)
July 20, 1944
Davies, Bob (player)
January 15, 1920
Davis, Johnny (player)
October 2, 1955

Dawkins, Darryl (player)
January 11, 1957
Dean, Everett (contributor)
1898
DeBusschere, Dave (player/contributor)
October 16, 1940
Dehnert, Dutch (player)
April 5, 1898
Devlin, Corky (contributor)
December 21, 1931
DiBernardi, Forrest (contributor)
February 3, 1899
Diddle, Ed (coach)
March 12, 1895
Dierking, Connie (player)
October 2, 1936
DiGregorio, Ernie (player)
1951
Dischinger, Terry (player)
November 21, 1940
Dove, Sonny (contributor)
August 16, 1945
Drew, John (player
September 30, 1954
Dukes, Walter (player)
June 23, 1930
Egan, John (player)
January 31, 1939
Ellis, Leroy (player)
March 10, 1940
Embry, Wayne (player/contributor)
March 26, 1937
Endacott, Paul (contributor)
1902
Enright, John (contributor)
April 3, 1910
Erickson, Keith (player)
April 19, 1944
Erving, Julius (player)
February 22, 1950
Feerick, Bob (player)
January 2, 1920
Feerin, Arnie (player)
July 29, 1925
Felix, Ray (player)
December 10, 1930
Finkel, Henry (player)
April 20, 1942
Fleischer, Larry (contributor)
January 17, 1917
Foley, Jack (player)
November 17, 1940
Ford, Phil (player)
February 9, 1956
Foster, Bud (contributor)
1906
Foust, Larry (player)
June 24, 1928
Fox, Jim (player)
May 7, 1943
Frazier, Walt (player/announcer)
March 29, 1945
Free, Lloyd (player)
December 9, 1953
Freeman, Don (player)
July 18, 1944
Friedman, Marty (player)
1889
Fulks, Joe (player)
October 26, 1921
Gabor, Billy (player)
May 13, 1922
Gallatin, Harry (player)
April 26, 1928
Gambee, Dave (player)
April 16, 1937
Garfinkel, Dutch (player)
January 18, 1925
Garmaker, Dick (contributor)
October 29, 1932
Gates, William (contributor)
April 12, 1920
George, Jack (player)
November 13, 1928
Gervin, George (player)
April 27, 1952
Gill, Slats (contributor)
1901
Givens, Jack (player)
September 21, 1956
Glammack, George (player)
June 17, 1919
Gola, Tom (player)
January 13, 1933
Goodrich, Gail (player)
April 23, 1943
Gottlieb, Ed (contributor)
1898
Grabowski, Joe (contributor)
January 15, 1930
Green, Johnny (player)
December 8, 1933

Green, Sihugo (player)
August 20, 1934
Greer, Hal (player)
June 26, 1936
Grevey, Kevin (player)
May 12, 1953
Groat, Dick (player)
November 4, 1930
Gruenig, Ace (contributor)
1913
Grunfeld, Ernie (player)
April 24, 1955
Guerin, Richie (player/coach)
May 29, 1932
Gullick, Luther (contributor)
1865
Guokas, Matt (player/coach)
February 25, 1944
Hagan, Cliff (player)
December 9, 1931
Hairston, Happy (player)
May 31, 1942
Halbert, Charles (contributor)
February 27, 1919
Hale, Bruce (player/coach)
August 31, 1918
Hannum, Alex (coach)
July 19, 1923
Hanson, Vic (player)
1903
Harris, Bob (contributor)
March 16, 1927
Harrison, Lester (contributor)
August 20, 1904
Haskins, Clem (contributor)
August 11, 1944
Havlicek, John (player)
April 8, 1940
Hawkins, Connie (player)
June 17, 1942
Hayes, Elvin (player)
November 17, 1945
Haywood, Spencer (player)
April 22, 1949
Hazzard, Walt (player)
April 15, 1942
Heard, Garfield (player)
May 3, 1948
Heinsohn, Tom (player/coach)
August 26, 1934
Hepbron, George (contributor)
1863
Hertzberg, Sonny (player)
July 29, 1922
Hetzel, Fred (contributor)
July 21, 1942
Heyman, Art (player)
June 24, 1941
Hickox, Ed (contributor)
1878
Hightower, Wayne (contributor)
January 14, 1940
Hinkle, Tony (coach)
1899
Hobson, Howard (contributor)
1903
Hoffman, Paul (contributor)
April 28, 1940
Hogue, Paul (player)
April 12, 1922
Hollins, Lionell (player)
October 9, 1953
Holman, Nat (player/coach)
1896
Holzman, Red (player/coach)
August 10, 1920
Houbregs, Bob (player)
March 12, 1932
Howell, Bailey (player)
January 20, 1937
Hoyt, George (contributor)
1883
Hudson, Lou (player)
July 11, 1944
Hundley, Rod (player/announcer)
October 26, 1934
Hutchins, Mel (player)
November 22, 1928
Hyatt, Chuck (contributor)
1908
Iba, Hank (coach)
1904
Imhoff, Darrall (player)
October 11, 1938
Irish, Ned (contributor)
1905
Issel, Dan (player)
October 25, 1948
Jabali, Warren (player)
August 29, 1946
Jackson, Lucious (player)
October 31, 1941

Jackson, Phil (player/coach)
September 17, 1945
Jeanette, Buddy (player/contributor)
September 15, 1917
Johnson, George (player)
December 18, 1948
Johnson, Gus (player)
December 13, 1938
Johnson, John (player)
October 18, 1947
Johnson, Mickey (player)
August 31, 1952
Johnston, Neil (player)
February 4, 1929
Jones, Bobby (player)
December 18, 1951
Jones, Caldwell (player)
August 4, 1950
Jones, James (player)
January 1, 1945
Jones, John (player)
January 1, 1945
Jones, K. C. (player/coach)
May 25, 1932
Jones, Larry (player)
September 22, 1941
Jones, Sam (player)
June 24, 1933
Jones, Wah Wah (player)
July 14, 1926
Jones, Wally (player)
February 14, 1942
Jones, William (contributor)
1906
Julian, Doggie (coach)
1901
Kaftan, George (contributor)
February 26, 1928
Karl, George (coach)
May 12, 1951
Kauffman, Bob (player)
August 30, 1947
Keaney, Frank (contributor)
1886
Keller, Billy (player)
July 13, 1946
Kennedy, Matthew (contributor)
1908
Kennedy, Walter (contributor)
June 8, 1912
Kenon, Larry (player)
December 13, 1952
Keogan, George (contributor)
1890
Kerr, Johnny (player)
August 17, 1932
Klotz, Red (contributor)
October 21, 1921
Knight, Billy (player)
June 9, 1952
Kojis, Don (player)
January 15, 1939
Komives, Howard (player)
May 8, 1941
Kundla, John (coach)
July 3, 1916
Kurland, Bob (player)
1924
Ladner, Wendall (player)
October 6, 1948
Lambert, Piggy (coach)
1888
Lanier, Bob (player)
September 10, 1948
Lapchick, Joe (coach)
1900
LaRusso, Rudy (player)
November 11, 1937
Lavelli, Tony (player)
July 11, 1926
Layden, Frank (coach)
January 5, 1932
Leaks, Manny (player)
November 27, 1945
Lee, Butch (player)
December 5, 1956
Lee, Clyde (player)
March 14, 1944
Lee, Ron (player)
November 2, 1952
Lehman, George (player)
May 1, 1942
Leonard, Bob (player/contributor)
July 17, 1932
Levane, Fuzzy (contributor)
April 11, 1920
Lewis, Fred (player)
January 7, 1943
Litwack, Harry (contributor)
1914
Loeffler, Ken (contributor)
1902

Logan, John (player)
January 1, 1921
Loscutoff, Jim (player)
February 4, 1930
Loughery, Kevin (player/coach)
March 28, 1940
Love, Bob (player)
December 8, 1942
Lovellette, Clyde (player)
September 7, 1929
Lucas, Jerry (player)
March 30, 1940
Lucas, Maurice (player)
February 18, 1952
Luisetti, Hank (player)
1916
McAdoo, Bob (player)
September 25, 1951
Macauley, Ed (player)
March 22, 1928
McClain, Ted (player)
August 30, 1947
McCracken, Branch (coach)
1908
McCracken, Jack (contributor)
1911
McDaniels, Jim (player)
April 2, 1948
McDermott, Bobby (contributor)
1928
McGill, Bill (player)
September 16, 1939
McGinnis, George (player)
August 12, 1950
McGlocklin, Jon (player)
June 10, 1943
McGuire, Al (player/coach)
September 7, 1928
McGuire, Dick (player)
January 25, 1926
McGuire, Frank (coach)
November 8, 1916
McKinney, Bones (player/coach)
January 1, 1919
McMillan, Jim (player)
March 11, 1948
Malloy, Mike (player)
May 10, 1949
Maravich, Pete (player)
June 22, 1948
Marin, Jack (player)
October 12, 1944
Martin, Slater (player)
October 22, 1925
Maxwell, Cornbread (player)
November 21, 1955
May, Scott (player)
March 19, 1954
Meanwell, Walter (contributor)
1884
Melchionni, Bill (player)
October 19, 1944
Meschery, Tom (player)
October 26, 1938
Mikan, Ed (player)
October 20, 1925
Mikan, George (player)
June 18, 1924
Mikan, Larry (player)
April 8, 1948
Mikkelsen, Vern (player)
October 21, 1928
Miles, Eddie (player)
July 5, 1940
Miller, Larry (player)
April 4, 1946
Mix, Steve (player)
December 30, 1947
Moe, Doug (player/coach)
September 21, 1938
Mokray, Bill (contributor)
1907
Moncrief, Sidney (player)
September 21, 1957
Money, Eric (player)
February 6, 1955
Monroe, Earl (player)
November 21, 1944
Morgan, Ralph (contributor)
1884
Morganweck, Frank (contributor)
1875
Mount, Rick (player)
January 5, 1947
Mullaney, Joe (coach)
February 3, 1923
Mullin, Chris (player)
1963
Mullins, Jeff (player)
March 18, 1942
Murphy, Calvin (player)
May 9, 1948

Murphy, Stretch (player)
1907
Naismith, James (inventor)
1861
Nater, Swen (player)
January 14, 1950
Natt, Calvin (player)
January 8, 1957
Naulls, Willie (player)
October 7, 1934
Neumann, Johnny (player)
September 11, 1951
Newell, Pete
August 31, 1913
Newlin, Mike (player)
January 2, 1949
Nixon, Norm (player)
October 10, 1955
Noble, Chuck (contributor)
July 24, 1931
Nostrand, George (contributor)
April 5, 1924
Nucatola, John (referee)
November 17, 1907
O'Brien, John (contributor)
1888
O'Brien, Larry (contributor)
March 29, 1912
Ohl, Don (player)
April 18, 1936
Olsen, Harold (contributor)
1895
Otten, Don (player)
April 18, 1921
Otten, Mac (player)
December 16, 1925
Page, Pat (contributor)
1887
Palazzi, Togo (player)
August 8, 1932
Paulk, Charlie (player)
June 14, 1944
Paultz, Billy (player)
July 30, 1948
Petrie, Geoff (player)
April 17, 1948
Pettit, Bob (player)
December 12, 1932
Phillip, Andy (player)
March 7, 1922
Podoloff, Maurice (contributor)
August 18, 1890
Pollard, Jim (player)
July 9, 1922
Porter, H. V. (contributor)
1891
Porter, Kevin (player)
April 17, 1950
Quigley, Ernest (contributor)
1880
Ramsay, Jack (coach)
February 21, 1925
Ramsey, Cal (player/announcer)
July 13, 1937
Ramsey, Frank (player)
July 17, 1931
Ray, Clifford (player)
June 21, 1949
Reed, Willis (player/coach)
June 25, 1942
Regan, Richie (player)
November 30, 1930
Reid, William (contributor)
1893
Reiser, Chuck (player)
September 18, 1923
Richardson, Michael Ray (player)
April 11, 1955
Riordan, Mike (player)
July 9, 1945
Risen, Arnie (player)
October 9, 1924
Robbins, Red (player)
September 30, 1944
Roberts, Anthony (player)
April 15, 1955
Robertson, Oscar (player)
November 24, 1938
Robinson, Flynn (player)
April 28, 1941
Robinson, Truck (player)
October 4, 1951
Rocha, Red (player)
1924
Roche, John (player)
September 29, 1949
Rodgers, Guy (player)
September 1, 1935
Rollins, Tree (player)
June 6, 1955
Roosma, John (contributor)
1900

Rosenbluth, Len (player)
January 22, 1933
Roundfield, Dan (player)
May 26, 1953
Rowe, Curtis (player)
July 2, 1949
Rule, Bob (player)
January 29, 1944
Rupp, Adolph (coach)
1901
Russell, Bill (player/coach)
February 12, 1934
Russell, Campy (player)
January 12, 1952
Russell, Cazzie (player)
June 7, 1944
Russell, Honey (coach)
1903
Sachs, Leonard (contributor)
1897
Sailors, Ken (player)
January 14, 1922
St. John, Lynn (contributor)
1876
Sanders, Satch (player)
November 8, 1938
Saperstein, Abe (contributor)
1902
Sauldsberry, Woodie (player)
July 11, 1934
Schabinger, Arthur (contributor)
1889
Schaus, Fred (player/coach)
June 30, 1925
Schommer, John (contributor)
1884
Scolari, Fred (player)
March 1, 1922
Scott, Charlie (player)
December 15, 1948
Scott, Ray (player)
July 12, 1938
Sears, Ken (player)
August 17, 1933
Sedran, Barney (contributor)
1891
Selvy, Frank (player/coach)
November 9, 1932
Senesky, George (contributor)
April 4, 1922
Seymour, Paul (player)
January 30, 1928
Shackelford, Lynn (player)
August 27, 1947
Shaffer, Lee (player)
February 23, 1939
Sharman, Bill (player/coach)
May 25, 1926
Shirley, Dallas (referee)
June 7, 1913
Shue, Gene (player/coach)
December 18, 1931
Siegfried, Larry (player)
May 22, 1939
Silas, James (player)
February 11, 1949
Silas, Paul (player)
July 12, 1943
Simpson, Ralph (player)
August 10, 1949
Sloan, Jerry (player/coach)
March 28, 1942
Smith, Adrian (player)
October 5, 1936
Smith, Bingo (player)
February 26, 1946
Smith, Elmore (player)
May 9, 1949
Smith, Phil (player)
April 22, 1952
Smith, Randy (player)
December 12, 1948
Snyder, Dick (player)
February 1, 1944
Sobers, Ricky (player)
January 15, 1953
Sojourner, Willie (player)
September 10, 1948
Stagg, Amos Alonzo (contributor)
1862
Stallworth, Dave (player)
December 20, 1941
Steinmetz, Christian (player)
1882
Stokes, Maurice (player)
June 17, 1933
Stutz, Stan (player)
April 14, 1920
Taylor, Brian (player)
June 9, 1951
Taylor, Chuck (contributor)
1901

Thompson, David (player)
July 13, 1954
Thompson, John (contributor)
1906
Thompson, John (coach)
September 2, 1941
Thorn, Rod (player/contributor)
May 23, 1941
Thurmond, Nate (player)
July 25, 1941
Tobey, David (contributor)
1898
Tomjanovich, Rudy (player)
November 24, 1948
Toney, Andrew (player)
November 23, 1957
Tower, Oswald (contributor)
1883
Trester, Arthur (contributor)
1878
Twyman, Jack (player)
February 18, 1944
Unseld, Wes (player/coach)
March 14, 1946
Van Arsdale, Dick (player)
February 22, 1943
Van Arsdale, Tom (player)
February 22, 1943
Vandeweghe, Ernie (player)
March 8, 1926
Van Lier, Norm (player)
April 1, 1947
Verga, Bruce (player)
September 7, 1945
Wachter, Ed (contributor)
1883
Walker, Chet (player)
February 22, 1940
Walker, Jimmy (player)
April 8, 1944
Walsh, Dave (contributor)
1883
Walton, Bill (player)
November 5, 1952
Wanzer, Bobby (player)
1926
Washington, Kermit (player)
September 17, 1951
Webster, Marvin (player)
April 13, 1952
Wedman, Scott (player)
July 29, 1952
Weiss, Bob (player/coach)
May 7, 1942
Wells, Clifford (contributor)
1896
West, Jerry (player/coach)
May 28, 1938
Westphal, Paul (player)
November 30, 1950
White, Jo Jo (player)
November 16, 1946
Whitehead, Jerome (player)
September 30, 1956
Wicks, Sidney (player)
September 19, 1949
Wilkens, Lenny (player/coach)
October 28, 1937
Wilkes, Keith (player)
November 30, 1950
Williams, Charles (player)
September 5, 1943
Williams, Freeman (player)
May 15, 1956
Williams, Gus (player)
October 10, 1953
Williams, Ray (player)
October 14, 1954
Williamson, John (player)
November 10, 1952
Willoughby, Bill (player)
May 20, 1957
Winters, Brian (player)
March 1, 1952
Wise, Willie (player)
March 3, 1947
Wohl, Dave (player/coach)
November 2, 1949
Wooden, John (player/coach)
1910
Yardley, George (player)
November 3, 1928
Zaslofsky, Max (player)
December 7, 1925

Selected Bibliography

Axthelm, Pete. *City Game: Basketball, from the World of Madison Square Garden to the World of the Playground.* New York: Putnam-Berkley, 1982.

Barry, Rick, and Bill Libby. *Confessions of a Basketball Gypsy.* Englewood Cliffs, NJ: Prentice Hall, 1971.

________. *Rick Barry's Ratings.* Chicago: Bonus Books, 1989.

Barzman, Sol. *505 Basketball Questions Your Friends Can't Answer.* New York: Walker and Company, 1981.

Bee, Clair. *Making the Team in Basketball,* rev. ed. New York: Grosset and Dunlap, 1960.

Bee, Clair F. *Winning Basketball Plays.* New York: Ronald, 1963.

Bell, Marty. *The Legend of Dr. J.: The Story of Julius Erving.* East Rutherford, NJ: Coward, McCann & Geoghegan, 1975.

Bellotti, Bob. *Bob Bellotti's Basketball Analyst: New Ideas About an Old Game.* New Brunswick, NJ: Night Work Publishing, 1990.

Berger, Phil. *Big Time: A Novel.* 1990.

________. *Heroes of Pro Basketball.* New York: Random House, 1968.

________. *Miracle on Thirty-Third Street: The N.Y. Knickerbockers Championship Season.* New York: Simon & Schuster, 1990.

Bevington, Raymond H. *Basketball Record Book.* Danville, IL: Interstate, 1953.

Bruns, Bill, and Dave Wolf. *Great Moments in Pro Basketball.* New York: Random House, 1968.

Bunn, John W. *Basketball Techniques and Team Play.* Englewood Cliffs, NJ: Prentice Hall, 1964.

Byerk, Cornelius. *Simplified Multiple Offense for Winning Basketball.* Englewood Cliffs, NJ: Parker, 1970.

Caudle, Edwin C. *Collegiate Basketball: Facts & Figures on the Cage Sport.* Winston-Salem, NC: John F. Blair, 1960.

Cooper, John M., and Daryl Sidentop. *Theory and Science of Basketball: For Coach and Professional Student.* Philadelphia, PA: Lea and Febiger, 1969.

Cousy, Robert. *Last Loud Roar.* Englewood Cliffs, NJ: Prentice Hall, 1964.

________, and Albert Hirschberg. *Basketball Is My Life.* Englewood Cliffs, NJ: Prentice Hall, 1958.

Dickey, Glenn. *The History of Professional Basketball Since 1896.* Briarcliff Manor, NY: Stein and Day, 1982.

Earle, Jimmy. *Coaching Basketball's Red-Dog Defense.* Englewood Cliffs, NJ: Parker, 1971.

Forker, Dom. *The Ultimate Pro Basketball Quiz Book.* New York: New American Library, 1982.
Fox, Larry. *The Illustrated History of Pro Basketball.* New York: Grosset & Dunlap, 1974.
Halberstam, David. *The Breaks of the Game.* New York: Ballantine, 1981.
Harkins, Mike. *Successful Team Techniques in Basketball.* New York: Prentice Hall, 1966.
Harrell, B. *Championship-Tested Offensive and Defensive Basketball Strategy.* New York: Prentice Hall, 1967.
Harris, Delmer. *Multiple Defenses for Winning Basketball.* Englewood Cliffs, NJ: Parker, 1971.
Harris, Merv. *On Court with the Superstars of the NBA.* New York: Viking, 1973.
Heuman, William. *Famous Pro Basketball Stars.* New York: Dodd, 1970.
Higdon, Hal. *Find the Key Man.* New York: Putnam, 1974.
Hirschberg, Al. *Basketball's Greatest Teams.* New York: Putnam, 1966.
Holzman, Red. *Red Holzman's Pro Basketball Guide.* New York: Aurora, 1970.
Jagger, B., ed. *Basketball Coaching and Training.* Philadelphia: Trans-Atlantic, 1971.
Klein, David. *The Making of a Basketball Rookie.* New York: Cowles, 1971.
Koppett, Leonard. *The Essence of the Game Is Deception.* Boston: Little, Brown, 1973.
________. *24 Seconds to Shoot.* New York: Macmillan, 1968.
McGuire, Frank. *Team Basketball: Offense & Defense.* Englewood Cliffs, NJ: Prentice Hall, 1966.
McLendon, John B. *Fast Break Basketball—Fundamentals and Fine Points.* Englewood Cliffs, NJ: Prentice Hall, 1965.
Meyer, Ray. *Basketball as Coached by Ray Meyer.* Englewood Cliffs, NJ: Prentice Hall, 1967.
Miller, Kenneth, and Rita Horky. *Modern Basketball for Women.* Westerville, OH: Merrill, 1970.
Morris, D. *Kentucky High School Basketball.* Englewood Cliffs, NJ: Prentice Hall, 1969.
Neft, David S., and Richard M. Cohen. *The Sports Encyclopedia: Pro Basketball.* New York: St. Martin's Press, 1975 and 1989.
Padwe, Sanford. *Basketball's Hall of Fame.* Englewood Cliffs, NJ: Prentice Hall, 1970.
Pepe, Phil. *Greatest Stars of the NBA.* Englewood Cliffs, NJ: Prentice Hall, 1970.
________. *The Incredible Knicks.* New York: Popular Library, 1970.
Perry, Richard M. *Men's Basketball.* Englewood Cliffs, NJ: Goodyear, 1969.
Rupp, Adolph. *Adolph Rupp's Basketball Guidebook.* New York: McGraw-Hill, 1967.
________. *Rupp's Championship Basketball.* Englewood Cliffs, NJ: Prentice Hall, 1957.
Santos, Harry. *How to Attack and Defeat Zone Defenses in Basketball.* Englewood Cliffs, NJ: Prentice Hall, 1966.
Sharman, Bill. *Sharman on Basketball Shooting.* Englewood Cliffs, NJ: Prentice Hall, 1969.
Strack, Dave. *Basketball.* Englewood Cliffs, NJ: Prentice Hall, 1969.
Van Ryswyk, Ron. *Complete System for Winning Basketball.* Englewood Cliffs, NJ: Prentice Hall, 1978.
Ward, Charles R. *Basketballs Match-up Defense.* Englewood Cliffs, NJ: Prentice Hall, 1979.
Wilkes, Glenn. *Winning Basketball Strategy.* New York: Grosset-Dunlap, 1955.
Winter, Morrice. *Triple-Post Offense.* Englewood Cliffs, NJ: Prentice Hall, 1962.
Wolfe, Herman. *From Tryouts to Championships.* Englewood Cliffs, NJ: Prentice Hall, 1972.
Wooden, John R. *Practical Modern Basketball.* Ronald, 1966.

Index